BOOK THREE IN THE CO

The New Covenant

THE HEART OF GOD'S PLAN FOR YOUR LIFE, AND FOR ALL OF HUMANITY

MARK JOHNSON, MD

Carpenter's Son Publishing

The New Covenant

Published by Clovercroft Publishing, Franklin, Tennessee

Published in association with Larry Carpenter of Christian Book Services, LLC
www.christianbookservices.com

Edited by Bob Irvin

Cover and Interior Layout Design by Suzanne Lawing

978-1-952025-35-8

THIS BOOK IS DEDICATED TO THOSE WHO MENTOR

This book is dedicated to those in the Body of Christ who mentor others. These people have embraced the plan of God in substantial ways. They have implemented God's truth in significant ways. They have walked the path of God long enough to be shaped in His image in visible ways. And these people recognize our responsibility to help others on their journey.

Good preaching and teaching are essential. Personal study of God's Word is vital. It is imperative that we recognize the nature of these writings: truths revealed by God, to be applied in our lives. But more is required if we are to implement and become these truths. We can hear and understand, yet not act or become. A process is required to implement these truths, to grind them into the fabric of our lives so that we become these things. The New Covenant makes these changes possible, but we must be taught how to grow and change. We only discover the need to change or see the benefits of change in the context of a relationship. The New Covenant and Marriage are *relationships* that are intended to point the way to needed growth and transformation.

The mature Christian life is like a large tree from which hangs good and nourishing fruit. One may desire to be such a tree. But we can only build this life by building the root system that allows such growth. These roots are out of the public eye. These are the unseen things one does to build an intimate relationship with God. Mentors lead others down a path of growth and transformation they have already walked. They share lessons of growth and transformation, of building intimacy, of loving in challenging situations, of being faithful against all odds. All who walk far down God's path have such people in their lives. May you find your mentors, and may you ultimately become one.

Contents

A Personal Welcome! 7

What Is a Relationship with God Supposed to Look Like? 13

How Would You Describe the 'New Creature'
We Become in a Relationship with God? 17

What Is a Covenant? 39

Why Do We Need Covenant? 81

The New Covenant 139

Life in the New Covenant 205

Personal Growth and Transformation in Covenant 251

Building an Abundant Life 293

A PERSONAL WELCOME!

Since I became a Christian forty-plus years ago, I have spent countless hours talking with people about their lives. Talking about applying God's truth to the real-life situations we encounter day by day. About dealing with the inner confusion, uncertainty, and lack of peace that plague all of us. About how to find the quality of life we all seek as Christians. About the deep and powerful relationship we all want with God, and how to build such a relationship. I wish you and I could spend an hour a week for a year or so eating breakfast and talking about your life. If we could do this, I would impart to you the things you are about to read in this book. My finite life does not allow this many breakfasts! But we all have an open invitation to spend time with another Mentor, one who is far better—the Spirit of God. This teacher and friend dwells within each of us if we are in a Covenant relationship with God. As you read through this material, discuss it with this Teacher. Let Him show you what is needed to build the life God planned for you before the foundation of the world. If you are not in a Covenant relationship with God and want to better understand this relationship, or learn how to enter it, you will find those answers within these pages. May your time be richly blessed! [Author's note: though the word *Covenant* is not normally capitalized, it is my desire to place particular emphasis on the unique nature and the divine origin of this relationship. Therefore, I will capitalize this word when referring to the *New Covenant* and to the *Covenant of Marriage*. – MJ]

The New Testament describes dramatic changes in the lives of many people who entered a New Covenant relationship with God. This corresponds with scriptural imagery about this relationship—"new birth, death of the old, new life, be transformed ... " But even in the early church the lives of some Christians evidenced little such transformation. They continued to live as they always had. A good deal of New

Testament teaching is directed toward people who were in this new relationship but still lived the "old life." Most people who enter a relationship with God today want something about their life to change. Many wait and pray and hope that at some point God will change their life. But many do not experience anything that resembles the radical transformation we read about in Scripture. We are told: "God does it all." So what about this life transformation? Does God transform some lives but not others?

Current teaching is not clear regarding what happens as we enter this relationship. The terms we use offer little help: "saved," "made a decision," or "converted." But what about us *changes*? How do these changes impact our lives? Why do life outcomes vary so widely among those who call themselves Christians? In Scripture God tells us to do certain things and not to do other things. Teaching in the church today focuses on obeying God—on "not sinning." Is this the sum of our Christian life? Are we simply to obey while we await God's transformation? Or does obedience even matter in our modern world? Even among those who scrupulously follow the rules—like the Pharisees—at times something is clearly missing. So what is a relationship with God really about? If God "does it all," what are we supposed to be doing? We are called to love God and love others. Does this mean to just be nicer, participate in church, and be a little more generous? Should there be more to a relationship with the Living God than we see when we look around the Christian community … or look in the mirror? More impact *within us,* more impact *on our lives,* and more impact *of our lives*? If we are joined to a Being more powerful than anything in our universe, should His power not be more evident in our lives?

So what is a relationship with God really about? If God "does it all," what are we supposed to be doing?

A clear answer to these questions comes from a surprising source: the *nature of the relationship* we enter with God—a Covenant relationship. God created this form of relationship. He offers us two versions of this relationship: Marriage, and a New Covenant relationship with Himself. The historic understanding of Covenant—the topic of this book series—answers the questions just posed, and many others. Unfortunately, this understanding has gone largely missing in our day.

How are we transformed when we enter a New Covenant relationship with God? There are actually two distinct transformations that occur at different times and in different ways. The first occurs at the time we enter this relationship. At this point we are changed in the core of our being into a *new creation,* joined to God in the most intimate of bonds and indwelled by the Holy Spirit. But other parts of us may not be impacted by this inner transformation. We may feel different in some ways. We may see some things differently. But most of the things we have built into our lives over our lifetime—things which form our guidance system for living, our experience of living, and our character—these, for the most part, are unaffected by our initial transformation.

Therefore, as we begin our Christian life two parts of us predictably come into conflict. Our new nature and identity—this new creature we have become—versus three elements we bring forward from our pre-Christian life. The first element we bring forward consists of the *beliefs, values, priorities, and other things* we thought we knew about how to live. Together, these form our internal guidance system. This frame of reference directs every choice we make. The second element we bring forward is our *character*. Our character is the sum of everything we have decided to become as a person. These choices reflect our beliefs about the kind of person we need to be or want to be. The third element is our *self-image*—who do we believe ourselves to be, and where do we think we fit in the overall scheme of things.

Why do these come into conflict with the new being we have become? Even a quick reading of Scripture reveals many things God tells us to do and not do. Many of these things conflict with our guidance system. God tells us many things we are to be or not be. Some of these we simply *are not*—like consistently loving. He tells us things about who we are. Yet our perceptions and beliefs about ourselves may differ

> God tells us many things we are to be or not be. Some of these we simply *are not*—like consistently loving.

from God's revelation. If we disagree with God, who is right? What do we do now?

At this point some pull out an eraser or editor's pen and amend what God has clearly stated in Scripture. Some reason that ancient rules and sayings have no relevance in our modern world. They assume God's grace will make up the difference between what God says and what we are and do. Others make a serious attempt to do what God says to do and be what God says to be. However, as we attempt to obey, if we look at God's instructions as merely a *list of rules*, we miss something vital. What rules can we follow that will make us loving? Yet God clearly expects this of us.

Fortunately, God does not leave us hanging. Covenant is not just a relationship. It is a plan. This plan draws from elements God built into our mind, heart, and will—powers we will examine and learn to use. This plan centers upon faithfulness to our Covenant partner (in this case, God) and *the relationship we have entered with Him.* Through history this form of Covenant requires very specific things from each participant. We will learn about the requirements that are part of this relationship. Faithfulness to this plan is the key to bringing our life, character, and everything else about us into harmony with two things. First, God's plan is designed to bring our *external life* and our *experience of life* into harmony with the new being we have become when we entered this Covenant. Second, God's plan is designed to bring us into harmony with His Word, His heart, and His plan for our lives. God is inviting us to build a life that authentically expresses who we are at the deepest levels of our being, and a life that authentically reflects Him.

In order for our lives to *actually be* transformed in these ways, though, we must understand several things. First, God does not "do it all." There are some things God does and other things He delegates to us in this relationship. Covenant is an *all-in* thing on the part of both parties. This is as true in a New Covenant relationship as it is in Marriage. Covenant relationships, properly conducted, require us to offer everything we have, everything we are, and everything we can become to love the one, or One, to whom we are joined. We are to offer each other our very best. But even our best at times falls short of what is needed.

> Covenant is an all-in thing on the part of both parties. This is as true in a New Covenant relationship as it is in Marriage.

The second thing we must grasp is that faithfulness to our Covenant is about more than making correct in-the-moment decisions. It is about growing our new life to maturity. In this process we develop new capabilities and strengths. Faithfulness is about *playing the role we have been assigned in our transformation* so that our character and guidance system cease to pull us away from God's plan.

God's Covenant plan is deep, broad, and detailed—touching literally every element of self and life. This book can only provide an overview of such a plan. We will highlight three vital elements. First, *the things God graciously offers to us.* Among these are a new life that is joined to God and shared with Him, and His truth revealed in Scripture. Second, *the things God delegates to us.* God transforms our nature and identity as we enter Covenant. But, the way we live and the way we experience our lives often changes very little. A second process of transformation must occur if we are to live differently and experience the abundant life God offers us. Our guidance system, character, and self-image must be revised in order for these visible life changes to occur.

This second transformation requires the third element: *our choices.* Specifically, to build what God desires we must choose to be faithful to God's plan—in whole and in every detail. In order to carry out this plan we must know several things. We must understand what about us has already changed in a relationship with God, and what still needs to change. We must understand *why* these changes are vital if we are to build our best life, and we must know *how* these changes occur.

Specifically, we must know the role God assigns to us in this second transformation. But knowing every detail of this plan will not make it happen. We must then choose to follow this plan, do everything in our power, and learn to develop new powers under God's guidance to fully follow God's plan.

Our choices produce the transformation needed to build our best life and most powerful relationship with God. Though the choices are ours, the *foundation for these choices* must shift from our previous belief system to *truth revealed by God*. We walk hand in hand with God through this process. Our path to God's choicest blessings is faithfulness. God will not pour the blessings of a transformed life into our life in the face of neglect or disobedience. He lays His plan before us and offers us a choice. Will we choose to follow Him and His plan? Will we be faithful to the God we *say* is now our Lord?

If you or I have become a Christian, and wonder why our lives have changed so little, where should we look for a solution? Might the best approach be to search out God's plan for our relationship with Him and our lives? God's plan informs us about what to do, motivates us to conform, and transforms us as we follow it. God's plan enables us to actually do the things we are called to do and be what we are called to be. And what are we called to do? What are God's greatest commandments? To love Him with our whole heart, mind, soul, and strength; and to love our neighbor as ourselves. It is on this foundation that everything else worth having in life is built. We are also called to build the new life we have been given to maturity so that we become reflections of God.

The word *Christian* means "little Christ." God makes an offer to each of us, an offer accompanied by a plan to bring these things into existence in our lives. But God's *intended* life will only become reality in our lives if we choose this life, and choose to build it.

DANCING WITH GOD

What Is a Relationship with God Supposed to Look Like?

Have you seen skilled ballroom dancers up close, in person? Leading and following with incredible power, precision, and skill? Bodies form into shape after shape at impossible speed. Brains and bodies work as one to create something of transcendent beauty. Something so appreciated at a distance is produced by myriad subtle movements. Vast numbers of muscles are in play each second. The dancers are perfectly trained so each finger is in a specific position, along with head, arms, torso, legs, and feet. These combine to form a perfect picture, but it is not a static sculpture. The dancers move through space creating picture after picture in perfect harmony with the music. Athleticism, speed, timing, and control appear effortless as two people physically express a piece of music.

How much training, effort, time, energy, and heart went into creating what we see?

There is teamwork: the man leads, the woman follows. Each is extraordinary; together they are magnificent. The leader is firmly in charge—and yet showcases his partner. The woman, reading his cues, maintains proper position as they move in

The leader is firmly in charge—and yet showcases his partner. The woman, reading his cues, maintains proper position as they move in synchrony. Her movements are expression and response.

synchrony. Her movements are expression and response. They communicate through a nuanced language of touch, but there is also an intimate knowledge of one's partner. What is possible for each, and how can a particular series of pictures be created? Dances may be choreographed. Those with higher skills, though, can create a dance to a piece of music in the moment. Instant by instant, minds and bodies innovate, create, read, and respond at lightning speed to render both a perfect physical expression of a song and a perfect expression of a form of dance—salsa or tango or waltz.

Our relationship with God is supposed to look like this. A partnership that creates. A working relationship between us and our Lord that is beautiful to behold and offers something of great value to the world.

How are such high-level skills possible? The best way to achieve this state of wonder is to try dancing. There is something called a "dance school." These schools take normal humans and turn them into dancers. A finely honed training process produces this transformation. One only needs to submit to this process and spend the necessary time and effort.

Now imagine another picture. The leader moves and offers cues. But his partner never attended the training process. Muscles are not trained. She does not know what the dance is supposed to look like, or how to move across the floor, or how to put the correct foot down on the correct beat. So the leader graciously picks her up and drags her across the floor from point to point. Even with this encouragement, his partner makes no effort to learn. She is content to let the leader do what she has been told he would do—"everything."

Does this spectacle inspire anyone to dance with the Master? Is this dancer a constructive part of the Master's plan? Is she experiencing the abundant life as she is dragged across the floor? How do these two pictures relate to a relationship with God? One may fault the dancer, but there is a deeper problem. While there is a clear-cut path to become an expert ballroom dancer, there is an amazing lack of clarity about how one becomes a skilled dance partner for God.

How do you or I move from where we begin to living a transformed, fruitful, abundant life that reflects the mind and heart of God? Is this about merely "saying no to sin"? Does God transform our life while we patiently sit listening to message after message week after week? We wait for an all-powerful, all-knowing, perfectly loving God to do … what? Or is there another plan by which our relationship with God can grow into something of great beauty and power? If so, what is this plan?

Let's voice the questions most are afraid to ask. Why are so many frustrated and baffled by the mismatch between what we *thought would happen* and *what we experience* after we join ourselves to Him? Is God not as loving, powerful, and attentive as we expected? Does a "personal relationship" with the Living God exist? Does He even exist? Do these questions—and the lack of clear answers from pulpits and the lives of those in the Christian community—explain the exodus of young and old from the ranks of believers? Perhaps God does have a clear and precise plan that many, tragically, have never heard. They hear the plan of salvation and eternal security, but what about the plan of God to build the life they long to live, in the relationship with God they long to have?

Do these questions—and the lack of clear answers from pulpits and the lives of those in the Christian community—explain the exodus of young and old from the ranks of believers?

Maybe we need to find God's school of dance. Maybe we need to understand the plan of God and our part in this plan. Entering a relationship with God is not an endpoint. It is the beginning-point of an entirely new life. At least it is intended to be this. Another thing is also clear. Throughout the Scriptures there is a tug-of-war in individual lives. We see this battle played out in the nation of Israel in the Old Testament and in the Body of Christ in the New Testament. This tug-of-war is between *faithfulness to God* and *unfaithfulness*. Once in a relationship with God, outcomes depend on our decisions and actions. This is true not only for eternity but also in this life. If the quality of our life depends on faithfulness, what is faithfulness? Faithfulness to whom, and what?

In this book we are going to pay a visit to God's school of dance. We can look in the mirror and see where we are now. We can look at the lives of mature, godly believers whom we know or read about—those who truly dance. But what does the process look like that gets us from here to there? What are we supposed to do? How do we grow? How are we transformed? How do we become different, and what needs to become different in each life? At the end of this process, is the reward truly worth the effort? What is this reward other than a seat on the bus to Heaven when we die? The one who ignited the stars and set our universe in motion also created each of us! He designed a unique life for every unique individual. This life perfectly suits us and is designed to bless us more than we can imagine at the outset. But we must become equipped to live the life God intends for us, and to learn how to *enjoy living it.* This is the abundant life: an intimate relationship with our Creator, Lord, and Lover of our soul.

God's plan is more complex than a dance school curriculum. In dance school one repeats certain steps over and over until they become engrained within that person. God's process of transformation does far more and requires far more from us. His school is called Covenant. It is designed to change everything about us so we live differently, love differently, and think, feel, and relate differently.

His school is called Covenant. It is designed to change everything about us so we live differently, love differently, and think, feel, and relate differently.

And, not least, that we learn to dance with God. But all of this can only occur within a very special kind of relationship that is conducted in particular ways. What is this New Covenant He offers us? I'm glad you asked.

A NOTE TO THEOLOGIANS AND PASTORS

How Would You Describe the 'New Creature' We Become in a Relationship with God?

From Augustine to Calvin to the Wesleys and countless others, leaders and teachers of Christianity have struggled with several key questions. First, we become new when we enter a relationship with Christ. But what is different about the new creature we have become? Second, if we are made new, joined to the Creator of the universe and indwelled by His Spirit, why is this new being still so imperfect? Why does the way of life and experience of life change so little for so many? Third, once we become a Christian it is clear that Scripture still instructs us to change. What additional change is required within us to conform to God's plan, and how does this change occur? Fourth, we are instructed to be faithful in our relationship to God. But faithful to what, and to do what?

If "God does it all," as is often said, why does He not do more to transform individual lives? And why in Scripture are we instructed to do things that oppose not only our desires, but at points seem to oppose our nature? Yet the language of Scripture is clear; God intends that we comply. What are we to do as Christians? Why are we to do these things? And, how can we possibly do, and be, what God requires of us?

Is the pattern of radically transformed lives seen in Scripture still possible in our day? And, if possible, is it desirable? Is our best life now, as then, found in this transformed life? What role does God play in engineering this new and different life, and what role do we play? Consider the following thesis statement. If we better understood:

the transformation that occurs when we enter Covenant;
the nature, structure, and function of this relationship;
and God's plan to build this relationship ... would it help us?

The reason these questions remain questions is that the language of Scripture is at points indistinct. In the book of Romans, Chapter Seven, do the struggles with sin that Paul relates refer to life before becoming a Christian, or after? What is our "old self"? Is this something God alone can deal with, or something we are supposed to deal with? Is Calvin correct in saying that every fiber of our being as a Christian remains thoroughly tainted by a sinful nature, therefore we remain desperately wicked in every respect? In our attempts to obey, are we instructed to fight a nature we cannot hope to actually overcome? Is our only hope some ongoing transformative process that God doles out as He pleases? If so, is His grace as capricious as it appears when we consider how few truly godly men and women we know? Or, does our faithfulness—*our choice* to obey—play a key role in our relationship with God and the development of our life? The language of Scripture leaves room for many opinions on these points. But, if we understand the nature, structure, and function of a Covenant relationship and view God's Scriptural injunctions through this lens, these no longer remain questions.

When asked about Marriage in the conversation recorded in Matthew 19, Jesus referred the questioner back to the *original blueprint* for this relationship: "In the beginning ..." He invited this person to understand the one flesh nature of marriage, for if one understands and carries out *the plan inherent in the nature of this relationship,* divorce would not be a question ... and not simply because people should not divorce. If two people build a marriage according to God's plan, they will not *want* to divorce.

In the same way, would we benefit from understanding God's original blueprint for a relationship with Himself—Covenant? Today, we often hear that a Covenant is "a contract, but one written by God." In this book series we have already seen that Covenant differs from a contract in many important respects. A contract is entered by agreement and stipulates behavior. In sharp contrast, a Covenant is entered by an exchange of identity. It alters the identity of each party and joins the two via a bond of shared identity. The historic practices of Covenant create a relationship of love-in-action, and a heart of genuine love for each other. Those historic practices are reflected perfectly in God's Scriptural injunctions about how we are to approach God in a relationship and how we are to approach others in the Body of Christ.

In the contractual view of Covenant, where obedience is understood as mere rule-keeping, would something vital go missing? The most vital thing which would go missing is the larger plan of God for a person's life. Many things we are told to do and be are simply beyond our ability at the outset. What do we do then? Do we edit God's word to conform to our abilities or preferences? Do we wait for Him to change us into people who willingly and capably do as He directs—and in the meantime trust God's love, grace, and mercy to make up the difference while we continue to live as we choose? Or, do we follow God's plan and walk His path of growth and development? Do we recognize and embrace the guiding principle that *faithfulness to God and to our Covenant with Him* means that we *will be radically transformed* in our heart, mind, and will? Do we recognize that this is the path which leads to a new and very different life?

How does focusing only on external obedience build an intimate love relationship with God or a heart of love for others?

To walk this path, though, we must understand the *what, when, why, and how* of transformation. These are not academic and intellectual questions. These are imminently personal and practical questions. A correct answer will direct our growth according to God's plan. Or misconceptions will stand in our way as we try to follow God.

Are we not, after all, supposed to become reflections of Him? To grow to maturity in Him? Are these accomplished through rule-keeping? How does focusing only on external obedience build an intimate love relationship with God or a heart of love for others?

Do God's love and grace make obedience to ancient commands unnecessary in modern life? Are we truly free before God to be guided by our own well-intended lights? Was Jesus serious when He instructed His followers to teach others to obey *everything* He commanded? As we confront this question, we must recognize that Jesus had something in mind beside each of us emulating the life of a first century Jewish peasant. He intends that we follow *His plan of growth and development* so that we come to express the heart and mind of the eternal God in our daily lives in any culture, at any point in history.

Was Jesus serious when He instructed His followers to teach others to obey *everything* He commanded?

Inherent in the nature, structure, and function of a Covenant relationship is a plan to accomplish this exact outcome. God's intent is that we conduct our relationship with Him so that this relationship is built to its potential, and so that we are built to our potential. Let me outline in brief the plan we will discuss in detail in the rest of this book.

Blood Covenants were a part of most cultures in the ancient world, including in Israel during the time of Jesus' earthly life. The historic understanding of this relationship is founded on the belief that within one's blood is one's life, a view echoed in Leviticus 17:14. If blood is exchanged, life is exchanged. In such an exchange the very essence—the identity—of the persons are exchanged and shared going forward. If the core of one's life is shared in this way, then everything else in life is reasonably shared. Families, friends, enemies, assets, debts, and every other aspect of life is shared between the two. All of the ancient practices of Covenant are logical extensions of this sharing of life and identity.

In the conversation recorded in John 6:25-70, Jesus' hearers were familiar with these concepts. This is why they reacted so strongly when Jesus invited His hearers to "eat His flesh and drink His blood" (John 6:53). They were not baffled by these words—quite the opposite. They understood exactly what He was offering. He was inviting them into a Blood Covenant with One who was establishing His claim to be the Son of God. The crowd reacted as they did because this idea was the furthest thing imaginable from their concept of a relationship with God. They understood the offer. But they could not fathom why Jesus would make it. Let's take a closer look at Jesus' offer in light of the historic practices of Covenant.

—Jesus poured out His blood for us, not just as a sacrifice, but also as an offer of His life. We receive Him—His life—into ourselves (drink His blood) by *believing in Him*. That is, by accepting Him in His proper role in our life (as Lord and Savior), by accepting a relationship with Him on His terms (Covenant), and by offering up our life to Him in return with nothing held back (at which point our old life is put to death and we are reborn as a new creation). In this process of death and rebirth the identity of God—the Holy Spirit—comes to live within us. We are now in *Christ*, and He is within us. This is the New Covenant exchange of identity and nature.

—We are not only new and different creatures, we are now in a unique bond with God. Since God is within us and we are within God, we are now in a state of "oneness" with Him (John 17:20-23). The Greek word translated as "one" in John 17, as the "one flesh" of the Covenant of Marriage, and as "God (the Trinity) is one," does not refer to a singular item. Instead, this term refers to multiple things joined by a common nature or identity. This sharing, alteration, and joining of nature or identity is the hallmark of this kind of Covenant. It is also clear from these uses of this word that the model for Covenant is also the Author of this relationship—the Trinity.

—If the essence of our beings is shared in this state of oneness, every other aspect of life is logically shared (John 17:10). There is no more "my life," or "mine" and "yours." There is only "our life" and "ours." This full sharing of life is perhaps the main reason that Jesus became fully human. And why, once in Covenant, we are no longer "of this world" (John17:16).

—The historic practices of Covenant include many duties, obligations, and responsibilities. All of these are logical extensions of this sharing of life in the depth of our beings. Our highest duty is to honor the other in every way. Then, to provide, protect, and defend with every resource at our disposal. We are to promote the interests of the other in the same way we would care for our own. But Covenant includes more than a discreet list of duties. Instead, Covenant is a blank check: "whatever you need; whatever I have, am, or can become" is at the disposal of the other. The sum of these things can be simply stated: "love in action." We are to love the other as we love ourselves because the other has literally become an extension of us. Every injunction in Scripture reflects some aspect of loving God, loving others in the Body of Christ, or loving those made in God's image who are not yet in Covenant with Him. Upon what basis are we called to obey these injunctions? In John 14, love for God and obedience to God are made synonyms. Obedience is not simply to satisfy a contractual obligation. Through obedience we learn to love, build relationships, and build ourselves.

—The highest imperative of Covenant is *faithfulness*. Faithfulness consists of wholehearted devotion to one's Covenant partner and scrupulous adherence to the principles of this relationship. Historically, Covenant relationships have been understood as the highest priority in life. Everything else in life integrates around this center-point. Ancient literature is full of stories about the lengths to which people would go to honor a Covenant obliga-

> tion. Such effort was counted the height of heroism, while refraining from fulfilling these obligations was counted the height of dishonor.

Is a corresponding level of commitment inherent in the New Covenant (or the Old)? We are assured that God is always faithful. He supplies our every need. He provides abundantly, beyond anything we could ask or think. He came so that we could have life to the full. But, what about us? How are we to approach this relationship? What is the First Commandment, and what is Jesus' parting injunction in Matthew 28:20? We are called to love God with every fiber of our being and to worship and serve Him only. We are called to scrupulous obedience to His every word.

This is what the New Covenant is supposed to look like. This is how we are supposed to order our priorities and conduct ourselves. Why, then, do I describe this relationship as a *plan* instead of simply a relationship? Because, at the outset no one is capable of doing or being the things required by God in this relationship. Fortunately, *within the nature of this relationship* is a plan to transform us so that we can do and be these things. God intends that we grow the new creature we have become to maturity—that is, that we live out the initial transformation of Covenant that was accomplished entirely by God. However, in order to do so we must engage in a *second transformation.* In this process we play a key role. The extent to which this second transformation occurs largely defines the quality of our relationship with God and our life. This, in turn, largely depends on our faithfulness or the lack thereof. Let me briefly describe this second transformation and the critical role it plays.

First, we must understand the various parts of ourselves. We were created by God. Our ultimate potentials and our hard-wiring were set in place by Him. These things *God created, that we cannot change about ourselves*, represent our true nature or our identity. But at any point in time can any of us fully describe who we are? This identity resides so deeply within us that we spend a lifetime trying to figure out who we really are. This quest is important, because any deep satisfaction arises from authentically living out our God-created identity. But at any point the answer to the question "Who am I?" can be elusive. Why is this?

Our God-created identity may be difficult to see because it is surrounded by a character, guidance system, and self-image that *we created.* These elements of self are created over the course of our life through decisions we make—decisions about *what we believe to be true.* We make decisions about the best way to live, about who we need to be or want to be, and about who we are and how we fit into the overall scheme of things. Our embraced beliefs about any of these questions may be absolutely correct, far off base, or anything in between. That we have decided something is true in no way assures that it is true. This is a different question altogether.

These *embraced beliefs* play perhaps the most significant role of all in fashioning our lives and determining our experience of life. These beliefs form our self-image—who *we think* we are; our character—how we interact with other people and life; and our guidance system—our values, goals, ideals, priorities, and other elements which direct our decisions on every other topic. When we embrace such ideas, they become a part of us. These beliefs become the things *we assume to be true* about self and life. The sum of these beliefs form our sense of reality, for better or worse. Thus, we defend these ideas in the same way we would resist someone who was trying to cut off our arm. *In our perception* these embraced ideas feel like the very essence of us.

We easily confuse these parts of us which were *created by us* with the unchangeable parts of us which were created by God. What is the vital difference between what God has made and what we have made? These embraced beliefs can be changed at our discretion if we have sufficient reason to do so. If we change one of these beliefs, the self-image, character, or internal guidance built upon this belief will also change. Therefore, the way we express our life, build our life, and experience our life will change. It is here that the genius of God—in fashioning Covenant—shines most brightly.

Why did God not simply forgive us and drop off any additional instructions? Why did He show up in person, spend three years 24/7 with a small group of people? Jesus spent three years challenging and adjusting the embraced ideas of His disciples, so they would be able to fulfill their assigned roles in His Kingdom. What would the disciples lives have been like if Jesus had not spent years dealing with these misconceptions?

Our minds, hearts, and lives are challenged for another reason. Each newborn person is not only made in God's image; each also contains the nature of God's enemy, and is therefore under the sentence of death stated in Genesis Chapter Three. If God simply forgave our sins this nature would remain within us. Upon entry into Covenant, we enter the Kingdom of God and are indwelled by His Spirit. The nature of God and the nature of Satan cannot cohabitate within His Kingdom, or within an individual. In light of this reality, is there a compelling reason why Covenant was designed so it begins with our death, then rebirth as a new and different creature?

Many contend that the "sin nature" remains within us after we are Christians, and it is this nature which drives behaviors that oppose God's will. Though several New Testament passages are indistinct and can be construed in this way, the understanding of Covenant set forth in this book argues against the nature of Satan and the nature of God simultaneously inhabiting us. Consider the analogy in a similar Covenant. Adultery—sexual intercourse with someone not our spouse—breaks one Covenant as it initiates another. One "oneness"—shared identity—is broken as another is created. In a similar manner, the original state of humanity—oneness with God—was replaced by a breach between humanity and God. Humanity was joined to Satan and his rebellion, the nature of Satan came to reside in the original humans and all their descendants, and dominion over the earth was transferred from Adam and Eve to Satan in a Covenant exchange (Luke 4:6).

As we enter the New Covenant, our old life is put to death (carrying out the sentence of death of Genesis Chapter Three), and the temple of the Holy Spirit (I Corinthians 6:19). We are reborn as a new creature, indwelled by God and joined to Him in a state of oneness (John 17:20-23). This new creature is within the Kingdom of God (John 17:14).

Therefore, this new creature must no longer contain the nature of the enemy of God.

If a sin nature no longer resides within, why does this new creation still live such an imperfect life? We are basically restored to the pre-Fall state. In this pre-Fall state Adam and Eve were still subject to deception, as are we. But, in contrast to their sinless beginning, we bring with us a character, guidance system, and self-image that are largely unchanged as we enter God's Kingdom. Are the beliefs that formed these elements of ourselves all based on *actual truth*? Or are the previous beliefs of those who enter God's Kingdom largely based on something else? How many times in life have we followed our best lights to wrong conclusions? Perhaps more important, throughout history have the enemies of God powerfully influenced humanity to get things wrong? If we embrace these deceptions, what impact might this have on our being or the course of our lives?

Since we cannot perceive much of our true nature at any point, the day after we become a new creature how much of the reality of this creature can we perceive? Therefore, what we perceive as us once we are in the New Covenant still consists largely of elements we created in our pre-Christian life. In our perception, this is *our life*, and we tend to continue living it.

But God calls us to live a different life based on His truth, example, and leadership. What now? God calls us to obey and to love. Is it truly in our best interest to do so? Is our best life actually found by following God in an exacting way? Many say, "No." Why? Is it not true that everything God calls on us to do and be builds the best

Everything we are called to do and be according to the historic practices of Covenant, and everything God calls on us to do and be in Scripture, are the logical outworkings of the transformation and joining accomplished when we entered Covenant.

relationships, accrues the best consequences, and leads to a life blessed by Him? Why, then, do we resist His path? Because in our mind decisions have already been rendered for many key questions about life and self. Remember, from our vantage point our embraced ideas *represent reality*. Yet, it is these very ideas which lead us to disobey God and act in unloving ways. God asserts that His Word is truth. If our view differs from His, who is right? And, where did these alternate beliefs that we value so highly come from in the first place?

By entering the New Covenant we become a being with incredible potential and access to potentially unlimited resources. How could we NOT love the God who makes this possible with every fiber of our being? Yet, our love for Him remains a possibility, not a certainty. Everything we are called to do and be according to the historic practices of Covenant, and everything God calls on us to do and be in Scripture, are the logical outworkings of the transformation and joining accomplished when we entered Covenant. God simply calls on us to authentically live out this new life in Him. But He also recognizes the challenges we face in doing so. His Covenant plan provides a way to overcome these challenges. One challenge we often fail to recognize is the difference between *our perception* of truth and reality—based on buying into particular ideas—versus actual truth and reality.

Another challenge we face is understanding the various parts of ourselves. We have a true identity created by God, then re-created as we enter Covenant: we become a new creation with a new identity wholly distinct from our pre-Covenant self, now joined to God. We cannot alter the elements of this created nature. But we have a character that *we formed* by embracing various ideas. We may be irresponsible, thoughtful, entitled, generous, destructive, bitter, or many other things. We can change these characteristics. We have a guidance system formed by our beliefs

As we become aware of the things that need to change within us, we begin to recognize the role deception has played in our lives.

that points us toward some behaviors and away from others. Do we value key relationships above all, or will we sacrifice those around us for financial gain, power, or popularity? What appetites do we cultivate, including sexual tastes and preferences? Can key priorities or powerful appetites change? If one becomes a diabetic, can one re-direct an intense love for sweets in a healthier direction? Despite our current culture's assertions to the contrary, desires, appetites, and emotions are not expressions of our true identity—for all of these are subject to change.

It is vital to clearly differentiate the part of *self* which is created and unchangeable from the parts which are created by positive affirmations or by our response to life circumstances. All of the latter are subject to change, and we may be directed to do this in God's plan. The former is what we want to authentically express. Think back to the original questions in this section. When we become a Christian, what changes? What remains the same? Why are we still so imperfect? Does this distinction, in light of the realities of Covenant, bring clarity?

Why, then, is there confusion about our imperfection and transformation? We read terms like "the flesh," "the body of sin," and "the old person" or "old self. What do we understand these to be, in light of the changes we are discussing? What did God change, what are we to change, and how do these changes occur? Consider the following passages.

Therefore, if anyone is in Christ this person is a new creation:
II Corinthians 5:17

For we know that our old self was crucified with Him so
that the body ruled by sin might be done away with,
that we should no longer be slaves to sin—because anyone
who has died has been set free from sin. Romans 6:6-7

You were taught with regard to your former way of life, to put off your old self, which is being corrupted by its deceitful desires; to be made new in the attitude of your minds; and to put on the new self,

created to be like God in true righteousness and holiness.
Ephesians 4:22-24

Did you note that our old self in the Romans verse was crucified so the rule of sin in our lives would be broken (by stripping from us Satan's rebellious nature)? This death, rebirth, and transformed new life is wholly engineered by God; we play no role beyond submitting ourselves to this process. Then, this *same term* (old self) was used to describe elements of our old life which *we are instructed to alter.* Both of these elements of self—our fixed identity and the self-created aspects of self—comprised our old being. The former part of ourselves is made new upon entry into Covenant. What about the latter? These parts of self that we created come forward into Covenant largely intact. What are we to do with these aspects of ourselves if they lead us to stray from God's path? Does it help us to recognize that the entirety of these elements of ourselves are formed of ideas we have *embraced* as true, and firmly *believe* are true? What if, instead, these ideas are deceptions sold to us by the enemies of God?

In these verses we see several key truths. As we enter Covenant the old self was put to death, and by this we have been *set free from sin.* From other verses we know this means that we may on occasion commit rebellious acts, but our relationship to sin (rebellion) has fundamentally changed by entry into Covenant. We are no longer its slave. What does it mean to be a slave? One has no choice except to obey. When the rebellious nature of Satan was within us we could not wholeheartedly obey God at any point. How does this change once we are in Christ?

We can choose to obey—to follow God's path and plan, and to be faithful. Or, we can choose not to. Hence, the instruction we receive in the verse in Ephesians. We are to *put off the old self.* This picture of obedience suggests more than simply changing behavioral choices. We are to deal not just with our choices; we are to deal with *our self.* That is, we are charged with altering the self-created parts of ourselves, which fashion the ways we express ourselves and direct our lives. The

Ephesians verse notes that these parts of ourselves have been corrupted by *desires*. What is the relationship between desire and deception?

God's plan is not founded on rules, but relationship. What is God plan to deal with all of this? He invites us to play a key role in a *second transformation*. God instructs us to dismantle what *we built*—our character, guidance system, and self-image—to the extent that these differ from His truth. Then, to rebuild our expression and experience of life under His guidance. How do we do this? By embracing a new set of character-building and life-directing ideas based on His Truth. Why do we do this? To build relationships.

Do not conform to the pattern of this world, but be transformed by the renewing of your mind. Then you will be able to test and approve what God's will is—His good, pleasing, and perfect will.
Romans 12:2

We are now in an intimate relationship with God. But we only learn to love as we build this relationship and other relationships in the Body of Christ. At the same time, as we try to build these relationships we will encounter things within ourselves which oppose love and lead us to disobey. Some of our beliefs that form values, priorities, goals, our sense of self-interest, and *our path to our best life* will lead us in different directions. These ideas must change if they oppose love and faithfulness, or we will continue to be unloving and unfaithful. As we become aware of the things that need to change within us, we begin to recognize the role deception has played in our lives.

To deal effectively with deception—and fulfill our role in this second transformation—we must first understand deception. In the Garden of Eden the first humans were offered a deceptive path. Jesus was tempted. He was offered a deceptive path to rule the earth. Jesus declined this offer, but every human has been offered—and embraced—vastly more deception than any of us realize. What is deception, and where does it come from? The first two offers of deception just mentioned were made directly by Satan. I believe this is the ultimate source, directly or indirectly, of every human deception.

Deception is more than something not true. The best place to study the full nature of deception is in Genesis Chapter Three, which we will do in a later section. In essence, deception starts by convincing us that there is something we need for our best life—which lies outside of the life God ordains. Satan offered Eve the opportunity to become "as God." She desired this upgrade, then acted to obtain it. Every deception is founded upon a desire. We are offered an opportunity to enhance our lives in an important way.

Such enticements will not work unless a person embraces the importance of this offer for his or her life. This is necessary, because one soon discovers that the path to obtain this now-needed thing involves a moral compromise. One must violate God's Word in some way to receive this benefit—and thus damage one's relationship with God (which is the true motivation behind these offers). One's eyes must be so firmly fixed on the prize that he or she is willing to overlook any possible cost. The person must brush past God and His guardrails to reach for something so important, so vital … until one realizes that the promised benefits never materialize, and the cost of the compromise is vastly greater than anticipated.

A deceptive offer is by definition one we would never agree to if the terms were clearly laid out. Instead, benefits are exaggerated or fabricated and true costs are concealed. Eve grasped these realities quickly as she stood before God. He described the consequences of her decision. She simply replied, "The serpent deceived me, and I ate" (Genesis 3:13). In other situations, though, the full impact of deception is not evident for years or decades. This is especially the case when we embrace deceptions which become part of our character, guidance system, or self-image. These ideas become a gift which keeps on giving, as we continue to pursue illusory benefits offered to us by the enemies of God.

As we confront issues of faithfulness or obedience, the strength of our opposition to God comes from our undying optimism that the beliefs we have chosen and the course these have charted for our lives will ultimately lead to the benefits we sought by embracing these ideas in the first place. This, plus the perception that God is asking us to violate something of ourselves by requiring what He requires of us. God unduly restricts; Satan offers unbounded gratification. These are our perceptions. But are they accurate?

God has given us His revelation of Truth, the Scriptures, as a reference point for actual truth. We can then compare anything we *feel, think, desire, do*, and *are* with His truth. If any element is out of sync with His Word, what does this mean? We can stand next to Eve and simply say, "We have been deceived."

What is the solution to this problem—the problem of *what we want, what we have become,* and *who we believe ourselves to be*? The first step is to acknowledge our capacity to be deceived. By definition, deception is a false idea that we believe is true. We must recognize the limitation of our perceptions about what is real and true, especially in comparison to God. Second, we must carefully consider the cost of deception in our lives thus far, and the cost going forward. By following deceptive guidance we oppose God and incur predictable negative consequences in the moral universe He created for us to inhabit. More importantly, in the end we will give a personal account to Him and see our eternity impacted by our faithfulness, or lack thereof. Third, we must realize that we come into the Kingdom of God already equipped with a lifetime supply of deception woven into our being. Our task is to rid ourselves of this deception. We are also at continual risk of embracing more such beliefs. Thus, we must learn to guard our minds and hearts.

Romans 12:2 directs us to the process of identifying and rejecting these lies, then embracing God's truth about each issue of self and life. When we reject the old ideas *because they are lies*, and embrace new ideas, we form anew a character, guidance system, and self-image based upon truth. This second transformation is a lifelong process.

In the terminology of Scripture, we *take off* these manifestations of the old life. Then we *put on* elements of life based on truth, faithfulness, love, and the reality of our connection to a divine Other. Obedience is a much broader question than making correct in-the-moment decisions. Obedience in a larger sense is to follow God's path of growth and transformation. As we encounter one issue of relationship and life after another, we are offered the opportunity to conform ourselves to God's plan and His path at every point. We can choose to love, or learn to love. We can choose to obey, or learn to obey. Or, we can continue to be guided by deception. This choice is ours.

If we are faithful to shift the foundation of our lives from deception to truth on an ongoing basis, our resistance to the ways of God will fade. Our relationships will improve. The consequences of evil in our lives will gradually be replaced with good consequences and God's blessings. We will fall more and more deeply in love with Truth and its Author. Our affinity for the deceptions of our old life will be replaced by an abhorrence of deception and its cost, and a desire to uproot these things from our life at any cost. God's goal is that our outward expression and inner experience of life accurately reflect what His transformation initially created in the core of our being. God simply invites us to authentically express the being we have become in Covenant with Him. We are to "live up to what we have already attained" (Philippians 3:16). Who can argue when God invites us to be ourselves?

External obedience to a set of injunctions is not the same thing as doing what is necessary to build a love relationship with God . This point was graphically illustrated in the lives of many Pharisees.

Though this process appears simple, consider its far-reaching implications. Literally any element of our life that is out of accord with God's plan is subject to change. Both our way of life and our experience of life can be radically transformed by the combination of the two transformations of Covenant.

God's goal for us goes beyond learning to love Him and others. He also wants us to enjoy this life more than any other. He loves us, and delights in showing His love. Part of the enemy's deceptions are aimed at keeping us from recognizing and appreciating the many things God has done in our lives. As we replace a never-satisfied discontent with contentment and appreciation, our experience of life will begin to resemble that of the godly men and women in Scripture.

Covenant also integrates the historic practices of Christianity into a seamless whole. From prayer, to the ways we are supposed to treat each other, to giving, to the Lord's Supper—and literally every other practice and principle of our faith—all of these flow from *the nature of the relationship we have entered with God*. Covenant is the vehicle through which God displays His love toward us and requires our love in return. Therefore, our confidence in God's intervention in our lives can be based on more than a "faith" consisting only of wishful thinking and the assumption that God shares our view of the best outcome. God is faithful to His Covenant with us. His displays of love will fall within the parameters of Covenant. He has obligated Himself to seek our best interests and has unlimited resources to carry out this intent. One question remains: "What is truly in our best interests?" Do we trust God's love to the point that we allow Him to answer this question?

What is the source of this understanding of Covenant? In 1885 noted Christian leader H. Clay Trumbull wrote a book entitled *The Blood Covenant: A Primitive Rite and Its Bearing on Scripture* [1]. In this book Trumbull first examines the fundamental nature of another covenant: a blood covenant. Like Marriage, this relationship is noted worldwide throughout recorded history. This form of relationship was well known in Israel during biblical times. Trumbull noted the defining feature of this covenant—the exchange of identities, and the shared life which results. He then studied its nature, structure, and function. Next, he examined the New Covenant in light of this understanding. The New Covenant shares this defining feature, and has an analogous nature, structure, and function. (As does Marriage.)

As Trumbull considered the New Covenant, his understanding of blood covenant shed new light on many aspects of God's offer and behavior. "The blood of Jesus poured out for us" is usually viewed as only a sacrificial act, one intended to pay our penalty for sin. While this is obviously true, the ancient understanding of the offer of blood as an offer of one's *life*—specifically the offer to join one's life to another via Covenant through the agency of this blood—also fits the biblical picture (John 6:56). Thus, Christ's outpoured blood was also an offer of new life—as a new creature who incorporates the life of God via His Spirit (Romans 6:4). While forgiveness is an indispensable part of entering this relationship, the most important aspect of Covenant is our new life that is now joined to God (see John 17, the entire chapter; Romans 8:9-11). And, our most important task is to build this new life and relationship, instead of simply confining ourselves to a checklist of approved behaviors.

The ultimate goal of Covenant is consistent love-in-action. By faithfulness we build our relationship with God into a lifelong love affair. God's intent is that our growing capacity to love be extended to those in the Body of Christ, then to those not in this Covenant. Every aspect of Covenant, along with aspects of our internal wiring system, are designed by God toward these ends. A byproduct of relationship building, and paradoxically the element which allows it to most fully succeed, is the ongoing second transformation of Covenant. The success of this transformation is in turn predicated on the reality of the first transformation. We need a new life to solve our truly unsolvable problem. God graciously offers us one. His gift is free, but paradoxically also requires everything of us. We must consistently apply every resource God has placed at our disposal over a lifetime to build this relationship to its potential, and build ourselves to our potential. Covenant is an "all-in" thing. The passive gratitude

I apply this understanding to three tasks: building a relationship with God, building the new life received by entry into the New Covenant, and playing our assigned role in the "second transformation" of our character and guidance system.

engendered by the notion that "God does it all" is far from the posture called for in Covenant.

God's ultimate intent is that we reflect His love, and build lives in His Kingdom that express His truth before a world that desperately needs to see the reality of God. As we approach these tasks we find ourselves on a battleground between truth and deception. The outcome of this battle in each life comes down to a series of decisions on our part about what is true. Do we believe in Jesus, and thus accept His offer of Covenant? And, if we do, will we follow His plan in whole and in every part? Or will our lives be reduced by continuing to embrace deception?

This question is played out on a daily basis as our culture embraces beliefs that are moving further from God's Word. Many who profess Christ also embrace and champion these ideas. Are new cultural beliefs the path to the best life for all of us, or simply the latest wave of deception washing across the landscape? The belief that *one's chosen beliefs represent reality* is certainly true in the eyes of the beholder. Is there a transcendent truth, though, by which our lives will be judged? On this matter God allows us to draw our own conclusion, at least for the moment. But our conclusions, as always, do not define or determine reality. God does these things, and He has spoken on these questions very clearly.

What does it mean to obey God? We certainly do not want to offend God through disobedience. But external obedience to a set of injunctions is not the same thing as doing what is necessary to build a love relationship with God. This point was graphically illustrated in the lives of many Pharisees. If our lives are to be a reflection of God, we do well to note that He created Covenant. This relationship is the vehicle through which He displays His love toward us and requires our love in return. It is entry into Covenant which grants us access into the Kingdom of God, and it is faithfulness to Covenant which equips us to become good citizens in our forever-home. I believe that obedience entails following God's example of Covenant faithfulness. In this we find not only the *what* of obedience, but also the *why* and the *how*. This is God's plan for our future—now and for eternity. Obedience, I believe, is synonymous with choosing to carrying out God's plan—His Covenant plan—in our lives.

This author has accepted Trumbull's scholarship and analysis of Covenant relationships at face value. In this volume I apply this understanding to three tasks: building a relationship with God, building the new life received by entry into the New Covenant, and playing our assigned role in the "second transformation" of our character and guidance system. Nothing is added to Scripture as we approach these tasks. This work and this series simply revolve around an historically correct definition of the word *Covenant*. Scripture interprets itself, but we must properly define the words and concepts it contains—ideally, using definitions current at the time words were spoken or penned. Trumbull's definition of Covenant appears to represent this understanding, though it is freely acknowledged that a scholarly proof of this is beyond the scope of this author.

This author's particular interests for more than forty years have been developing an intimate relationship with God, spiritual growth, mentoring, teaching, and building Marriage and family according to God's plan (as outlined in this three-volume series). This view of Covenant has been the integrating point for these pursuits for thirty-seven of those years. Everything said in this book has been tried and proven in one life or many. While this does not prove this view of Covenant at an academic level, the author bears witness of the fruit produced by this understanding.

What we *assume to be true* is one of the most powerful forces directing our lives—and one of the least recognized. God had a plan for the Israelites—from which they often departed. Jesus introduced the New Covenant to His followers in the conversation recorded in John 6. Most who heard His words were so disconcerted that they turned and walked away. When we hear the exacting nature of God's plan for our lives and note the departure of this plan from our desires and preferences, we are taken aback or offended. People's view of the fundamental nature of a relationship with God was an issue in ancient Israel, as it was in Jesus' day. It remains so in our day. Covenant seems always to present a problem for people. Is the answer to this question

Covenant is the heart of God's plan for humanity. It appears that the nature of this relationship—as Trumbull describes it—is the very heart of hearts of God's plan.

to refashion God's offer in accord with what we assume to be true?

Covenant is the heart of God's plan for humanity. It appears that the nature of this relationship—as Trumbull describes it—is the very heart of hearts of God's plan. A correct understanding of the various transformations we undergo, how they occur, and the role we are assigned by God for each step is critical. This key will unlock the potential of God's plan in individual lives and in the body of Christ. But this understanding is not commonly held among the Body of Christ in our day. This perhaps explains many things of concern in the landscape of Christendom. This is a plan we all struggle to understand and implement even if we are aware of it. Yet this plan is *God's only plan for our life.*

Our only hope resides in a relationship of growing intimacy with God. But faithfulness to our Covenant is a prerequisite for such intimacy. The transformation of our nature—as well as the transformation of our mind, heart, will, and character—is vital if we are to develop a passionate love for God. This love for God is in turn a prerequisite for such a degree of faithfulness. The growing capacity to love that results from our faithfulness is vital if we are to fulfill God's plans for us in the Kingdom of God. We must be filled with this same love to reach a lost and dying world. In other words, for any of God's plan to work as intended we must faithfully implement His plan in whole and in every part.

Therefore, I appeal to my brothers and sisters in Christ who devote their lives to mastering God's Word: rightly divide God's Word in this matter. See if the foundation upon which this book is built—this understanding of Covenant—represents the mind and heart of God, as I believe it does.

CHAPTER ONE

WHAT IS A COVENANT?

WHY ARE WE NOT JUST FORGIVEN?

I wish my life was ...
I wish I was ...

Scripture speaks of a new life when we enter a relationship with God. Thus, when we enter this relationship, what do we expect? A huge change in what goes on inside us and what happens in our life? We just joined God's family. Our eternal address is assured. But many who have done as instructed by current teaching and Christian friends are still waiting for something. They "made a decision," prayed the "sinner's prayer," and attend church. Now they are waiting for the new, different, and better life they expect God to create for them. They want the victorious life described to them on Sunday mornings. They are waiting for the abundant life ... and waiting ... and waiting ... as they continue to drown in frustration, confusion, uncertainty, or adversity. Non-Christian friends say we are fools for buying into the idea of a loving God who offers us a better life. Are we?

Are we forgiven through the sacrifice of Jesus—only to keep living the same life? If we were merely forgiven, and left unchanged, there would be no reason to expect different lives going forward. However, the language of Scripture says we are different. "New creature," "new creation," "born again." If we are changed, though, why do our lives still look so much the same? What does this new life mean if there is little difference in the way we feel or live? We hear phrases like "God does it all." "We live under grace, not law." "Christ's sacrifice paid it all." And from some we hear, "We are all terrible sinners, totally corrupt, with nothing good inside us and nothing worthwhile to offer." Do any of these teachings point the way to a new, different, and better life?

If God does it all, what do we do? Do God's rules even matter? If not, why not live the way I always have?

Is the Christian life just a fire insurance policy? If God does it all, what do we do? Do God's rules even matter? If not, why not live the way I always have? If all my sins are paid for, and my eternal home is secure, who cares whether what I do is right or wrong? Who even has a right to tell me which is which? Is Christianity a false promise of a new life? Or does it sell us a life that doesn't work as well as our old one? Why do the Scriptures keep talking about the "new person" we have become?

We may see few people around us living radically transformed lives, if any. What, then, does this new life under God's leadership mean ? What are we waiting for? And how does this change we seek—whatever it is—come about?

The promises in Scripture about a new and better life are real. The offer of a transformed life is real. The offer of a much different—and much better—experience of life is real. But these things do not come about by praying a prayer and "accepting Jesus as our Savior." These things do not come about through *rules*, whether we try to keep them or do not bother to try.

The new life we seek comes about through entering a Covenant relationship with God on His terms, then choosing to be faithful to that relationship. The things we want come about through building a relationship with God. In this relationship God offers us many good and important things—things that are vital if we are to live our best life. While God's love is unconditional, His gifts and blessings are *absolutely conditional.* In a Covenant relationship certain things are required of us for best results.

Unfortunately, in Christian teaching these days it is often unclear what God does require. If anything, we may be told to "not sin." While avoiding wrong behaviors is of benefit, is *rule-keeping* the path to the life we seek? We do what we do for reasons, ones we have decided are good reasons. Is the "abundant" life about refraining from doing things I enjoy? If not, what is the path that actually leads to a transformed and abundant life?

To answer these questions we must understand Covenant. Covenant is the type of relationship God designed to *relate to us* and *transform us*. Many people, after becoming Christians, wait for God to transform them and their lives. If we understand Covenant, we understand why this rarely happens. As we enter a relationship with God, He transforms us as much as He is ever going to in the depths of our being (at the level of identity and nature). But this initial transformation does little to change the way we live. For the way we live to change a *second transformation* must occur—a transformation of our perceptions, guidance system, character, beliefs, priorities, goals, ideals, desires, and many other things. These must change for the life we experience to change, and for the ways we relate to other people to change. This second transformation is something *God delegates to us* under His leadership. The revolution we wanted to see in our life when we entered a relationship with God can certainly happen—but only if we follow God's plan to transform our lives.

We must take very specific steps under God's direction to *dismantle the old life* we built, and then *build a new one* that authentically expresses the new creature we have become.

Covenant is a detailed plan designed by God to join us to Himself, then teach us to love as He loves. Our identity and nature became new and different as we enter Covenant with Him. The Spirit of God lives within us. The love, power, and resources of God are available to us. But we must take very specific steps under God's direction to *dismantle the old life* we built, and then *build a new one* that authentically expresses the new creature we have become—a creature who reflects God, and our new relationship with Him.

In Covenant God is now with us, but are we with Him? Will we do as He says to build the life He has made possible?

DON'T CHRISTIANS ALREADY KNOW ALL THIS?

If what we are saying about the nature of our relationship with God is so important, surely every knowledgeable Christian understands these things, right? Unfortunately, this is not the case. In our culture and our "modern" world, in contrast to most cultures throughout history, there is no relationship between people that resembles Covenant. The one exception used to be Marriage—which is also a Covenant given to humanity by God. In recent decades, sadly, concepts of Marriage have shifted far from the historic understanding. Thus, we have no cultural frame of reference for Covenant other than the vestiges of traditional marriage which remain. How, then, are we to understand the two Covenant relationships given to humanity by God?

Today most people within the Christian community view these two Covenants as a form of contract. I have heard the same sound bite from a number of Christian teachers: "Covenant is a contract, but one written by God." Why is this confusing? These covenant relationships and a third highlighted in this book series—a Blood Covenant—are not contracts. These are different in nature, structure, and purpose from a contract. If we misunderstand these two relationships as we try to build them, might this impact the success of the relationship? Is the success of Marriage or relationships with God an issue today in our Christian culture?

WHAT IS A CONTRACT?

Let's first look at what these relationships are *not*. What is a contract? We are all familiar with formal and informal contracts. Contracts hold our society and world together. Our legal system, the rules and regulations of modern life, our social expectations ... in short, everything that is deemed acceptable or unacceptable in daily life arises from this model. We enter and remain in these agreements to promote our self-interest—to make our world a more sane, safe, orderly, and enjoyable place to live. Contracts attempt to define what we must do to live the best life, and what we must not do to avoid tearing our world or our lives apart. To this extent contracts are useful.

Contracts are agreements between separate parties. People do not make contracts with themselves. There are rewards for engaging in certain behaviors and penalties for not obeying the terms of the contract. Contracts involve *an exchange* of property or other resources. Contracts are about promoting self-interest. The ideal is to offer something but receive something of greater perceived value. Contracts are kept in force by ongoing agreement of the parties. If one does not fulfill the terms of the contract, the other is free to walk away.

The contract model has weaknesses. Contracts are a weak glue, held together only by agreement, willingness to comply, and an ongoing belief that the benefits of this arrangement are *enough* to stay in the relationship. When dealing with the messiness and sacrifices involved in a Marriage, at times it's unclear if one is getting a "good deal," even in a good Marriage. If one has no other reason for staying in the relationship, and we seem to be giving more than we are getting, what often happens?

In a New Covenant relationship with God we are told many things that we will not agree with in the beginning. We are told to do many things we will not initially want to do. We are even told to do things that seem to violate our very nature. What now? If we are just in this thing to promote our perception of our self-interest, how do we respond to God's Word and His directions?

At first glance, God's laws—the Ten Commandments and the rest of His injunctions in Scripture about behavior—seem to fit this *con-*

tractual pattern. "Here is a list of things to do: you are rewarded for obeying, and punished for disobeying." As we will see later, this is not actually the case. But this misunderstanding at least makes sense.

IS A COVENANT A CONTRACT?

A contract only determines what we are to do. The type of Covenant we are studying *transforms who we are.* A contract is between separate individuals, while a Covenant joins us in a unique bond to another being. One is about rules, the other is about new life as a new creation, now in a unique relationship to another. Contracts trade rule-keeping for reward. In Covenants the focus shifts to *building our new life and our new relationship*. Covenant is about loving our Covenant partner through action. What might go missing if we have a contractual viewpoint of Marriage or a relationship with God? What if we try to build these relationships by doing only what we want to do? Why is this not the best approach? Because we will miss the very heart of what God is offering us in a Marriage, or in a relationship with Him. Covenant is the tool God uses to build new, different, and better lives.

What might go missing if we have a contractual viewpoint of marriage or a relationship with God? What if we try to build these relationships by doing only what we want to do?

In Covenant we are given new life. We are joined to another by a bond of identity and nature. What does this mean? The other being is in us, and we are in them. This is the "one flesh" of Marriage, or the "oneness" produced by our being "in Christ" and by the indwelling Spirit of God. We are told by God to "love others as we love ourselves." In Covenant, God makes this easy for us by making the other party literally an extension of ourselves. But this is only the beginning. Next we are to learn and apply God's definition of love (which is far beyond our own) to love the other.

What terms could we write into a contract that could even define love, much less produce it? What terms can we write into a contract that will transform us, or give us new life, or join us to another in a bond of shared identity? The first thing to realize about Covenant is that, by entering one, we change. This, in turn, changes everything. This transformation becomes the reason for everything else that occurs in the relationship. This reality is the key to our new, different, and better life. This internal change occurs when we enter the relationship. But this inner transformation only makes a new life possible. It is up to us to build this new and different life hand-in-hand with God.

Let's think for a moment about God's injunction that we love others. How do we comply with this? At the outset we cannot do, and will not feel, and cannot see things in a way that allows us to love others perfectly. In fact, we will not even get close. We will have trouble doing or being many of the things God says in the beginning. What now? In the contractual view there is no prospect of our lives being actually transformed—other than by trying harder. If you have tried this approach you already recognize its limitations.

In the beginning we will fall short in our contractual obligation, and there is nothing we can do about it. If we cannot do what we are told to do, what do we do next? We cease taking God's Word seriously. The words in Scripture become metaphors and myths … not a solid foundation on which we can build our new life. God's injunctions become just another great idea—like world peace—that cannot be achieved. Thus, we obey as best we can, or when we feel like it, and hope that God understands.

Or we go off in search of another answer.

Of course, the alternative is to follow God's actual plan.

COVENANT IS ABOUT BUILDING OUR NEW RELATIONSHIP

Covenant is not about rule-keeping. Instead, it is about *relationship-building*. Doing what is necessary to build our relationship with God requires more adjustment on our part than we realize. We must change the ways we choose to express our life. Part of this is simply choosing to do different things. Part is learning to grow the new person we have become to maturity. And part is to go back and dismantle our old self. What Scripture refers to as the "old self" is the guidance system and character we developed through our choices in our old life. We made these choices based on what we believed to be true about self and life. However, those things we chose to believe based on the influence of other people and our culture may not actually be true. God's plan involves embracing new truths and rejecting things about ourselves that are no longer true—if they ever were true. Why? Because God wants our lives to be *an authentic expression of the new being we have become.*

COVENANT IS ABOUT NEW LIFE

Let's think for a moment about the new life we received. It is from God. We now contain the Spirit of God. Christ is in us. What would an authentic life look like for this being? God equates love for Him and obedience (John 14:15-24). Jesus' last command was to teach others to "obey all that I commanded you" (Matthew 28:20). Jesus is *the Word*—God's revelation lived out (John 1:1). We are to be one with Jesus just as Jesus is one with the Father (John 17:20, 21). So, would it make sense that our new life is to perfectly reflect what is in God's Word? The truth He has revealed to us becomes our goal and our guide.

But success requires more than merely saying, "I want to."

COVENANT IS ABOUT FAITHFULNESS

As we will see, there is another goal and guide for our lives: *faithfulness to our Covenant.* The Scriptures are full of injunctions—things we are to do and be. If not a "to-do list," what are these things? Here a proper understanding of Covenant helps us immensely. According to the historic understanding of Covenant, there are many things we must do in this relationship. The sum of these things is an excellent definition of "love in action." The things God tells us to do build the best possible relationship with Him and with other people. Contracts tell us only what to do. Covenant brings many new reasons into the picture for doing things we are simply told to do in Scripture. In addition, Covenant tells us how we become able to do what God tells us to do. Covenant is about doing for the sake of *loving, building,* and *growing*. The highest priority in a Covenant is to be faithful: faithful to do all the things we are called to do in Covenant, and faithful to the one with whom we are in Covenant. Why? Because everything we are told to do is constructive. Anything different will damage the relationship or damage the other party. We are to learn how to build consistently. That is, we are to learn how to love consistently.

Once I realized everything in Scripture is essentially about building relationships and learning to love others, and once I saw that there is a plan through which I could actually grow into doing these things, everything changed for me. Covenant opens the door to this understanding.

LOVE IS ABOUT MORE THAN RULES

Let's think about rule-following in light of another Covenant: Marriage. Imagine for a moment that you just looked into the eyes of the person you will eventually marry. It registers in both of your hearts: "This is the one." So, you take out your pen and write down the ten or so things this person really despises. Then you devote yourself to *not doing* each of these things for the next year … and this is about all you do in the relationship. At the end of the year, how is your relationship going? Not very well, because you have not done anything to build a relationship! Not offending someone is part

You take out your pen and write down the ten or so things this person really despises. Then you devote yourself to *not doing* each of these things for the next year … and this is about all you do in the relationship.

of building a relationship, but much more is involved to build a love relationship to the point that you want to join together in Marriage. If most people devoted the attention and effort to their Marriage that they devote to building a relationship with God, what kind of Marriage would they have? Try devoting only an hour a week of polite attention to your wife, and take no further action based on what she says. See how this turns out.

Consider the command: "Love the Lord your God with all your heart and with all your soul and with all your mind and with all your strength" (Mark 12:30). According to Jesus this is God's greatest command, but how can we actually do this? How can we make ourselves feel love for God with our whole heart even if we want to? If we are married, or have ever had a serious relationship with someone, or even a strong relationship with a parent or relative, we know something about building and maintaining a relationship. Instead of treating our wife or husband the way most people treat God (the hour-a-week plan), what if we took our relationship-building skills and applied them to building a relationship with God?

Covenant is about love in action. This requires that we actually do loving things. God knows how a heart of love grows. He created the hearts that feel and express love. The four elements that create the deepest experience of love are trust, respect, commitment, and investment. God's Covenant plan is to trust, trust in, commit, be joined, and then fully invest in the life of the other. His plan is specifically designed to produce love-in-action, love-in-experience, and love-for-a-lifetime. This is true for Marriage and true for a relationship with Him.

God's Covenant plan is more broad and extensive than this introduction. Think for a moment what your life would be like if your people skills improved dramatically. What would happen to your character if counterproductive things were stripped away and replaced by constructive things. What if your direction system in life was stripped of things you thought would be good for you that instead prove *not* to be good for you? What if these were replaced by guidance toward things that offer true satisfaction? And what if you walked hand-in-hand

This offer is not just words or empty metaphor. This is the promise and plan of the Living God for your life.

with the God of the Universe, One whose agenda is to do things in and through you that only God could do? This offer is not just words or empty metaphor. This is the promise and plan of the Living God for your life. But something very special and, frankly, rather difficult is required of you. In return, you must give Him *everything*. Covenant is an all-in relationship: everything we have, everything we are, and everything we can become. All of this is offered to our Covenant partner according to the historic understanding of Covenant. But there is wonderful news! This works both ways. We are all in, but so is God! Jesus has already shown us what this looks like on His part, with more to come.

Would you be interested in a plan in which God transforms you in your deepest being and joins you to Himself? Then uses this relationship with Him and other people to teach you how to build the life you really want, and the relationship with Him you really want? How do you think we will feel about God as we commit ourselves to Him and His plan, enter a relationship with Him, watch this plan unfold, then experience its amazing benefits? Enthusiastically obeying His first and greatest commandment is the only response that makes sense. God has a plan. But this plan must be properly understood and faithfully implemented to produce the results God intends, and the results we most deeply desire—even if we do not yet realize it.

MY INTRODUCTION TO COVENANT

I became a Christian in 1977 during my first year of medical school. I soon joined a church with an outstanding teacher and became involved in a Navigator ministry, an organization that focuses on spiritual growth and mentoring. With input from these sources I learned much and grew much in the next few years. The next major step in my Christian life was attending a Kay Arthur Bible study on

Covenant in 1983[2]. (Don't let these dates scare you. You don't need a degree in archeology to read this!) Kay referenced a book by H. Clay Trumbull as a key source for understanding Covenant. I found a copy of this book, *The Blood Covenant, a Primitive Rite and Its Bearing on Scripture*[3], initially published in 1885, and was captivated by what I read. Initially, I found an explanation for everything in the Christian life. Until this point there was no obvious relationship between the many things we do—baptism, the Lord's Supper, treating each other well, prayer, giving, helping, worship services, sharing Christ with others, being careful to obey God's commands, and all the other aspects and practices that make up Christianity. All of these things in isolation are good things. But the only reason for doing them seemed to be "because God says so."

Each ritual and practice relates to some aspect of Covenant. There is a reason for each part and a reason behind the whole plan.

However, we do each of these things *because of Covenant.* These things are not about obedience per se. Each instruction in Scripture has to do with either relationship-building or personal growth and transformation—all for the sake of building better relationships. The entirety of Scripture is about faithfulness to our Covenant and our God. Each ritual and practice relates to some aspect of Covenant. There is a reason for each part and a reason behind the whole plan. Over the next few years I applied this understanding to every aspect of my Christian life and to teaching and mentoring others. As I did so, deeper realities became evident. Covenant is a plan. A definite series of steps must be followed if we are to grow and develop as God describes in Scripture. Growth and transformation are required for our relationship with God and our other relationships to improve. That is, our ability to love as God instructs depends directly on the extent to which we grow and transform.

One of the most important discoveries of all was the role that the transformation which occurred when I entered Covenant plays in obeying God's commands. Some of God's commands were far removed from *my* ideas about how to build the best life. These commands seemed to violate my self-interest. However, at a certain point I realized that who I am had changed when I entered the New Covenant. If I became a new and different person, what happened to the self-interest I was so anxious to promote? Had my self-interest also changed? Yes. But, what does the self-interest of this new creation look like?

I found that God's commands did not oppose my new nature. In fact they perfectly reflected my new nature!

Also, it became increasingly clear to me that many things I thought were true about life were simply wrong. Initially I thought I was being asked by God to ram a square peg of obedience into the round hole of my nature—where it did not fit. Then it dawned on me that I had a new nature. Perhaps I did not know the "new me" as well as I thought. I found that God's commands did not oppose my new nature. In fact they perfectly reflected my new nature! These were the things I wanted to do all along; I just had not realized it! It became increasingly evident that many ways I was choosing to live my life, brought forward from my old life, were now out of sync with the being I had become. Forty years later God is still inviting me to match the ways I live with the reality of who I am.

We must not only realize these realities are real, we must learn to harness their power. It also became evident that God created certain parts of us that are designed to interact with Covenant and with God's truth in Scripture—our mind, heart, and will. It is only by properly combining all of these elements—according to God's plan—that we can grow and be transformed according to the pattern God shows us in Scripture. Thus, I say: "Covenant is not just a tie that binds; it is also a plan."

This plan is the heart of God's plan for each person and for all of humanity. A plan to build a life that is truly worth living.

REDISCOVERING THE HISTORIC UNDERSTANDING OF COVENANT

THE BLOOD COVENANT

Jesus said to them, "Very truly I tell you, unless you eat the flesh of the Son of Man and drink his blood, you have no life in you. Whoever eats my flesh and drinks my blood has eternal life, and I will raise them up at the last day...Whoever eats my flesh and drinks my blood remains in me, and I in them" ... On hearing it, many of his disciples said, "This is a hard teaching. Who can accept it?" ... From this time many of his disciples turned back and no longer followed Him (John 6:53-66, excerpts).

I suspect when you read this Scripture passage for the first time you may have had the same reaction I had when I first read it. We were puzzled and a bit disconcerted. We were not sure quite what to make of what Jesus was saying. As Christians we know this has something to do with the church ritual of Communion. But, to say the least, we do not fully understand these statements. Then we note the reaction of His followers, who were obviously disturbed by these words. We assume they were as baffled by what Jesus said as we are, but this is completely incorrect. Jesus' followers did not erupt, then storm out of the room, because they did not understand what He meant. Many turned and walked away *because they understood exactly what He was saying*. The problem? These were the most mind-bending words they could imagine coming from someone who claimed to be God Himself. What did Jesus' hearers that day understand that we do not?

To best answer this question, let's go back to H. Clay Trumbull (1830-1903) and his story of discovery. Like any good detective story, this one started with what looked like an unexplainable coincidence. Let me first introduce you to the man. He is termed a world-famous author (fifteen books) and editor. Often called "the father of Sunday school," he pioneered the American Sunday school movement, then became president of the American Sunday School Society. He was a good friend of noted evangelist D.L. Moody and grandfather of internationally known missionary Elisabeth Elliot, whose story was recounted in the 2005 movie *End of the Spear*.[4] Thus he was a man of immense credibility. His deep and fruitful relationship with God impacted many lives in his generation.

At one point Trumbull lived in a location frequented by missionaries on furlough (those temporarily returning from the mission field). He heard one of these missionaries tell of a strange ritual of the tribe he lived among. Two people would take each other's blood into their bodies. This was accompanied by a public ceremony that included vows of deepest commitment spoken before each other and their gods. Each person was also cut in a way that would cause scarring; this was intended to be an ever-visible reminder of this joining. Gifts of clothing, weapons, and food were exchanged. Then there was a feast for the participants and assembled witnesses. The two people were now joined by the deepest and most sacred bond. They became part of each other's families. They shared friends, enemies, debts, obligations, and resources. They were to come to each other's aid at the risk of their lives, and they were to regard the interests of the other party equal to, if not more important than, their own. It became their most sacred duty to uphold the honor of the other. This bond was indissoluble except by death. The missionary had not been allowed to witness this rite until he had gained the trust of the tribe, for this represented one of its oldest and most sacred traditions.

The two people were now joined by the deepest and most sacred bond. They became part of each other's families. They shared friends, enemies, debts, obligations, and resources.

Soon after hearing this account, Trumbull was speaking with another missionary who worked among a primitive tribe in a remote

make any sacrifice to fulfill these vows. Their lives and futures are to be inextricably joined.

- *Blood is taken from each and taken in by the other via several possible techniques. The blood of each is understood to contain the identity of each, and the offering of it to represent the offer of one's life to the other.*
- *A mark is generally made on the body to be a visible, permanent token of these vows. Alternately, an amulet or other ornament becomes the symbol of this joining, and is to be worn henceforth.*
- *Clothing is exchanged to signify the exchange of identity.*
- *Armor and weapons are exchanged to signify the obligation of mutual defense.*
- *A meal is eaten by the parties and the assembled witnesses to signify the obligation of mutual provision.*
- *Gifts are exchanged to signify the obligation of mutual blessing. The two often compete to give the most extravagant offering.*
- *Now that identity is altered and joined, relatives are shared. Full familial obligations are in force toward the other's extended family.*
- *Friends and enemies become mutual, as do obligations of friendship or vengeance.*
- *Debts, assets, obligations, and resources are shared.*
- *Basically, any asset, resource, capability, or potential of one is at the other's disposal as needed.*
- *The honor of each is at stake in fulfilling these vows. The highest honor is found in upholding the honor of the other party.*
- *Temporal and supernatural consequences for unfaithfulness are assumed. For thieves or others whose character could not be trusted in any other circumstance, these bonds are held most sacred and almost never violated. It is counted the height of foolishness to incur a divine enemy in such a way.*

While these details of Covenant ceremonies are of interest, the thing we must understand to truly comprehend Covenant is the underlying principle: the changing and joining of identity through the exchange of blood. People's pledges and vows *do not* bind two together in Covenant. These vows state the parties' intentions to *live out the logical consequences of a new reality* which is about to come into being. What binds them together is *offering to another something which contains their identity—their blood—then receiving the other's blood into their body.* The identity—the very life—of each has entered the other. Each person now has an identity and nature which incorporates the other, creating a new, melded identity for each. Vows recognize that the other party will be treated as what they have become. If I enter Covenant with another person, I will treat that person as well as I treat myself, because this other person *is now a part of myself,* and *I am part of them* in a real and practical sense. Every other aspect of this relationship—in terms of behavior, attitude, and practice—is a consequence of the changing and joining of identity and nature.

What are the implications of this core principle of Covenant? Covenant may call for massive, even heroic sacrifice by one or both parties. On a more mundane level, the sharing of material goods and relationships involves every facet of the existence of both parties. Covenant basically says, "I will die for your sake, and I will live for your sake," which is perhaps even harder over the course of a lifetime. Former identities and natures cease to exist; these die and are replaced by new natures and identities which are now joined. Individuality is maintained in one sense, but identity and nature are shared at the very core of their respective beings.

With Trumbull's mature relationship with God and deep understanding of Scripture, one can easily see where he would next turn his attention: to correlating this particular understanding with the New Covenant. Might Jesus' outpoured blood on the cross, and His words about taking His blood into ourselves, be related to the ancient practice of Blood Covenanting? What about Jesus' death and resurrection? What about the imagery of our own death as we enter the New Covenant? What about being indwelled by the Holy Spirit as we are raised to new life as a new creature? What about being *in Jesus,* and *He in us*? Might His talk about "becoming one with Him" and "one with each other," as in John 17, be related to this Covenant concept? Or the fact that He became human in the first place, or took on our debt of sin and paid it? Or the fact that all who enter Covenant with Him are now family—not only with Him but with each other as well?

Over the course of Jesus' life on earth He experienced every human emotion, from most profound joy to deepest agony. Did He not also experience the spectrum of human relationship, from deepest love and affection, to harshest rejection and betrayal, to death by a "friend"? He took on our human life in every respect, to the extent that the God who created the cosmos was so physically weak He could not even carry His own cross to the site of His execution. The more one looks for the correspondence between the New Covenant and the historic practice of Blood Covenanting, the more corresponding elements are found. Beginning with the name Jesus offers for this relationship: the *New Covenant*.

"What must we do to do the works God requires?" (John 6:28)

Trumbull found that blood covenants were widely known and practiced in Palestine in Jesus' day. Those who heard Jesus teach were well aware of this relationship. So why did they react as they did? Because no one had ever envisioned being in this kind of relationship with God; this made no sense to them. The Jewish concept of a relationship with God focused on keeping rules—though the list of rules in Scripture was so long (and made even longer thanks to the religious leaders of the day) that no one could keep them all. Therefore, several people approached Jesus asking for the "short list"—the things God *really* cared about. They assumed that doing these things would keep them on God's good side.

Think back to the earlier conversation about viewing our relationship with God as a *contract*—which is all about keeping the rules. This misconception is not new. God knows that our best life requires far more than us just cleaning up our act. We need more than a shift in behavior or a new attitude. We need more than forgiveness for what we have done. We need to be *made new*—to have the life of God within us. We need to be transformed into people who can "do the works God requires." God's plan to create this transformation is Covenant. Throughout history, by contrast, people have wanted a contract with God that adds value and satisfaction to *their* lives. They want a relationship in which they do a few things for God. In return they expect God to do things in their lives only God can do.

This plan has never worked. It cannot build the life God has planned for us.

WHAT IS A COVENANT?

Before we go into the details of Covenant, let's pause to remember why we are doing this. The point of reading all of this is not to *know about* Covenant. It is to allow us to make our own choices wisely. It is about understanding so we can build what God has made possible in our lives. So, through the remainder of this book, I want you to keep several personal questions in mind. Please take some time and reflect on these questions. What I would like you to do is engage with God on these questions. Ask Him to show you a vision of what He intends your life to become, and what your Covenant with Him has enabled your life to become. Then, may you envision the decisions you must make to build this life in full cooperation with God.

1. What is God giving me in this relationship? What is this *new life I have*? Who am I now, and what life am I now capable of living? What does God intend for the person I have become? What are my dreams for this person I have become? What does *all of this mean for me?* What choices can I make that will build this life to its potential?
2. *What source of information am I going to trust more than any other* to teach me about life and reality? What does this source say I must do to live my best life?

3 *What is faithfulness?* This word sums up all we are to do in Covenant to make the most of a Covenant relationship. What could occur in my life if I followed God's plan faithfully? Where might my life end up? If the outcome of faithfulness is attractive to me, how do I become faithful? (I will offer a hint: faithfulness is produced by a decision to make faithfulness our highest priority, followed by a lifetime of decisions which back up this commitment, accompanied by an unshakable commitment to carry out faithful actions.)

If we simply read through Scripture we find several covenants mentioned. Among them: between God and Noah (Genesis 9:17); God and Abraham (Genesis 17:9); and with all Israel through Moses (Exodus 24:8). Unfortunately, none of these relationships are described in explicit detail. This is also the case with the Covenant of Marriage and the New Covenant. In the writings of ancient or modern cultures the definition of words and concepts is often assumed. If I write about attending a baseball game and catching a foul ball, my description would not include the rules of baseball and why the ball was "foul." Why not? Because people who read this in our culture understand baseball. These would be unnecessary words. But a thousand years from now someone reading these words would have many questions. What is baseball? What is *foul* about the ball? Did the ball … smell bad?

Several types of relationship in the ancient world were termed covenants. Treaties between countries, the relationship between a king and his subjects, and wills, as well as Blood Covenants and Marriages all fell under the general heading of the word "covenant." The men who wrote the Scriptures did not offer further details or distinguish between these types of covenants because readers at the time had a much better (though obviously not perfect) understanding of these various types of covenants. In contrast, in a world where this form of relationship has gone almost completely missing, we need an extensive explanation. It's almost like starting with, "What is baseball?" Then we can move on to the rules that apply in various scenarios.

Why does our Bible consist of an Old and New *Testament*? There is one Greek term that can be translated as "covenant" or "testament" depending on the context. The term "testament" is used for a will. A will is a form of contract. A will *does not alter the nature of our being*, as the New Covenant does. Thus, even the name for our Scriptures illustrates a bit of confusion. The original designations were "Old and New Covenant." These terms first appeared in print late in the second century, by Melito of Sardis. He pointedly used the word *Covenant*. However, when Jerome translated the Latin Vulgate in the fifth century, to translate this Greek word he used the Latin term *testamentum*. Unfortunately, this misnomer was used by later translators to name the entire book[5] and this same misnomer was used in some verses (e.g., Hebrews 9:16, 17). If you substitute the term "Covenant" for "will" in these verses, they now illustrate the death of the old self when one enters the New Covenant. Note, in the next verse, Hebrews 9:18, this same word in the original language is translated correctly as "Covenant."

What Is a Covenant? was the first volume of this series. It defines these identity-altering Covenants in much greater detail than we will offer here. That book was written as a preamble to the one you are now reading. It is strongly recommended that you read this foundational material for deeper understanding. Scripture offers some details about the two Covenants that are the focus of this series—Marriage and the New Covenant. But Scripture does not exhaustively define these relationships because a foundational understanding of these relationships is assumed by the writers. Thus, the picture of these relationships within Scripture is incomplete; this picture is like having eighty pieces of a hundred-piece puzzle. If the picture in the text has blank spots, how do we fill in these gaps to fully understand these relationships? We can do this by applying the historically correct understanding of these relationships; the alternative is to simply use our imagination or adopt the imagination of other people. The latter approach has created much of the confusion about these relationships we note today.

Marriage and the New Covenant are two examples of the same type of relationship. Does Marriage alter our identity in a way analogous to the New Covenant? According to God it does. Scripture terms this a "one flesh" relationship. The term "one" in the original language does not refer to a *singular* thing, but to two or more things connected by a common nature. This same word is used to say, "God [the Trinity] is One" (Mark 12:32). Within the Trinity are three distinct Persons, all of whom are joined by a common nature and identity. Each is fully God. Together, they are all God.

Thus, the core reality produced by three relationships is the same. If you have read *The Covenant of Marriage* (by this author) or its accompanying Study Guide, you are aware of the many similarities between the Covenant of Marriage and the New Covenant. But to fully understand these relationships we must be aware that these two relationships are modeled on a third relationship. The "one flesh" of Marriage reflects the oneness of its Author. The New Covenant brings us into a oneness with God that He compares to the Trinity. Also, inherent in the New Covenant is a similar joining among believers. In John 17 this same word "one" is used to describe the relationship among the Trinity, between believers and Jesus, and among believers.

If these relationships share a common foundation and a common Author, would it be fair to draw from the things Scripture says about Marriage to better understand the New Covenant? God does this. He often uses Marriage imagery when discussing His relationship with His people in the Old and New Testaments. If God uses Marriage as a teaching tool for the New Covenant, it is reasonable that we do the same. Thus, we can learn things about one relationship by reading what God says about the other. This will help us fill in some gaps.

If God uses Marriage as a teaching tool for the New Covenant, it is reasonable that we do the same. Thus, we can learn things about one relationship by reading what God says about the other.

H. Clay Trumbull quickly realized that the New Covenant *is* a Blood Covenant. So, is it reasonable to also draw from what Trumbull learned about blood covenants to better understand the New Covenant? Can we use this relationship for a teaching tool in the same way God uses Marriage? We must be careful about using cultural practices—past or present—to over-write Scripture. We should not use current ideas about Marriage to revise or delete what God says in Scripture about the real thing. But here we are doing something very different. We are doing exactly what theologians have always done. We are identifying the concepts that were current when a word was spoken or written—in this case, the definition and concepts associated with this variety of Covenant. Then we are using these concepts to flesh out the true meaning of the words and concepts in Scripture on this topic.

"Very truly I tell you, no one can enter the kingdom of God unless they are born of water and the Spirit. Flesh gives birth to flesh, but the Spirit gives birth to spirit" (John 3:5, 6).

While we can draw from common elements to better understand all three relationships, we must also keep in mind their distinctions. One can only be in a Marriage with one other person (adultery ends one Marriage Covenant by creating another), but Jesus can enter myriad New Covenant relationships. A person can be in multiple Blood Covenant relationships. However, in most cultures, if a male and female are in a Blood Covenant, Marriage between them is viewed as incestuous and prohibited. Two people exchange something physical from themselves to enter Marriage or a Blood Covenant. Though these covenants involve a physical *representation* of this exchange of life, the actual joining and alteration of identity occur in the spiritual realm. Regarding Marriage, Scripture says, "What God has joined together … " (Mark 10:9), not "what biology has joined together."

Jesus, being God, is not bound by time, space, or the limits of a physical body. At any time in the last two thousand years, at any place on earth, any individual can receive His offer of relationship and new life. Receiving Jesus' offer of relationship involves a prayer of repentance and commitment. But Jesus also said, *"Unless you eat the flesh of the Son of Man and drink His blood, you have no life in you"* (John 6:53). Yet receiving the symbolic representation of His flesh and blood—the Lord's Supper, or Communion—has always been understood as a periodic celebration of this relationship, not the act that initiates it.

Therefore, receiving the life of Jesus into ourselves appears not to *require receiving a physical material into our physical body*, as is the case with the other two covenants. Yet we do *receive* Jesus to enter this Covenant. *"To all who did receive Him, to those who believed in His name, He gave the right to become children of God"* (John 1:12). The criterion for entry into the New Covenant is a certain state of mind and heart that leads us to fully *trust* Jesus, and fully *entrust ourselves* to Him. We will examine this state of mind and heart more carefully farther down. For now, think of two people who offer themselves to each other at the altar of Marriage. Each offers all that he or she is. Each is open to receiving the entirety of the life of the other. Their identities are then exchanged and merged as they enter Covenant through intercourse.

Though entry into the New Covenant involves a transaction we cannot see, this entry is to be publicly evidenced by a physical act. In the New Testament baptism is consistently depicted shortly after an expression of commitment to God. Some believe that baptism actually initiates this Covenant, because the Spirit descended on Jesus as He emerged from the water of baptism (Matthew 3:16). However, God apparently intends that entry into this Covenant not rely on a particular ritual or scripted prayer. This transaction occurs between One who sees the depths of our hearts and one who wholeheartedly desires to give his or her life to God. This desire is typically expressed in a prayer to God that includes an acknowledgment of our prior rebellion against God, grateful acceptance of His offer of new life and forgiveness, and wholehearted acceptance of His Lordship over our lives.

FOUR CHARACTERISTICS OF THIS FORM OF COVENANT

We have said that the New Covenant, Marriage, and Blood Covenant represent a single kind of relationship. What makes these relationships different from all others? Four characteristics put these relationships in a unique category, different from any other human relationship.

"*... giving us a new birth and a new life through the Holy Spirit*" (Titus 3:5).

"*If anyone is in Christ, he is a new creation; old things have passed away; behold, all things have become new*" (2 Corinthians 5:17, NKJV).

1. NEW LIFE

One evening Nicodemus, a respected religious teacher, came to Jesus with a question in mind. He wanted to know the inside track to a relationship with God, the "short list" of "must do" things that would ensure God's favor. Jesus did not even give him time to articulate his question, though. He simply answered it: "*No one can see the Kingdom of God unless they are born again*" (John 3:3). In this answer Jesus began to unveil His plan of a New Covenant. Judging by Nicodemus's response, this was the last thing he expected to hear. Nicodemus had worked very hard for many years to build the best life for himself. He was a respected teacher, a religious leader, and a member of the Sanhedrin, the center of Jewish political power. He sought Jesus for the same reason most people seek God, at least in the beginning: my life, made better.

In this answer Jesus began to unveil His plan of a New Covenant. Judging by Nicodemus's response, this was the last thing he expected to hear.

We see a few things wrong with our lives. We want these fixed, but finally realize we do not have the power to do so. At this point some reach out to God for help. But God knows more than we do about the depth and breadth of the problems in our lives. Others seek God realizing that more is wrong with their lives and wrong with them. Some are considering ending their lives and reach out to God as a last hope. But whatever the perceived need might be, the desired solution in everyone's mind is the same: my life, made better. We must realize that God wants a better life for us than even we can envision. He approaches us all—regardless of our perceptions—with the same solution: an offer of new life in Covenant with Him.

If we accept His offer, this new life—this transformed identity and nature—does not appear fully formed. Being *born again* is much like our initial birth. From the time we are a one-cell fertilized egg, in the depth of this being resides everything it is possible for us to become. But almost all of *us* is in the form of *potential* as we float in our mother's womb or lay in our crib. Is our inherent potential always fully realized in life? Throughout life this potential may be recognized and developed—or not. This is also true for the new being we have become. The processes of growth and development are much the same. But one thing is different. This new us comes wrapped in all the things we built in our *old life*—habits, viewpoints, beliefs, values, and all the other elements that form the lives we live. *We* are new, but *our life* is going to look very much like the old life we have been living. It will look this way from the outside and feel this way from the inside. Unless …

"Whoever eats my flesh and drinks my blood remains in Me, and I in them" (John 6:56).

" … if indeed the Spirit of God lives in you. And if anyone does not have the Spirit of Christ, they do not belong to Christ" (Romans 8:9).

" … you are in Christ Jesus …" (1 Corinthians 1:30).

"*... which is Christ in you, the hope of glory*" (Colossians 1:27).

"*... I in them and You in Me—so that they may be brought to complete unity. Then the world will know that you sent Me and have loved them, even as you have loved me*" (John 17:23).

2. BOND OF IDENTITY AND NATURE

In Covenant, the identity—or life—of each party enters the other and remains. It is easier to envision this occurring between two humans than between a person and God. Why did Jesus become human, born of a young peasant girl, raised to adulthood in the same way as the rest of us? Before His incarnation He appeared to a number of people in essentially human form; why did He not simply make a more extended appearance in this *humanlike form* and offer His instruction to humanity ? He *became human* because of Covenant—the exchange of life and joining of life. Just as He entered our human life, He invites us to enter the life of God. Not that we become God by joining Him any more than I become female by marrying my wife. Yet, at the same time, I am *in her* and she is in me. Each becomes in a real sense an extension of the other. Why is this reality so important?

Because in Covenant our external lives are also to be merged. We become part of each other's families. Material resources are fully shared. Friends, enemies, debts, and assets are shared. This melding of lives is simply the logical result of the merger of identities that occurs as we enter this relationship. But there is an even more important impact of this reality. Though I have something that *might be* of use to the other, or there *might be* an effort I could make for his or her benefit, I still must *decide to provide or to do*. This means that my heart must be willing to make a choice for the sake of the other. Making this choice is the essence of faithfulness. Said another way, true faithfulness to Covenant means I am willing to love the other person *in action* (not just in theory) as I love myself. My choice to love makes this potential a reality.

God makes it easier to develop this mind-set and heart toward the other person. How? He makes the other person *literally a part of us, as we are part of them*. What we do for the other person, in a very real sense we do for ourselves. Our highest duty in Covenant is to honor the other person and enhance and support their reputation and name. This is, once again, a logical move because our name and reputation are wrapped in theirs. When one is honored, honor is shared. When one is strengthened, both benefit. When one gains, both gain. In every possible sense there is no more "mine" or "yours," only "ours."

The same is true for any reversal of fortune; thus we seek the best for each other at every point as if our own life depends on it. For it does.

How does the picture of Covenant between two people (in a Blood Covenant or Marriage) apply to our relationship with God? What is our highest duty before God? To honor and worship Him above all others (Matthew 22:38). The second commandment? To protect His name against defamation (Exodus 20:7). The Jews (based on experience) viewed God at a distance (Exodus 19:12). He was the fire atop the mountain. If you touched the mountain, you died. If you saw His face, you died. What they did for God was part duty, part appeasement, part fear. The idea of a deeply personal, intimate communion with God was not part of this picture.

The New Covenant picture could not be more different. God is *not* distant or unapproachable. We are *within Him* and He is *within us*. We are joined to God by a shared identity and nature. What does the word "Christian" literally mean in Greek? "Little Christ." We are to reflect our Covenant Partner. When people looked into the eyes of Jesus they looked into the eyes of God in a human face. Jesus conveyed all that He heard from the Father—for they are

What does the word "Christian" literally mean in the Greek? "Little Christ." We are to reflect our Covenant Partner.

one (John 15:15). We are to teach others all that Jesus taught us for the same reason: we are *one with Him* (Matthew 24:20).

In the same way, the life of God—His heart, character, truth, and kingdom—are exactly what to us? These become *our life*. God is now an integral part of every part of our lives. We are indwelled by His Spirit. What does it mean that your identity is wrapped up in God? Now consider that your identity—every potential and every possibility—was also authored by God. We often hear this phrase in our culture: "This is my life!" One may believe this if the person is not in Covenant with God. But this is absolutely untrue if he or she is in Covenant with God. And even for those not in Covenant, did they create themselves? Is their life not a gift from God that is subject to recall at His discretion?

"If you keep my commands, you will remain in my love, just as I kept my Father's commands and remain in His love" (John 15:10).

"My command is this: love each other as I have loved you" (John 15:12).

"All authority in heaven and on earth has been given to Me. Therefore go and make disciples of all nations, baptizing them in the name of the Father and of the Son and of the Holy Spirit, and teaching them to obey everything I have commanded you" (Matthew 28:19, 20).

"Not everyone who says to me, 'Lord, Lord,' will enter the Kingdom of Heaven, but only the one who does the will of my Father who is in heaven" (Matthew 7:21).

" ... whatever you did for the least of these brothers and sisters of mine, you did for me" (Matthew 25:40).

3. DUTIES, OBLIGATIONS, AND RESPONSIBILITIES TO LOVE ANOTHER AS SELF

In the historic practices associated with a Covenant between two people, the general obligation to love each other in action translates into a number of duties, obligations, and responsibilities. Family duties are assumed. We are obligated to defend and protect each other. We are responsible to provide for each other as needed. What of this applies to our relationship with God?

God also has interests to protect, defend, and promote: His kingdom, His Name, and His people. He intends that the gospel be preached and disciples be made in every nation. His name is honored or dishonored before a watching world by the behavior of those in Covenant with Him. Though He is the very definition of self-sufficiency, He asks us to contribute resources and effort into the efforts of the Body of Christ in a way consistent with Covenant. We are to stand up for truth, including God's moral truths; we are to defend the oppressed and help the helpless. We are to provide for the needy. Basically, we are to adopt and live out the love of God in a lost and dying world.

And we are called at times to suffer at the hands of this world, joining Jesus even in this way. Within this general obligation to serve those made in God's image, we have a much stronger obligation—a full Covenant obligation—to our brothers and sisters in the Body of Christ. If in Covenant we are all within God, and if Jesus is within each of us, are we not also all joined by a shared identity and nature? Did early Christians, more versed in the nature of Covenant than we are, understand their relationship in this way? See Acts 2:44-47, and consider why the early believers handled their resources in this way.

But our obligation to love God has another vital element. Between two humans, we love each other as best we can in light of our limited understanding and capacities. God, who knows all things and is the Author of all things, loves perfectly. One unique aspect of our Covenant with God is our obligation to learn to love as He loves. This is far more involved than it might appear at first glance. We will be discussing this process through the rest of this book. What keeps us from loving perfectly in the first place? The answer is not a sound bite. God's Covenant plan is designed to specifically address each part of the answer to this question. The first thing we must understand is the amount of *deception*, or lack of truth, upon which we have built our character and personal guidance system for living—and even our image of ourselves. The second thing we must understand is the vital role truth plays in our transformation. The third thing we must comprehend is that our transformation *changes us into* people who are capable of loving as God directs.

Now, to get from here to there, we must realize that we and God will differ at points. When we differ, who is right and who is wrong? Whose agenda and direction is based on truth, and whose is based on a highly questionable foundation? So, whose directions should we follow for best results: ours or God's? God is not trying to get in the way of our best life and ruin our good times. He is trying to show us the difference between a life based on truth and love and a life misdirected by deception, no matter how well-intended. He says, *"Then you will know the truth, and the truth will set you free"* (John 8:32). Free from what? Keep that question in mind as you read the rest of this book.

Because He loves us, God commands us to obey Him. We are to obey Him in general, and in the smallest detail. There are two other things He requires of us: faithfulness and love. Faithfulness is a Covenant term. It means to carry out each obligation, duty, and responsibility inherent in our Covenant in broad strokes and in every detail. Love is a many-faceted thing. It involves what we feel and think. It involves what we do and why we do it. It involves getting to know ourselves and each other. It involves growing and developing. It involves building relationship and intimate companionship. The path to our experiencing, doing, and being all of these things is faithfulness to our Covenant. Covenant is a plan, and it is also a path. So, faithfulness also means to carry out God's plan, and walk on a specific path. To do all of this with enthusiasm we must realize where this path leads. It leads to our *best life,* and it leads to the best *us*, refashioned and transformed hand-in-hand with a loving God. Thus, God tells us to obey Him.

"You shall have no other gods before Me" (Deuteronomy 5:7).

"He who loves father or mother more than Me is not worthy of Me; and he that loves son or daughter more than me is not worthy of Me" (Matthew 10:37).

4. THE PLACE IN LIFE OCCUPIED BY OUR COVENANT AND COVENANT PARTNER

We view various things as priorities in our lives. We actually get to determine the role a given thing plays within our mind and heart. But as humans we are prone to brush past important things in pursuit of things that are much less important. If we are in a Covenant relationship the priority of our Covenant partner and our relationship are clear according to God's plan. Given that our partner inhabits the very center of our lives and every part of our lives, building our "together life" is reasonably our first priority—always. This is the historic priority of Covenant, and reasonably so if we are joined to another person in this way. This central role in life is even more reasonable if our Partner is God.

Two things about Covenant are most important. *First is the transformation and joining* that take place, for every other aspect of this relationship flows from these realities. *The second refers to faithfulness*—each party to the other, and each to the relationship. Faithfulness is the choice we make—overall and in each detail—to comply with the reality of this relationship. Faithfulness means that we choose to be devoted to the other with mind, heart, and will. Faithfulness means living out this relationship in accord with God's plan and building the relationship to its potential. Faithfulness also means choosing to grow, and to follow God's plan for our transformation so that we fully develop our potential. The genius of God is seen most clearly here—for our potential can only be fully developed through *building* this relationship. So, how do we become faithful? One decision at a time.

The first decision we must make is the place God and our relationship with Him are to occupy in our life. Then we make daily decisions that confirm this decision. Or we make a different decision. In this case our life moves in a different direction, and relationship suffers.

BUT YOU DON'T UNDERSTAND, MY LIFE IS ALREADY FULL!

During first year medical school a staff member of the Navigator ministry moved to Birmingham to begin a ministry on the undergraduate campus. But seeing the fifty or so Christians in our class of 165, Jim changed course. He moved in with four of our classmates and focused his ministry efforts on our class. This was Jim's first ministry assignment following his return from the Vietnam War and discharge from the Marines. First year medical school is designed to overwhelm people with photographic memories and a compulsive work ethic. The Navigator ministry focuses on intense Scripture study, memorization, personal application of Scriptural truths, and training to minister in the lives of others through evangelism and mentoring. All of the above meant that our weekly assignments for medical school and ministry were considerable.

My strongest memory of Jim was looking into his eyes as he was looking into mine. I felt the back of my head begin to heat up as Jim's gaze started boring holes in the back of my skull—because I had not completed my assignment. This neglect of duty happened only once, as I recall. As medical students, let's just say we were somewhat impressed with ourselves and the importance of what we were doing. Jim was impressed by the place Jesus should occupy in our lives. After staring down the barrels of enemy rifles for the last few

As medical students, let's just say we were somewhat impressed with ourselves and the importance of what we were doing. Jim was impressed by the place Jesus should occupy in our lives .

years, seeing friends die, and having to face the hardest questions in life, he was less impressed by us. Jim taught me that my relationship with Jesus was always to come first in my life. Part of my obligation to Jesus was to properly prepare for my career, but this must remain in proper context. An even greater obligation was to learn a more important body of truth—God's Word. And, to prepare for an even more important assignment—a lifetime of following Jesus wherever He leads—while developing into a person who can be used by Him in more and more ways.

So, thank you, Jim. This system of priorities has served me extremely well for decades.

ENTERING A COVENANT

Entry into Covenant is an intensely personal matter, but historically also a public matter. This is true regarding Marriage and Blood Covenants, as well as the New Covenant. Weddings often include a beautiful public ceremony and a party for the assembled. Vows are spoken before God and each other that reflect the realities and implications of Covenant. Rings are exchanged as a permanent and visible token of Marriage. A blessing is spoken over the couple, and the joining is publicly proclaimed. But none of these preliminaries bring the Covenant into existence.

A Marriage Covenant is created the first time the couple has sexual intercourse (1 Corinthians 6:16). God has created us so that the ultimate celebration, the most intimate and delightful of human experiences—sexual intercourse—is the vehicle for the exchange of life between the parties. This results in the creation of a new and different identity—a new and joined life—for each. Incidentally, this same act can also combine the identities—the genetic material—of the two to create a brand-new child. Historically, intercourse first occurs following the wedding and party. If a wedding were to take place but for some reason intercourse never happens, the marriage could be *annulled*, or deemed by church authority to have never occurred. This outcome is entirely in keeping with the historic view of the means of entry into Covenant, and with God's commands regarding sexuality in Scripture.

To enter a Blood Covenant the participants and a group of witnesses also come together. Vows are spoken that outline the realities and consequences of the Covenant. These vows are spoken toward each other, and toward the reigning local deity (who is to enforce these vows). Speeches are made and blessings offered. The two parties exchange gifts, often trying to outdo each other's generosity. Gifts often include weapons, food, and other valuables to symbolize the various obligations each assumes toward the other. The assembled then witness an exchange of blood between the two. This creates the covenant. As an ever-visible reminder of this relationship, a wound is often made on each party in a way that produces scarring, most often on the wrist or hand. Alternately, the token may be an amulet or other object that is always to be worn. Then there is a feast for the assembled to celebrate this sacred and momentous joining.

ENTERING THE NEW COVENANT

"Then the Lord God formed a man from the dust of the ground and breathed into his nostrils the breath of life, and the man became a living being" (Genesis 2:7).

"Jesus said, 'Peace be with you! As the Father sent me, I am sending you.' With that He breathed on them and said, 'Receive the Holy Spirit'" (John 20:21, 22).

"If the Spirit of Him who raised Jesus from the dead is living in you, He who raised Christ from the dead will also give life to your mortal bodies because of His Spirit who lives in you" (Romans 8:11).

Some aspects of entry into the New Covenant have already been described. The overall process is similar in many ways to the above two Covenants. These include a desire to offer one's life to the other party and receive theirs in return. Vows of commitment are made. Jesus placed His commitment to us in writing: in Scripture. We offer ours in return via prayer.

Two transformations that occur in different ways are key parts of God's Covenant plan. The first occurs at the point of entry into Covenant as the life of God—His Spirit—enters us. When this occurs, Scripture describes the death of the old person and rebirth of a new creature with a new identity and nature—one now joined to God. This creates a new creation in the depths of the person, but may do little to alter one's way of life or experience of life. There is a second transformation—of the external life—which occurs over time as we voluntarily conform to God's Covenant plan. Many want their lives to change when they enter Covenant with God. But people often do not understand the nature of the change that occurs upon entry into Covenant, nor do they understand the process by which the life changes they desire actually occur. In other words, many do not understand God's plan. This plan involves our transformation and joining to God, His truth, and our decisions. Understanding this plan truly brings the account of Jesus' life, death, resurrection—and what happened next in the lives of the disciples—to life. And this understanding offers those who enter this relationship today a realistic promise that their lives can be similarly transformed and powerful.

Though there are parallels between the New Covenant and the historic practices of Blood Covenant and Marriage, there are some obvious distinctions. One is the straightforward physical approach to entering Marriage or a Blood Covenant versus entering the New Covenant. For our timeless and eternal God, the first part of this Covenant ceremony and exchange occurred two thousand years ago with Jesus' outpoured blood. The second occurs when each individual responds to Jesus' offer of Covenant. While there is no face-to-face physical exchange, all the elements of Covenant are represented. For the disciples who ate a symbolic Covenant meal with Jesus the night before His crucifixion, actual entry into the New Covenant occurred three days later. Jesus rose from the dead on Sunday morning, then appeared to His disciples that evening. At this time Jesus breathed on them, and the Holy Spirit entered each person (John 20:22). Receiving His Spirit was the disciples' point of entry into the New Covenant (Romans 8:16), the point at which they became Christians.

What about the rest of us? Let's look at the bigger picture. Near the beginning of His ministry Jesus was baptized by John the Baptist. In Jewish culture (Numbers 35:30), for a matter to be confirmed as true the testimony of two or three witnesses was required. In the first chapter of the books of Mark and John we see a threefold public witness that Jesus was the Messiah who would baptize His followers with the Holy Spirit. First, John publicly identified Jesus as the one who would offer a New Covenant to humanity. Second, the Holy Spirit descended on Jesus in a visible form and remained on Him. Third, God spoke audibly, identifying Jesus as His Son.

Prior to His crucifixion, as Jesus ate the Passover Feast with His disciples, He offered them a representation of His blood and body—though not the real thing—which they received. Jesus told them to repeat this Covenant meal—now referred to as the Lord's Supper, or Communion—as a token of the New Covenant. This is analogous to God instructing a married couple to engage in intercourse frequently, as a token of their Covenant; or two with visible scars made at the time of entry into Covenant viewing these scars on a daily basis. These are to be ever-present reminders of the obligations of Covenant. These things were but a preamble, though, akin to a wedding ceremony.

The next day an all-too-public offering of blood was made as Jesus hung naked on a Roman cross pouring out His very life—the life of God offered to us. That offer was first consummated when the Holy Spirit entered the disciples three days later, as previously described.

When Thomas questioned Jesus' post-resurrection identity, what did Jesus show him? A wound in His side and another on His wrist—the place where Romans actually placed crucifixion nails. The same place that a scar is typically made as a token of a Covenant. Thomas's response to seeing this token? "My Lord and my God!" (John 20:28)

The more carefully we examine the facts of Jesus' life on earth, the more we see of God's Covenant plan. His death, burial, and resurrection; the offer He makes to each of us; and the life we are called to live in Scripture are all completely consistent with a Blood Covenant pattern. Everything Jesus did, and everything we are called to do, is because of Covenant. Covenant is God's love language. Covenant is the framework within which God shows His love for us and requires our love in return. In light of this, should we not do everything possible to understand God's Covenant plan and carry it out?

"We were therefore buried with Him through baptism into death in order that, just as Christ was raised from the dead through the glory of the Father, we too may live a new life" (Romans 6:4).

"… this water symbolizes baptism that now saves you also—not the removal of dirt from the body but the pledge of a clear conscience toward God. It saves you by the resurrection of Jesus Christ" (1 Peter 3:21).

BAPTISM, A PUBLIC PROCLAMATION OF OUR COVENANT

The public celebration of entry into the New Covenant is baptism. This is analogous to both a wedding ceremony and a wedding ring. This ceremony physically depicts several elements of the New Covenant. First, we see a picture of our death and burial through immersion. Rising from the water depicts being raised from death to new life. Second, the cleansing power of water depicts the washing away of the old. We are cleansed of the penalty for sin by the blood of Jesus, which creates a clean conscience. But we are cleansed in another vital way when we receive our new life joined to God. The nature of Satan, often termed our "sin nature," stays behind, within an old nature that ceases to exist.

Some in the Body of Christ believe the Covenant actually comes into being and the Holy Spirit enters a person at the time of baptism. Others believe we are to baptize infants in the hope that they will one day enter a New Covenant relationship. God does not precisely identify the point at which His Spirit enters a person. He does say clearly that we *do not belong to Christ*—thus, are not in a New Covenant relationship—*if the Spirit is not within us.* One is either a Christian—in this New Covenant relationship, with a new life that is joined to God and indwelled by God's Spirit—or one is not. There is no halfway point and no third category. How can we know whether God's Spirit is within us? Romans 8:16 tells us to pose this question to God. He will answer us if we ask Him.

One is either a Christian—in this New Covenant relationship, with a new life that is joined to God and indwelled by God's Spirit—or one is not. There is no halfway point and no third category.

MATCHING THE CURE TO THE DISEASE

I am a surgeon by training. When I proposed an operation to a patient, it is amazing how often I heard the same question in responses: "Do I really need this operation?" What people were really asking was this: Is the problem worth the pain and recovery period of surgery? Does the risk justify something so dramatic? Is the way this may *change my life* a price I want to pay to *cure this problem*? Is the problem really *that bad*?

To answer this important question (and all the underlying, unspoken ones) I always went back to the disease. What problem are we trying to solve? How serious and how dangerous is it? Different cancers and conditions pose unique risks. Does your particular bladder cancer justify removing your bladder and building you a new one using part of your intestine? A life-altering move to be sure, and an operation with multiple inherent risks. The treatment must match the risk of the disease in a patient's mind before he or she will agree to radical surgery, or any other course of action.

Most of us begin seeking God because we want *something to change*. Something within us, or some life circumstance that is beyond our power to resolve. God's love meets us where we are at this point of need. But our idea of what is needed and God's idea are usually different. We want to solve a problem in our life; God wants us to have a new life in Him. God offers to perform a more radical procedure on each of us than anything I ever did with a scalpel. Before we can really appreciate His offer, or even understand it, we need to first understand our current condition. We must make sure we understand the problem that needs to be solved. We see a *symptom* we want God to make go away. A little blood in the urine or a little pain in the side. We do not realize that we have cancer. We cannot know this until we are evaluated by an expert who knows how to see things within us that we cannot perceive. And even if we know we have cancer, what does this really mean? For a medical issue we have to trust the opinion of an expert and put our life in his or her hands. What about a spiritual issue—something we cannot fully understand using our senses and our mind?

Do spiritual realties pose a threat to us? Threats—within ourselves and in our world—that escape our notice?

Do spiritual realties pose a threat to us? Threats—within ourselves and in our world—that escape our notice? Might these threaten us in ways we do not fully understand even if we realize they exist? Why would we even consider undergoing something so radical as the death of our old self and the creation of a new being? Let's take some time to think about our lives, and life in general.

CHAPTER TWO

WHY DO WE NEED COVENANT?

DISCOVERING THE RIGHT QUESTIONS

"There is nothing new under the sun" (Ecclesiastes 1:9).

THERE ARE NO NEW QUESTIONS—AND NO NEW ANSWERS

Covenant provides many answers for the questions of life. But we first need to make sure we are asking the right questions—about life in general and about our life. Perhaps we've asked this one: "How is God going to help me get famous enough, rich enough, or ____ enough to be really happy?" Perhaps this is not the right question. One of the most important journeys in my life has been figuring out, not the right answers, but the right questions. We will never find the right answers until one asks the right questions. For me, these questions often become apparent while I am grappling with serious life issues. Once these questions are fully formed, God has answered one important question after another. But only after I understood *why* the question was important, then sought the answer from the right source—which always ended up being God. Let me share some of these questions. Feel free to add yours to the list. This book is not just about my journey. It is about something much more important to you: *your journey.*

See if God's plan of Covenant is not also the answer to your most important questions about life.

DOES A SPIRITUAL REALM EXIST?

Let's start with one of the most important questions today for our culture. If you walk into most college classrooms today and begin talking about God, or the authority of the Scriptures, or Satan, what will likely happen? You will be treated like you are an idiot. Your views will be dismissed as imaginary, and you will be informed that the only source of truth in this enlightened era is science.

Your views will be dismissed as imaginary, and you will be informed that the only source of truth in this enlightened era is science.

Since the views of many have been attacked in such a way, and not just in classrooms, I want to offer a scientific, logical, and compelling rebuttal of this statement and others like it. These statements are intended to challenge Christianity and everything it stands for. You need not be intimidated by such challenges. The people who level these attacks are not standing on solid scientific ground, logic, or common sense. Their view is not a superior view in any sense, and we need to understand why.

Does a spiritual realm of life exist, or does life only consist of the matter, energy, and chemistry of our physical world? The scientific and educational establishments today label any thoughts about a spiritual dimension of life, spiritual beings, or spiritual truths as mere *mythology* or *superstition;* or they may use the new term *untestable thinking*. That is, any statement about the spiritual realm is a product of human imagination—period. Nothing is real beyond matter and energy that we can measure and the physics and chemistry we can study. This position is called *naturalism*. It is asserted that anything we can possibly understand about life will be understood through scientific study of the natural realm. It is therefore proclaimed that the hope for our future resides solely in science, technology, and education—end of story. Really?

The spiritual realm is by definition not part of our physical universe. It does not consist of things we can directly measure, observe, or subject to scientific study. However, things within that realm *exert an influence on this realm* in ways we *can* perceive. Humans, made in the image of God, have a physical dimension, but they also have a spiritual dimension. We can be impacted on a physical level, and we can be impacted on a spiritual level. Whether your life is worth living is a spiritual question.

On a physical level, what is your life worth? You are composed of elements and chemicals that are worth, at today's prices, about three dollars. If someone offered you five dollars for your child, is this a good deal? At some level we all understand that people are valuable in a way that is far beyond their chemistry and utility. Our intrinsic value comes from being made in the image of God. This understanding is a *spiritual truth*, not an idea derived from a naturalistic view of human beings.

You are composed of elements and chemicals that are worth, at today's prices, about three dollars. If someone offered you five dollars for your child, is this a good deal?

Top-tier scientists and people with the best minds in every realm of life in past generations saw no conflict between studying our physical universe, while at the same time acknowledging the reality of the spiritual one. Many prominent scientists today hold this position. Belief in the supernatural is not evidence of a lack of intellect or education. A belief in the supernatural simply reflects a reality freely acknowledged by most scientists until recent years—along with the vast majority of the human race throughout history. But in the past well-trained scientists also recognized the limitations of science. They did not try to speak as scientists about the many questions science cannot answer, in the spiritual realm or the natural realm.

Is science really capable of solving all problems and answering all questions? To understand the current debate, it is extremely helpful to define what science *is*, and what it *is not*. The *scientific method* requires two things. First, that a phenomenon is *directly observed*. Second, that the phenomenon in question is *reproducible*, typically in a laboratory environment. Does a beam of light bend when passing next to an object with a massive gravitational field? This phenomenon can be directly observed, and it occurs without exception. It is reproducible. Therefore the statement, "Gravity changes the course of photons" is a scientific truth. It is extremely important in science to distinguish among: 1) what is proven by the scientific method; 2) what is a *theory*—a proposed scenario which *could* logically explain an observed phenomenon, but has not yet been proven by the scientific method; and 3) what is *conjecture*—an idea about a matter for which there is no definitive evidence and no logical mechanism. The latter kind of statements represent only the imagination of a scientist, or reflects his or her personal bias about a matter.

Tragically, in an attempt to sell the idea that "science is the only source of truth," many scientists today offer supposed "scientific truth" about questions which are beyond the reach of the scientific method. They steal the credibility of actual science to make their personal biases sound authoritative. We are supposed to believe every word that flows from the mouths of these people because … they are scientists.

SCIENCE VERSUS SPIRITUAL TRUTHS

Let me share my background and why I am able to comment on these questions. I attended a prestigious private university on a full National Merit Scholarship, graduating with a degree in Chemistry and an acceptance letter to medical school. I have spent almost forty years caring for patients. In doing this I have drawn information from a vast number of scientific studies. I have also drawn from the experience of learned colleagues and my own experience to craft a plan of diagnosis and treatment for every patient who sought my care. In medicine there is a test for the truth of an idea: the outcomes in all the individuals in whom the idea is employed. As I have treated many thousands of patients I have seen great benefits from use of the scientific method. But I have also seen the limitations of this approach. The most glaring deficiency? Most important clinical questions have not been subjected to scientific study, nor will they ever be.

The scientific method can only study one variable in a study, or at the most two or three variables. Rarely can even an array of studies provide a comprehensive answer when dealing with an individual patient. Why? Because even simple problems involve many variables related to an individual's condition and care. Therefore, the experience of the practitioner and his or her success rate to date for a given problem become important. To properly care for an individual, one must draw from multiple sources of information and synthesize this information in the proper way. One must know how to adjust and occasionally innovate depending on an individual's response to treatment. Medical scientific studies offer only a fraction of the information needed for successful medical care.

If an answer is derived from a scientific study, is this the definition of truth? Not necessarily. For an important question multiple studies may be available. These studies rarely produce uniform results. If there are twelve studies, five may conclude one thing, four conclude something different, and three reach no conclusion. In order to sort out the truth, one must look at more than data. One must also look at the design of the study and perhaps at the motivation of the person conducting the study.

THE LIMITS OF SCIENCE

I have listened to many marketing pitches through the years: "This new thing is *the solution* to that problem!" These pitches are always backed by the latest scientific study. But over the years a more nuanced picture emerges. Most of these "next new things" end up in the trash can in a few years because initial studies did not reveal infrequent but major complications, less impressive results in a broader sample of patients, or other problems associated with the treatment. Scientific studies per se are not the most direct path to truth for every question, to say the least.

Standing with one foot firmly planted on scientific studies and the other firmly planted on the reality of patient outcomes offers me a unique vantage point. The bottom line? Science, the scientific method per se, scientific studies, and opinions of individual scientists or groups of scientists are *never* able to comprehensively define even the realities they can study. Science is an important tool. But as with any tool, one must understand its proper uses and limitations. How should we describe today's scientists who presume to speak about issues for which there is no scientific data? Or who attempt to cobble together extremely limited artifacts, plus conjecture, plus bias, then proclaim, "This is the true story of humanity." At least it's the story until they dig up the next fossil.

Standing with one foot firmly planted on scientific studies and the other firmly planted on the reality of patient outcomes offers me a unique vantage point.

In 1978 the law review *Forum* (according to snopes.com) contained an account of a man who used a lawnmower to cut a hedge. Several of his fingers were removed by the lawnmower blade, resulting in a lawsuit and large liability judgment against the lawnmower manufacturer. The lawnmower company was judged liable because it had not warned the user of potential damage which might occur by using the lawnmower in this manner.

What was the real problem here? The real problem was *this story*—which was employed for decades to make the point that liability lawsuits have gotten out of hand. This event apparently never actually happened. But this fact only became evident when extensive efforts were made to confirm the story several decades later. If one is trying to make a point, one can misuse journalism to do so. Unfortunately, scientific studies or the assertions of scientists can be misused in the same way. There is a saying in the scientific community: "The answer you get depends on how you ask the question." So the first question we must ask of any scientific statement is whether the scientist is looking for truth or trying to make a point.

Has the theory that "the spiritual realm does not exist" been proven by the scientific method? No. It would be correct to say: "I am aware of no evidence upon which I, as a scientist, can base an opinion." We must also be aware that the *absence of evidence is not evidence of absence.*

The fact that human beings have a spiritual dimension has been scientifically proven by a fascinating study detailed in *Erasing Death*[6] by Sam Parnia, MD. Parnia is an internationally recognized specialist in cardiopulmonary resuscitation at Stonybrook Hospital, SUNY. He studied patients who had undergone CPR in a hospital setting. In these patients, for a period of time blood pressure and blood oxygen levels were below levels required for brain chemical and electrical activity to occur. That is, patients were studied during a time when the electrical and chemical activity necessary to embed memory in brain cells was not occurring. Thus, it would be impossible for them to remember events during this period of time via any known physical process.

However, Dr. Parnia found that some patients do recall details that occurred during a time when memory is not possible. And the vantage point from which these patients described events in their room was not the bed upon which they laid. They correctly recall people and actions not visible from their bed (and not discussed by staff). What they saw was consistent with another vantage point. For one patient described in the book , this vantage point was the corner of the patient's room near the ceiling. Details this patient recalled included a nurse placing dentures in a particular drawer, specifics of hair and clothing of various staff members, and other facts that were later confirmed by the staff to the smallest detail. Dr. Parnia concluded that, though we as humans inhabit a physical body, we are capable of being apart from our body as a conscious being. We are capable of *creating memories that do not depend on the function of our brain.* That is to say, scientific evidence now shows that humans have a physical dimension, but also a spiritual dimension. This latter aspect of our being lies outside the physical realm and does not obey the laws of that realm.

IS SCIENCE THE SOURCE OF ALL TRUTH?

Naturalistic scientists do more than deny the spiritual realm. They set science—and themselves—forward as *the source* of all actual truth. Therefore, they sign up to answer the big questions, the ones we all care about. The answers to these questions have always been sought in the spiritual realm because they fall outside the realm of the scientific method. Why? Because *none of these things can be directly observed, studied, or tested.* Things like the origin of life and the origin of us. What is our place in the universe? What is the meaning and purpose of life? Does God exist? If so, how do we relate to Him?

OVERREACHING …

In their quest to be *the* source of truth about life, naturalistic scientists not only fail the commonsense test at many points, they violate the definition of science. For example, how did life come to be? Did a group of chemicals become a living and self-replicating being via random chemical reactions? This is asserted to be a scientific fact. But has this process been observed or reproduced? No. Is there any plausible mechanism by which a DNA molecule could form? No molecule with the complexity of DNA has ever been observed outside of a living being. If one did randomly form at some point in history, in order to produce even the most simple living being there must be *information within this molecule* that would produce the physical and operational structures of this organism. This information must be decoded and implemented in order to produce the physical and physiologic characteristics which define life, including the ability to replicate. This cellular machinery must therefore simultaneously appear alongside the first DNA molecule, in order to produce the RNA, epigenetic material, and cellular energy processes necessary to live and reproduce. The assertion that this is possible "given enough time" was made before the complexity of these chemicals and processes was fully appreciated. The Origin of Life Foundation is currently offering a one million dollar prize to anyone who can come up with a plausible theory for how this might have occurred. Not only is there no winner in over a decade, no theory has even been submitted for consideration. Why? Because to have this remarkably complex and interlocking group of chemicals and processes arise by random chance is frankly impossible, no matter the time frame[7].

MORE IMPOSSIBLE THEORIES

How about the origin of us? Regarding the "evolution of humanity" from a single-cell organism, there are additional major problems with the "serial mutations" plan. Mutations result from DNA *damage*. Information encoded within the DNA is either corrupted or lost. All observed mutations follow this pattern. Even assuming such loss or corruption produced a change that was helpful on occasion for the next generation, we must take another reality into account. For organisms of *increasing complexity* to occur, a larger body of DNA information must be present. For a single-cell organism to turn into a multi-cell organism with, say, a working eye, the DNA coding must somehow come into being for the physical eye, the retina, the neural transmission system—and for the brain that interprets this.

How, then, do we start with the genetic information of the *least* complex independent creature—e.g., a Mycoplasma with 525 genes—and end up with a human who contains more than 30,000 genes? This requires that we move from the DNA of Mycoplasma that has 580,000 base pairs to human DNA with the *three billion* base pairs needed to produce these genes. Where, then, would an additional length of DNA which contains the information necessary to produce all of this come from? People have observed molecules joining together to form longer chains, and years ago inferred that such a process must have occurred to turn smaller and more primitive DNA into larger and more complex DNA. This simplistic viewpoint was replaced by a sobering reality as molecular biologists learned more about the information coding and decoding necessary for life.

There is no situation in which a *coherent information gain* has been observed in any genetic system. To accomplish what mainstream scientists assert is a *scientific fact,* a strand of DNA would need to not only become much longer by an as-yet-unidentified process, it must also contain a huge amount of *new and perfectly coordinated* information. There is no proposed theory for how such a perfect addition, or any addition, might appear even once. Yet, this process is asserted to have occurred on a continuing and progressive basis throughout the history of life. When we look at the overall situation there is an insurmountable problem for the evolutionary viewpoint from a scientific perspective. These serial DNA additions, supposedly ubiquitous throughout history, have no current examples in any DNA sample ever sequenced. There is *no* random elongation, functional or not, hanging off the end of any DNA molecule ever studied.

Therefore, there remains no realistic or scientific explanation for life per se, or biodiversity, or us—except for God.

If one replies that evolution has been observed in the fossil record, and thus must have occurred in a macroevolution sense, we must go to the fossil record and see what this evidence proves. That question is far beyond the scope of this book. The reader is referred to two excellent analyses: *Darwin on Trial*[8], by Phillip Johnson, PhD (law professor at the University of California, Berkeley); and *The Greatest Hoax on Earth*, by Jonathan Sarfati[9]. One hint: when Darwin published his *On the Origin of Species,* he said his theory would be proven by subsequent fossil findings.

What we have found so far in the fossil record is the appearance of categories of creatures fully formed, which contain a full set of functioning organs. Structures which supposedly evolved in a sequence—like less complex to more complex eyes—have been shown to appear simultaneously in the fossil record. Several fossil finds have been proposed as "transition forms" between categories. But these have been removed, one after the other, as new evidence came to light. Archaeopteryx is a dinosaur fossilized in a way that clearly showed it had feathers. Therefore, it was set forth as a transition form between dinosaur and bird. That is, until it was noted that many dinosaurs had feathers! It is possible they all did. If one simply started with the current fossil record and tried to explain it, evolution as it is currently understood and taught would not occur to an unbiased examiner.

SCIENCE OR BIAS?

Naturalism itself is not a scientifically proven position, nor can it be proven. It is a bias, a belief *one desires to hold* that is not backed by a shred of evidence. If one says, "Evolution must have occurred because it is the only option," that person is expressing their opinion that a Creator does not exist. This statement is not scientific in any sense of the word. Every statement built upon this foundation is, likewise, merely building on the same foundation of bias. Why, then, is there such an urge to sell naturalism to students and our culture? That answer will become apparent farther down.

If one says, "Evolution must have occurred because it is the only option," that person is expressing their opinion that a Creator does not exist.

SCIENCE OR HYPOCRISY?

For now, note that people who deny there is a spiritual dimension of life do not live as if this is true. Why do I say this? The spiritual realm is about much more than what might be hiding in a dark corner of your room. It is about moral concepts like justice and moral values—things that we deem "right" and "wrong." If someone asserts that life is purely physical, and the only importance of an action is its relevance to evolution, they have just asserted that there is no such thing as right and wrong. Period. Any such thinking is merely mythology and superstition. Duly noted … But now try mistreating the person who asserts this position and watch what happens. They will describe this situation in moral terms. Their offender is being dishonest and oppressive. Their offender is a cheater, a liar, a hater, or simply wrong. Why does everyone reflexively express their *natural reaction to immoral behavior directed toward themselves* in such ways? Because we are all made in the image of God. We all agree at some level—perhaps in spite of ourselves—that right and wrong exist. A person on the receiving end of sexual immorality—adultery, rape, molestation—clearly perceives that something wrong occurred. But this same person may assert their right to engage in exactly the same behaviors *because they have been told they have such a right.* Rather than an issue of right and wrong, this scenario is simply a matter of wrong—and more wrong.

SCIENCE OR WILLFUL BLINDNESS?

Right and wrong are real and meaningful categories that *mirror the moral nature of our universe.* We live in a cause-and-effect world. Every action has consequences, and these consequences—when all have occurred—perfectly reflect God's moral law. These categories mirror the real-world impact of behaviors on people, and these categories mirror our internal wiring system.

THE IMPORTANCE OF WHAT WE *ASSUME* TO BE TRUE

Why do we devote so much attention to these questions? Because naturalistic science nominates itself to *refute and replace God's revelation as the source of ultimate truth.* Should we vote with the fraction of the scientists who believe this (for many scientists do *not* hold this view)? This philosophical assertion—echoed by thought leaders in education, media, politics, and law—has become the guiding principle of our culture. God and His Word, both of which were welcomed in public schools and the public square a few decades ago, are now forbidden as topics of serious discussion. Instead, a new trinity is held up as the hope for humanity—science, technology, and education. And another faux savior waits in the wings: politicians.

Who is offering truth and who is peddling mythology?

A new trinity is held up as the hope for humanity—science, technology, and education. And another faux savior waits in the wings: politicians.

Our answer to the original question—the existence of a spiritual dimension of life—forms our foundation for answering all other questions. How would you answer this question? The rest of this book will outline the reasons I believe this spiritual side of life not only exists, but dramatically impacts our natural lives. I believe the description of life offered by the Judeo-Christian Scriptures offers the only clear and correct view of this spiritual realm and the ways it impacts our lives and the world we inhabit.

Everything in our lives, and in our world as a whole, can only be explained by a Creator who loves us all and offers us a relationship with Himself, and a being in rebellion against this Creator and those who follow him. The *only* satisfactory explanation for the good things in people and our world, juxtaposed with the challenges, confusion, deception, pain, and occasionally horrific things, is a spiritual war in the heavens that has spilled over into our world—and into each of our lives. Over the four decades I have been a Christian, the Scriptures have done a far better job of analyzing current events than our news media. And a far better job of analyzing and explaining all of human history. More importantly from my perspective, the Scriptures have done a better job of explaining *me and my life* than any other source. These Scriptures have well-deserved credibility in many realms.

I want to show you how to use the truths of Scripture in the most constructive and helpful way in *your* life.

WHAT IS YOUR BOTTOM-LINE SOURCE OF TRUTH?

But how you will understand and apply these truths depends on another question. What is your bottom-line source for truth? If you hear conflicting things, what source do you trust most? Is this source your own perceptions? Is there a source you believe in so strongly that you will allow this source to overrule even your own perceptions? Or do you believe that truth in any absolute sense does not exist? Do we all have our own truth that is equally valid compared to all others? Let us turn this fill-in-the-blank question into a multiple choice question. In reality, there are only a few possible choices for our bottom-line source for truth:

a) *our* perceptions and analyses ;

b) the perceptions and analyses of *other people*;

c) the *Scriptures*, God's revelation of truth about ourselves, our realm, and the spiritual realm;

d) *other spiritual beings and writings* that purport to reveal answers on these topics—though the information provided in them conflicts with the Judeo-Christian Scriptures.

Keep your bottom-line source in mind as we work through the rest of the material in this book. Once you have considered all of this material, see if your bottom-line source remains the same or changes.

HOW DID I BECOME THE PERSON I AM, AND MY LIFE BECOME WHAT IT IS?

There are changes all of us would like to see within ourselves and our lives. But how can these changes come about? Or, are these changes even possible? Why do I make the decisions I make that cause problems? Why are there things about me that cause problems? Why do the things I *want* sometimes lead to problems? We often view ourselves as a *fixed thing*, a being who just showed up the way we are. We often view the problems in our lives solely as the fault of others. "If everyone would just ____, I would be OK."

What I have learned through the decades—mainly from dealing with my own issues—is that my *character*, the *guidance system* that directs my decisions, and even the circumstances of my life are not random things. I am far more the author of all of these than I realized at first. And it is in my power to change far more about my life than any of us realize if I am in a relationship with God and following His plan.

People and circumstances wound us as we go through life. Life is not fair. Our desires and needs can be dismissed. We can be rejected. Some are broken by these circumstances. But others are made stronger, grow deeper, and learn to love more through adversity. What is the difference? The difference is how we view our adversities and the resources we employ to deal with adversity. I want to show you the resources that are available to deal with our life if we are in Covenant with God. And I want to show you God's plan, which will allow you to build a life worth living here and now regardless of your circumstances.

WHAT ARE MY REAL NEEDS?

Our world spends a vast amount of energy trying to convince us that our best life requires one thing or another. We have all had the experience of getting what we think we want, and it not being the wonderful experience we hoped. Or we believe someone is standing between us and something we need for our best life, and we descend into a life of victimhood, resentment, and bitterness. Do you notice how much confusion is out there about the path to our best life? Do we really need a degree from a prestigious school, or a winning lottery ticket, or more social media buzz, or a certain watch? Have we arrived if people really think we are "hot"? Or do we really need love and acceptance? Or need a life filled with meaning and purpose? What really does lead to fulfillment?

Do you notice how much confusion is out there about the path to our best life? Do we really need a degree from a prestigious school, or a winning lottery ticket, or more social media buzz, or a certain watch?

Just as important, if we are clear about our needs and the path to a truly fulfilling life, how can we get there in our world? Even if we grasp the role we played in creating the mess we are in and want to fix things, how can we do this? Why is our guidance system so challenged? Why is our character such a mess? Why do we seem at certain points to be our own worst enemy, and what can we do about that? And why is our entire world such a confusing mess? Why is it a battleground, and why am I caught in the cross fire? These are key questions. Fortunately, these questions have answers.

WHAT IS THE PATH TO MY BEST LIFE?

Our world reduces this to two words: *more* and *better.* Do we follow our feelings? Do we pursue our preferences? Do we try to fit in, and at the same time to stand out? Whose guidance do we trust? Can we trust our own instincts? Should we trust social media to define us and guide us? Or do we listen to the progressive philosophy of our day and trust that science, technology, and education will solve not only the world's problems but also our problems? (Just a random thought—didn't science and technology create the plastic in our oceans and all the toxins that surround us?) We all wait for the newest thing, the latest development—as though the *next big thing* will be the answer… and waiting. Still waiting…

Is freedom to follow our desires the answer? What is holding us back from glory? When people can do whatever they feel like, sometimes what they feel like doing is beautiful. Sometimes it is baffling. Sometimes it is horrifying or terrifying. Is unleashing everyone to live however they want the answer? If not, what is the path to our best life?

WHY CAN'T WE ALL JUST LOVE ONE ANOTHER?

We all bear scars from a lack of love from our parents and family. From the lack of a father or mother, or of one who seemed to us to truly care. Or from a family member who couldn't stay off drugs or out of trouble. Or from people too wrapped up in their lives and cellphones to pay attention to us, much less train us to face our world successfully.

Why do people substitute sexual encounters for love? Why do the people around us really not care? If they notice us, why do some delight in hurting us?

Then we turn loose all these wounded people to figure it out as adults. Why do marriages often fail even if two people start out deeply in love? Do people not know how to build love? Have they ever seen a loving relationship up close? Why do people substitute sexual encounters for love? Why do the people around us really not care? If they notice us, why do some delight in hurting us? Where do we go to find actual love? Sadly, the answer may not reside within most churches. All those people who gather weekly to worship the God who is love may reflect Him poorly one-on-one. After experiencing a lack of love many have walked away from family, or from God's family. Within the depths of our hearts many of us blame God for the unloving world in which we live. We must realize that *this is not a failure on God's part.* By the end of this book you will see why people often are poor reflections of God, and how your life and my life can come to reflect Him.

> *"Do not be deceived: God cannot be mocked. A man reaps what he sows"* (Galatians 6:7).

WHAT IS THE NATURE OF OUR WORLD?

The longer I live the more evidence I see of the moral universe we inhabit. A cause-and-effect relationship is woven into the fabric of our world. If someone makes a habit of lying to promote his or her interests, this may actually work—but only for a while. At some point the consequences of lying will visit this person and things will fall apart. We see similar consequences flowing from adultery and every other moral breach. Every action sets into motion a series of consequences. Some occur in the moment, while other consequences are long delayed. These consequences are like the circular waves that result from throwing a rock in a pond. These spread out in all directions just like the consequences of our actions, impacting lives beyond our own. Depending on whether an action is right or wrong, these consequences help us, or further harm us. Now, envision everyone you know gathered on the shoreline throwing rocks into a pond. Given that much of human activity violates God's moral laws, the consequences of the actions of everyone around us will combine into larger and larger waves of negative consequences. Eventually these waves begin to wash over everyone on shore. This is the world we inhabit, one awash in behaviors that violate God's moral laws and the consequences of those actions. Of course, we see the same cumulative impact of good actions. But which kind of waves are bigger? This is why consistently making the best choices does not ensure a trouble-free life.

Our experience of life is formed to a significant degree by the consequences of our actions. A good part of our future is formed by consequences that have yet to arrive. We can choose our actions, but we cannot choose their consequences. People may reasonably believe that immoral actions have no consequences because we all live in a place called "now." At this singular point in time all the consequences of any action have not occurred. But these consequences *will* occur. And when all consequences of all actions have played out in full, including the eternal consequences meted out directly by God, we will all be forced to acknowledge the truths that God conveyed to us in Scripture.

We can choose our actions, but we cannot choose their consequences.

It should be noted that God's forgiveness, mercy, and grace do not necessarily remove the consequences of our actions. We may be forgiven for dishonesty, but trust issues remain and a job or relationship may be lost. We may be forgiven for adultery, but the divorce still occurs. Or the Marriage that survives may never become what it could have been.

Now that we have clarified the questions—and please add your own to my list—let's look at some realties that will help us answer these questions.

THE SPIRITUAL WAR

WE ARE THE BATTLEFIELD, TARGET, AND PRIZE

Throughout history there has been continual conflict in our world. Conflicts between countries, individuals, and ideas. There always seems to be two sides in these conflicts—right and wrong, good and evil, oppressor and victim—though it may not always be clear which side is which. The people engaged in these conflicts always see them in this way, and all believe their cause is righteous. Thus, what we see in our world is confusion. Do you have conflicts in your life? Why? Are you confused about these conflicts? Why?

The conflict and confusion in our lives and culture actually mirrors another conflict that has raged throughout human history: one in the spiritual realm. This conflict is between God and His enemies, but it is also played out in our world. Individuals are not just the battlefield upon which this warfare takes place, and the target of the attacks. We are also the prize in the battle. This is a battle of ideas, power, and allegiance. Our Creator and His love for us are on one side; on the other is an enemy sworn to overthrow God's rule and establish himself as the ruling authority in the universe. This enemy is called Satan. This term is not his actual name. *Satan* simply means "adversary." The actual name of this being is never mentioned in Scripture.

It is always good to know how and why a war started and what is at stake. Many think the Scriptures are out of date and irrelevant in our day. But let us go to the oldest story in the Bible and see if this is true. Let's see if the story of Adam and Eve is not also *our story,* here and now. Once we understand the sides in this war and the agenda of each side, see if this helps us better understand our lives and our world.

THE GARDEN OF EDEN: ADAM AND EVE, TRUTH AND DECEPTION

As we consider the following conversation, remember that this situation involved Adam and Eve. Though this is Eve's conversation, the mind and heart issues we will highlight are not a male-female thing. They are a human thing. Though Adam's thoughts are not revealed to us in this scenario, he made the choice along with Eve to turn from God and follow Satan's guidance.

> Let's see if the story of Adam and Eve is not also *our story*, here and now.

Eve was created in a one-flesh (Covenant) state with Adam in the Garden of Eden. She and Adam were also in a state of oneness with God. They were made in His image. At some point Eve had a conversation with a being who did not bother to introduce himself, which is recorded in Genesis 3:1-6. This being offered Eve what sounded like "insider information" about her Creator, the God she had loved and worshiped until now without question. What did Satan offer Eve? First, he pretended to offer the *truth about God.* Her Creator was withholding the best option from her. His skillful innuendo suggested that God is the kind of being who withholds good things from others (v. 1). Eve leaps to God's defense in verse 2—sort of. But we can see this innuendo about God's character bothered her. In her defense of God she actually misquotes Him. In fact, her words created a scenario in which she could appear to discredit God as well—by touching the Tree of the Knowledge of Good and Evil and not dying on the spot. What God actually said was *not to eat the fruit.* He said nothing about touching the tree. Adam and Eve could build a tree house in the tree if they liked! But if they *ate the fruit* they would die.

At this point, aware that Eve's confidence in God was shaken (Genesis 3:3), Satan unveils his real plan for her: *to disobey God.* He offered something seemingly wonderful if she would do as he suggested. Innuendo changed to accusation: God is a liar! "You will surely not die. For God knows that when you eat of it your eyes will be opened, and you will be like God, knowing good and evil." Note carefully the offered benefit: to become "like God." Would Eve desire this promotion? Does *this desire* explain the rest of the story? Let's see. Have humans aspired to this promotion ever since? In what ways in our world do you see people trying to play the role of God?

Eve's next step is truly fascinating, not only in light of her story, but in light of *all* of our stories. She engaged in the first scientific experiment ever recorded—at least science as it would be defined today. First, she discounted the reality of God's revelation (what He said would happen if she ate the fruit: death). What remains? She was left with her own powers of observation. Therefore, Eve examined the fruit. "When the woman saw that the fruit of the tree was good for food and pleasing to the eye, and also desirable for gaining wisdom … " (v. 6). If we do not take spiritual realities into account, what is the basis for our decisions?

Now we arrive at the focal point of the situation, the same point we discuss throughout the Covenant series, the same point at which each of us will find ourselves countless times throughout life: we come to the point of decision. Until this point it was just words. All of us go back and forth in our minds about situations. We consider, we ponder, we assess the relative merits of things we hear. We try to understand our desires and needs, along with the likely outcomes of various decisions. We assign weights to all of these factors, then try to make the best choice. In this entire process there is one defining moment: the moment when a decision is rendered and action results. At this point the consequences of the decision are unleashed, for better or worse. These consequences may follow us, shape and define us, or perhaps haunt us for the rest of our lives. Has anyone ever had buyer's remorse? Have we ever wanted something so badly that we ignored objections that we knew, somewhere down inside, were really true? We ran over this guardrail on the way off a cliff as we chased something so important, so desirable—or at least we thought it was. When the reality of the situation becomes apparent and we are headed toward a painful landing, what do we say? "If I had only listened to … " Have you ever had such a moment? How did you realize you had been deceived?

"If I had only listened to . . . " Have you ever had such a moment? How did you realize you had been deceived?

We can envision Eve leaning against the tree as she studied the fruit. Then she reached up and touched it. Perhaps she snapped off the stem and held the fruit in her hand, looking closely. She smelled it, felt it, perhaps even squeezed it a little. At a superficial level her decision was about one thing: whom did she really believe? She was already far down the path toward disbelief in God's words.

At a deeper level, though, her decision came down to choosing one of two ways of thinking: whom did she have the most reason to believe, or *whom did she most want to believe?* Did Eve have more reason to believe her Creator? Or should she trust this unfamiliar creature who suggested her Creator's intentions were not what she thought? Was God really not worthy of trust? Or was she being truly observant and analytical? Did she consider her entire life? From the time her eyes first opened beside her husband, lover, and best friend in a world perfectly suited to her, had there been any reason to not trust God? *The only time she ever questioned His love was right here, right now, based solely upon the words of this unknown being.*

The vital element in play here, beyond what is factual and what is not, is *desire*. Eve was open to Satan's ideas because *she thought her eyes were being opened to new and very desirable possibilities.* As a result, Eve narrowed her examination of reality to a single question. The answer she chose reinforced her move away from trusting God: *the fruit simply did not appear to be as dangerous as God said it was.* In fact, it looked ... good to her, thus good for her. This lined up with the words of her new best friend and confidant. Perhaps he was right when he said her God was holding back the best things! After considering all of the above, Eve exercised her most fundamental human prerogative (and all three of the powers we discuss in this book series). She made her decision, then raised the fruit to her lips (v. 6). Have you ever been thoroughly convinced you were right, only to find you were not? What role did desire play in your situation?

Rather than experiencing the wonderful new life she had been promised, Eve soon discovered that every idea offered by her new BFF was a *lie*. Truth and reality are synonymous at the deepest level. Truth is simply a statement of reality, an accurate description of the cause-and-effect universe God created us to inhabit. Eve would find that everything God said about eating the fruit was true. God's truth, His Word, has been conveyed to humanity throughout history. But since the very beginning there has also been another voice. This voice spews out innumerable reasons why we should *not believe* our Creator or His Word. He offers seemingly compelling reasons to pursue another agenda. We get to choose between these two voices. Unfortunately, we often embrace the words of the one who *appears* to offer the best future rather than the One who truly does. Does this pattern still exist in our life today?

THE POWER OF DECEPTION

If we are to defend our lives and build them to their potential, we must understand the power of deception. Deception is not just a lie. It is an offer of something we become persuaded is important for us, something that is necessary for our best life. In order to receive the promised benefit, though, this offer always requires us to *depart from God's path*. This, by the way, is the point of this entire exercise. To pull us away from God, Satan's representatives offer us something God does not offer in His plan. Something we decide justifies our brushing past God as we reach out for something so … wonderful … until we find that it is not. Promised benefits *never materialize, or are not at all what we expected.*

"… whoever is united with the Lord is one with Him in spirit" (1 Corinthians 6:17).

"… he who unites himself with a prostitute is one with her in body? For it is said, 'The two will become one flesh'" (1 Corinthians 6:16).

"In my sinful nature [I am] a slave to the law of sin" (Romans 7:25).

HOW SATAN'S REBELLIOUS NATURE BECAME PART OF US

More occurred in this story than a mistake that damaged the lives of Adam and Eve. When they turned from God and followed Satan two exchanges took place. First, they gained a new element in their nature: part of the nature of Satan. This rebellious nature not only continued to plague Adam and Eve throughout life, it passed into their offspring—that is, into all of us. If an exchange of nature occurred, what also must have occurred? For natures to be exchanged, a *covenant* must have been entered. Though this detail is not recorded in Scripture, if we examine the overall scenario a clear picture emerges: one Covenant (with God) was broken as a new one was formed (with Satan). This occurred in the same way that adultery breaks one Marriage Covenant as it creates another (1 Corinthians 6:16).

A second exchange also occurred that is characteristic of Covenant. Dominion over the earth, which had been conveyed from God to Adam and Eve, passed from Adam and Eve to Satan (Genesis 1:26). Jesus would later refer to Satan as "the prince of this world" (John 12:31). Both this exchange of nature and this "life exchange" would occur only within a Covenant.

This is why more than forgiveness for our sins is required to restore our relationship with God. This is why a New Covenant is required. Entry into this Covenant now breaks the covenant between Adam and Eve and the enemy of God. The New Covenant restores us to humanity's original state of oneness with God. This can only occur by putting our old nature to death, then raising us to life as a new creation that is now joined to God and indwelled by His Spirit. This is why *fixing our current life* is insufficient. Our old life and nature must die. We need a new life in Covenant with our loving Creator.

The problem is that, from our vantage point, none of us realize this. The problems of our world and our lives are obvious. But most do not welcome God's solution to the most fundamental problem in their life. Instead, most of humanity continues to buy into an ongoing series of deceptive offers: *our life, made better.* Is there anything in all of human history that inspires confidence in this plan? Still, few of us recognize that the first step on the path toward our best life is the death of the life we so much want to fix. From our vantage point, shouldn't we be trying to save our life?

"For although they knew God, they neither glorified Him as God or gave thanks to Him, but their thinking became futile and their foolish hearts were darkened" (Romans 1:21).

"They exchanged the truth about God for a lie, and worshipped and served created things rather than the Creator" (Romans 1:25).

"Because of this, God gave them over to shameful lusts" (Romans 1:26).

"Just as they did not think it worthwhile to retain the knowledge of God, so God gave them over to a depraved mind, so that they do what ought not to be done" (Romans 1:28).

To understand the nature which became part of us, we must understand who Satan is and what he is doing. As we describe his nature, see if we notice these same elements in people today. His primary desire is to *be worshiped as God.* His plan is to displace God as rightful ruler of the universe and install himself in God's place. This involves denying God's authority over our lives and our accountability to Him. Satan as ruler would become the one in charge of ultimate outcomes. For example: "you will surely not die." Of course, the outcome Satan is most interested in overwriting is God's ultimate judgment of him for his rebellion.

Ultimately, it is God who ordains every outcome. This is what it means to be God. Satan wants this power, and through it he wants to control every life. Do we see people trying to control the lives of others? Satan wants to be worshipped. Do we see in people a corresponding desire for adulation and fame? Satan wields power through fear, intimidation, deception, and shame. His goal is to dominate everyone. Do humans follow this pattern? Satan wants to rewrite the moral code of the universe. What God calls evil he calls good, and what God proclaims to be good Satan declares to be evil. Do some people vilify God's moral law and hold up what is evil to be admired and emulated? Satan promises us that our best life will be found by throwing off God's moral restraints. To have the best life we must *rebel*, often not realizing that as we do this we immerse ourselves more deeply in Satan's rebellion.

This path leads only to death, as it always has. He promises freedom. But his path enslaves us—to himself and to the behaviors we embrace as we follow him. Death came to humanity through Satan, along with every brutality and lie.

Our entire society has shifted during my lifetime. It has moved from publicly honoring God and basing large areas of public life on His Word to living out in "mainstream" culture the very progression referenced in Romans 1 above. It may be helpful to pause for a moment and read the entire chapter. We see these very things all around us.

"*... for when you eat from it you will surely die*" (Genesis 2:17).

THE SENTENCE OF DEATH HANGING OVER US

What are the consequences of Satan's initial rebellion, and of our joining this enemy? Death. This meant Adam and Eve, who were intended to live eternally like the angels, began the process of physically dying. Not at once, but eventually both died physically. But death has other dimensions. The word *death* actually means "separation." Adam and Eve were immediately separated from their oneness with God. But for each of us there will also be an ultimate judgment by God (Revelation 20:11-15). He will separate us into two groups—those whose names are "written in the Book of Life," and those whose names are not. Those whose names do not appear in this Book will be eternally separated from God. Whose names are in this book? For those who lived after Jesus offered us the New Covenant, I believe this book lists those who have received new life from God by entering this Covenant with Him. Those who have not chosen to enter the New Covenant will be allowed to remain in their chosen state of separation for eternity.

Humanity also became fractured and fragmented in other ways. "Human nature" now separates us from each other—in Marriages, families, and as a society. There can be no true unity among humanity because of this separation—a fact demonstrated consistently throughout history.

Parts of us are also separated within ourselves. Mental illness is one manifestation. We have great difficulty determining who we are, why we are here, and how to live our best lives. Therefore, we are more susceptible to the initial human failing: deception. Each of us is made in the image of God; we reflect elements of His character. But because of the ingrafted nature of the enemy of God, we also have the urge at points to kill, steal, and destroy. These urges compete within us, leading to internal conflict and shame. But there is another less-noticed, though highly corrosive outcome: the continual state of confusion in which our lives and our society are immersed. We have lost our ability to discern what is really true, or right, or best, or real.

We have great difficulty determining who we are, why we are here, and how to live our best lives. Therefore, we are more susceptible to the initial human failing: deception.

Therefore, more is required for each of our lives than "trying harder to do better." Our efforts cannot erase God's sentence of death over our lives, nor can our efforts break the hold that rebellious behaviors have on us. It is vital to understand the reality of our condition. What must God do, and what must we do, if the consequences of rebellion are to be fully undone? What would make us fit to inhabit eternity in oneness with God? What must God do, and what must we do to build a blessed, abundant, and properly connected life? We must enter the New Covenant to be sure.

But entering this Covenant does not eradicate all the problems that result from our rebellion. Entering Covenant is an essential first step, but *we also play an essential role in Covenant.* We must faithfully carry out our assigned role in this relationship if the impact of sin is to be reversed in our day-to-day lives. Covenant is the solution, but part of this solution comes in the form of an opportunity. Covenant is more than a relationship; it is a plan. It is faithfulness to God and our Covenant that determines the actual impact this relationship will have on our lives here and now, and on our rewards in eternity.

If we are in Covenant with God, we are assured of a place in eternity with Him. If this were all that mattered, we might as well die and enter our eternal home the moment we enter this relationship. But this is not God's plan. It is vital we understand why. When we enter Covenant the core of our being—our identity—is transformed and joined to God. But other parts of our being come forward from our old life largely unchanged. We have a guidance system—the part of us that directs our behavior. We spent our entire lives building the belief system that directs our decisions. We enter Covenant with a character we spent our lives building. This too is mostly carried forward from our old life. Though we are now different in the core of our being, the way we live and the way we experience life remains much the same—until something else changes within us.

To be sure, if we have actually entered Covenant with God by offering our lives to Him and accepting His offer of relationship on His terms, some things about us are immediately transformed. We will notice some of these changes. We may feel a new sense of peace. We may see ourselves and God differently. We may have a new desire to read and understand God's Word. Some things about us will change, but not most things. Some of our decisions will be different, but most will be a continuation of our old ways. If the things which form our daily lives shift only a little, how much of a change can we expect in our relationships, our circumstances, or the way we experience life? The transformation of life we seek by coming to God has only just begun. The massive and revolutionary changes that are God's plan for us exist only in potential at this point—that "abundant life" He promises those who come to Him. For these things to become reality in our lives something else is required: the plan of Covenant. And for this plan to be accomplished in our lives something is required of us: faithfulness to the Covenant we have entered.

"Anyone who chooses to be a friend of the world becomes an enemy of God" (James 4:4).

"The mind governed by the flesh is death, but the mind governed by the Spirit is life and peace" (Romans 8:6).

"The acts of the flesh are obvious: sexual immorality, impurity and debauchery; idolatry and witchcraft; hatred, discord, jealousy, fits of rage, selfish ambition, dissections, factions and envy; drunkenness, orgies and the like. I warn you, as I did before, that those who live like this will not inherit the Kingdom of God" (Galatians 5:19-21).

WHAT ARE 'THE WORLD' AND 'THE FLESH,' AND WHY DO THEY MISLEAD US?

In Scripture there are many references to "the world" and "the flesh." These references are always unfavorable. These *lead us away from God and His plan for our lives.* We noted that Satan rebelled against God, and Adam and Eve joined him and acquired part of his nature. This nature carried forward into every descendant of Adam and Eve—that is, into all of us. This alone would be enough to cause problems in our world. But is there more to this picture? People speak of being "tempted by Satan." Satan must really get around, since he is a created being, and thus capable of being only in one place at one time.

Is there anything else happening in the spiritual realm that plays a role in leading us astray? What is this influence and how is it wielded?

Eve believed in a promise of a better life, but this promise was a lie. By believing in and acting upon this promise her life was grievously damaged. Where do the deceptive ideas in our world come from? Satan sold one to Eve. "The world," under the influence and guidance of Satan and his followers, tries to sell us more deceptive ideas on a daily basis. "The flesh," or the parts of us that are constructed upon already-embraced deception, will continue to be an influence that corrupts and misdirects our new life, unless…

To rid our lives of this influence, God charges us with the task of renewing our minds. We must reject and eject the deceptions we have embraced, and replace these with God's truth. The problem with this plan from our standpoint is this: in our perception these ideas we have embraced *are true*, and any idea which opposes these ideas is false. To work our way through this maze successfully we must learn about deception—its source, the agenda of this source, and how to identify deception.

*"The Nephilim were on the earth in those days—
and also afterward—when the sons of God
went to the daughters of humans and had children by them.
They were the heroes of old, the men of renown. The Lord saw
how great the wickedness of the human race had become,
that every inclination of the thoughts of the human heart
was only evil all the time"* (Genesis 6:4, 5).

" … the sacrifices of pagans are offered to demons, not to God"
(1 Corinthians 10:20).

*"For our struggle is not against flesh and blood … but against the
powers of this dark world and against the spiritual forces of evil in
the heavenly realms"* (Ephesians 6:12).

THE FALLEN ANGELS

Several other books are referenced in Old Testament writings. These books were not viewed as infallible (in contrast to the way Scripture was viewed by Jewish teachers), but as reliable reference sources. One, the Book of Enoch[10], was quoted several times by New Testament writers. In Genesis Chapter 6 an event is briefly referenced: "sons of God" (perhaps better translated "sons of Heaven") came to earth and procreated with human women. Their offspring were the Nephilim, hybrids between angels and humans with superhuman powers. Genesis 6:4 uses language to describe these beings that sounds complimentary: "heroes of old, men of renown." The Book of Enoch describes this same event in much more detail. It is anything but complimentary toward these beings. The topic we are about to cover briefly is covered in much greater detail in Volume One of this series, *What Is a Covenant?* The purpose of this material is to help the reader understand the origin, nature, and agenda of the deception and confusion which permeate our world. If we understand the true nature and purpose of these ideas, we may become far less interested in holding on to them.

Satan was joined in his rebellion by one-third of the angels. We are not told the total number of angels, but this represents a large number of rebellious beings. The Book of Enoch describes two hundred of these fallen angels with twenty leaders coming to earth in the fourth generation from Adam. They procreated with humans and taught humans many things. In Enoch, seventeen things are listed that these angels taught humanity. First, as fallen angels, what do they desire? To be worshiped. These beings taught humans to worship them. They taught occult practices and astrology. Also, they offered a considerable amount of scientific and technical information to these early humans. They taught metallurgy to make weapons, metal jewelry, and mirrors. Makeup was introduced and other "arts of civilization" were taught. But there was more: under the leadership of these beings moral depravity was the rule, in keeping with the character and agenda of their ultimate leader, Satan. This led to evil among humanity so pervasive that God was ultimately moved to wipe human life off the earth. He sent a flood that was survived only by righteous Noah and his family.

This is an interesting and detailed account, but is there anything in the historical record that correlates with this story? In fact, a vast amount of evidence corroborates this account. There is only one point of conflict between the Book of Enoch and the Bible on one hand, and the writings and artifacts of the Sumerians (the first human civilization) and the archeologists and scientists who have studied these writings and artifacts on the other hand. *Who were these beings* who so obviously impacted this civilization?

This raises a corollary question. When were Adam and Eve alive? We must hold any conclusions we draw from artifacts that are thousands of years old, including the accuracy of our dating, with an open hand. But several corroborating lines of evidence—within Scripture, the Book of Enoch, secular archaeology, the history of the ancient world, and current science—in sum support the picture I am going to offer. This picture, in turn, supports a belief commonly held in the Christian community for centuries: that Adam and Eve lived around 4000 B.C.

The book of Enoch, in harmony with Genesis 6, identifies the beings who led the Sumerians as fallen angels. These angels taught humans, had offspring with them, and thoroughly corrupted them. The Sumerians identify these beings as gods. And how do mainstream archaeologists view these beings? As "the mythology of the Sumerians."

The book of Enoch, in harmony with Genesis 6, identifies the beings who led the Sumerians as fallen angels. These angels taught humans, had offspring with them, and thoroughly corrupted them.

How does the archaeologic record correspond with these assertions? For a couple of million years (per the dating schema of mainstream archaeology) hunter-gatherer groups wandered the landscape using fire and stone tools. Suddenly, at one location everything changed. Around 4000 B.C. the first cities appear in ancient Sumeria. The most prominent features in these early cities are temples, often in the form of pyramids (ziggurats). Culture and technology developed rapidly, leading to several city-states in this region. Writing appeared along with schools, libraries, sophisticated textiles and a legal system that included contracts and medical malpractice laws. Scientific knowledge appeared that seems far beyond the capacity or tools of the people who possessed it[11]. The question on the mind of everyone who has studied these artifacts is, "How did this group of people learn to do all of this?"

> *"They provoked Him to jealousy with strange gods,... They sacrificed unto devils, not to God;"* (Deuteronomy 32:16-17).

The Sumerians themselves are very clear about the source of their "arts of civilization." They got all of these things from their gods. They built temples to these beings and worshiped them. They described these beings and depicted them in carvings on temple walls. They were larger than humans, often depicted with wings, and absolutely terrifying. These beings had offspring with Sumerian women (a phenomenon also described in many subsequent ancient cultures). The same group, or pantheon, of these gods was worshipped throughout Sumeria. Different city-states had different patron deities but paid homage to all of them. Among these cities there was a continual state of warfare in the name of their gods.

Around 3200 BC civilizations began to appear in other areas—China, Japan, the Indus Valley, Egypt, and other places. Then civilization spread throughout the world. In the written records of virtually every civilization we have been able to translate, there are accounts of a pantheon of gods analogous to the gods of Sumeria. Stories from many of the oldest civilizations speak of a time when gods walked the earth with people and ruled them. The gods conveyed the "arts of civilization" to each of these early cultures, ruled them, and procreated with them. Often subsequent rulers claimed to be of the bloodline of these gods and ruled in their name. This pattern is seen throughout the ancient world, along with ancient temples, often in the shape of a pyramid, that are dedicated to these gods. While the names changed among the civilizations, the description of the various gods (e.g. "god of war, knowledge," et. al.) in these various cultures follow similar patterns. But how does this impact us today?

We claim to be part of Western Civilization. Where did Western Civilization come from? The cultural ideas we embrace about the path to the best government and the best life came down to us from ancient Greece by way of the Romans and their legacy in European countries. But where did the Greeks get their ideas? They say from their gods. And where did they get their gods and their way of life? The ancient Greeks say from ancient Babylon. And where did the Babylonians get their gods and their way of life? They say from Sumeria. For instance: Innanna, the goddess of fertility, marriage, and prostitution of the Sumerians became Ishtar of the Babylonians, who became Aphrodite of the Greeks, who became Venus of the Romans.

"You know, it's getting very simple now /
Since no one believes in me anymore"
"No One Believes in Me Anymore (Satan's Boast)"
–Keith Green song[12]

As noted, modern archaeologists and commentators refer to these gods as only *mythology*. A myth, by definition, is something not real. This designation correlates with a general move by "educated people" to dismiss as myth anything associated with the spiritual realm. But does this assertion properly explain the remarkably similar worldwide accounts of these beings—at a time when humans were supposedly too "primitive" to engage in intercontinental travel? Or the worldwide, massive efforts to build remarkably similar temples to honor these beings? Or the remarkably similar worship practices noted in Europe, Asia, Africa, and the Americas in the name of these beings? Or are these beings actually real, and did they actually influence people and their way of life? And, do these same beings continue to influence our way of life?

They provoked Him to jealousy with strange gods, with abominations they provoked Him to anger. They sacrificed to devils, not to God; to gods whom they knew not...
(Deuteronomy 32:15-16)

If one reads Scriptural accounts of the ancient Israelites, one is struck not by our differences from these people but by our similarities to them. Our tools and toys are different, but these people confronted the same issues of life we face, and in largely in the same ways. These were not primitive idiots. The premise that ancient people devoted remarkable resources and effort to build massive and beautiful temples across the ancient world to chase fairy tales is much harder to believe than the premise that these beings *actually existed* and influenced much of the way these people approached life. A way of life that has filtered down to us. These beings were appeased with offerings and obedience because ancient peoples thought these beings controlled the physical universe and held one's life and prosperity in their hands. And, to a degree, perhaps they did.

Of course, occult practices that seek supernatural protection and favor have died out in our modern world ... or have they? The Scripture refers to fallen angels who have some degree of control over our realm as "principalities and powers." Ephesians 6:12 informs us that the ultimate conflict in our world is not among humans, but with these angelic beings.

"The rest of mankind who were not killed by these plagues still did not repent...they did not stop worshipping demons, and idols..."
(Revelation 9:20).

Do these beings impact your life and mine today? Angels are immortal. If they were present and influential in the ancient world, why would this not be the case in our world? If you know any missionaries from third world counties, or any country other than our own, ask about their experiences with supernatural forces in their area. If we in the United States for the most part no longer believe in such beings, are we safe from their influence? If you are not aware of the presence of radioactive radon gas in your basement, are you and your family safe from its influence?

Consider Adam and Eve. They did not fall down and worship Satan; they did not build an altar and make a sacrifice to him. In order to be joined to Satan they merely had to follow his advice about seeking "their best life." They *listened*, they *believed*, they *believed in,* and they *followed.* As we look around our culture, is anyone following this same pattern? Are individuals or our culture as a whole being deceived in this same way?

WHERE DO ALL THESE IDEAS ABOUT LIFE COME FROM?

These realities have had many impacts on my life. I used to see the world in three categories: the things of God, human diversity that should be at least tolerated and probably more appreciated, and really evil things. My affinity for human diversity shifted when it became evident that ways of life which do not reflect God are not just about human creativity. Instead, when we look beneath the surface, things not of God all reflect the influence of the enemies of God. Once we understand the purpose of this influence and its outcome, these ideas lose their appeal. I now see only two sources for information about life: God and "other." Diversity simply represents the variety of deceptive pitches made to humanity that have been carried forward in various cultures and disseminated throughout history.

My affinity for human diversity shifted when it became evident that ways of life which do not reflect God are not just about human creativity.

One of the most important things we must understand about our life is that *our life is a battleground.* The weapons in this war are ideas. We talked about deception, which is intended to get us to embrace and act on wrong ideas based on false reasoning. How is this war waged within us? We will have to lay some more groundwork to fully answer that question. First, we need to learn some things about our internal wiring system. God gave us three powers as human beings. First, the power to decide what we believe is true and not true—the *power of assent and dissent;* second, the power of deciding what is more or less important—the *power of attention;* and third, the power to decide what, if anything, we are going to do about a given idea—the *power of intention.*

How are these powers used? Consider the use of these powers in the various people who interacted with Jesus. Some believed Jesus was God, but others did not. Some believed that following Him was the highest priority in life, and others believed other things were more important. Some left everything of their previous life and faithfully followed Him. Others chose to pursue different agendas. We see these different responses, but we may not realize that each response reflects a specific choice made by each individual. God allows each of us to make these choices, and holds us accountable for the choices we make. We each get to decide what we think is true, and embrace this belief. But what we embrace as true may or may not actually be true. We get to choose what we think is important or unimportant, but may over-value one thing and under-value another. We can choose to devote ourselves to doing good and right things, waste our lives on unimportant things, or pursue things that are frankly evil. Or we can have a life full of good intentions that were never carried out. For all three powers, note that *we get to decide how to use them.* Others can influence us in various ways, but no one can force us to believe something if we choose not to believe it; no one can make us value something if we choose not to do so; and no one can force us to act in a certain way if we are absolutely unwilling to do so, and are willing to pay the price for our choice.

Why did God give us these powers? These powers allow us to *identify truth, prioritize it, and then act based on truth as necessary*. These powers allow us to identify right things and make right choices. But as we use our powers to choose there is a much more powerful impact on our lives, one we may not realize is even occurring. As we choose to believe one idea or another about ourselves, or about the fundamental questions of life, these beliefs in turn form important parts of us. The sum of these beliefs form our *guidance system*, our *character*, and our *self-concept*. Thus, these decisions play a remarkably powerful role directing the course of our life. God intends that our belief system, actions, and self-concept be based on truth. What if, instead of embracing and living out truth, we embrace deception and are guided by lies? What if we build our self-concept on things that are *not true*? If our life is a battleground of ideas, might deceptive life-directing ideas be one of the enemy's most powerful weapons? Our three powers, designed to produce something of great benefit in our lives, can be hijacked and misdirected. And by this our entire lives can be misdirected—by the influence and deception of God's enemies. Do we see this occurring around us? Or in our own lives?

Much has been taught and written about what God does for us that we cannot do for ourselves. All of these things relate to Covenant. But we have highlighted another very important truth. Many outcomes in our lives after we enter Covenant depend on our decisions. This is true in a Marriage or our relationship with God. God offers many wonderful opportunities in our Covenant with Him. We can choose to make the most of these opportunities, or not. The focus in Christian teaching is often on choosing to do the right thing, or not sinning—that is, on simple behavior choices. But the choices God offers us in Covenant go far beyond in-the-moment behaviors. If our lives are not what we want them to be, could it be that we are casualties in the war of ideas and beliefs we mentioned above? Could many of the problems in our lives be due to ideas we have chosen to believe—ideas which, when embraced, formed our character? What if we are dishonest, defiant, or destructive? If our life is going in the wrong direction, why is this? If our experience of life is not what we want, why is this? If we are in a Covenant with God and these things are still true, why is this?

In the plan of Covenant God offers us a truly remarkable opportunity. That is, *through making new choices about what we believe to be true,* we can experience the abundant life God promises us. Given that our previous choices formed much of the very fabric of our being, this is a process of transformation that continues for the rest of our lives. Jesus said that to follow Him we must take up our own cross daily. The cross is a tool of execution. What must we put to death on a daily basis to follow Him? We must put to death our false beliefs, and the parts of us which are built upon these false beliefs. Why is this a vital thing to do? Because it is these beliefs which form us and direct us to not love and not obey God. It is these things that stand in the way of our best life, and our best experience of life. Why does God not simply remove these things from us? In His plan, He instructs us to disassemble the parts of us that *we built* through use of our three powers; then, we are to use these same powers to rebuild our lives hand-in-hand with God upon the foundation of His truth. When it comes to transforming and rebuilding our lives in Covenant, God does not do it all. He does His part. We must do our part. This is not easy. Nothing that really matters in life is ever easy. But it is doable. God has a plan that we can choose to follow.

Let's take a closer look at the nature of our three powers. Then we will see how to use them.

THE THREE POWERS GOD GAVE US

"If you hold to my teaching, you are really my disciples. Then you will know the truth, and the truth will set you free" (John 8:32).

"I know that you are Abraham's descendants, yet you are looking for a way to kill me because you have no room for my word. I am telling you what I have seen in the Father's presence, and you are doing what you have heard from your father" (John 8:37, 38).

"Do not conform to the pattern of this world, but be transformed by the renewing of your mind. Then you will be able to test and approve what God's will is—His good, pleasing, and perfect will" (Romans 12:2).

The three powers we are going to consider correspond to three terms we hear more commonly: our mind, heart, and will. I believe it is vital to recognize these as powers. Why? Because many people do not realize we actually control these parts of ourselves. Many believe they are at the mercy of their thoughts and feelings, and good intentions are substituted for determination and perseverance. Unless we see these as *powers we have the sole ability to direct*, we will not learn to use these powers as God intends. God intends that we use these powers to accomplish good things and to properly build and shape ourselves.

To carry out God's plan of growth and transformation we must learn to take charge of these powers. We cannot simply choose to do so, any more than we can choose to run a marathon, then get up off the couch and run 26 miles if we have not properly trained for this. Our ability to identify truth improves with practice, our judgment about what is most important sharpens with experience, and our will-power grows as we choose to use it.

"Sanctify them by the truth; your Word is truth" (John 17:17).

THE POWER OF ASSENT AND DISSENT: THE TRUE POWER OF AN IDEA

We get to decide what we believe to be true and not true. Many ideas come before us every day. We sort some into categories without a second thought; others require due consideration. But we end up determining whether, in our opinion, an idea is real, true, right, good, beneficial, or appropriate. Or, is it false, wrong, bad, harmful, or inappropriate? Think of Eve as she tried to decide whether to believe God or Satan. There is always a period in which we consider an idea.

Then, there is the point at which we decide. It is at the *point of decision* that this power is wielded. What we choose to believe is true not only reveals something about us, these embraced ideas also do much to form us.

It is vital to realize that our decision that something is true in no way determines whether that thing is *actually* true. That is a different question. We are merely deciding what we believe. Once we embrace an idea we are drawn to people with similar views. In fact, embraced ideas are one of the most powerful forces drawing people together or pulling them apart. Think of all the groups in our world that gather around ideas, or of families that are divided by ideology.

Once we embrace an idea we are drawn to people with similar views. In fact, embraced ideas are one of the most powerful forces drawing people together or pulling them apart.

Once we embrace an idea, this becomes *our truth*. For us this is now a settled question. It becomes part of our sense of reality: this is the way things are, the way things work, the way people are, or the way we are. Our sense of reality does not like conflicting ideas. If we strongly embrace a new idea, other things within us shift to accommodate the newcomer. Thus a single strongly embraced idea can impact prior beliefs, values, priorities, goals, and many other things within. For details, see that college freshman who comes home for Thanksgiving and he or she is … different. Also, similar ideas are now embraced more easily. People tend to embrace related groups of ideas and resist mixing them. People embrace conservative ideas or liberal ideas. Few people are part conservative and part liberal.

Embraced ideas impact emotions. Our emotions have two fundamental purposes. First, emotions serve as a sensory faculty in the moment. "What did that person *really* mean when he or she said that to us?" Second, emotions give us energy to move toward or away from things; thus they are a key part of our value system. We feel warmly toward our beliefs and those who hold them, and less warmly toward those who differ. We move away from things we fear or hate and toward things we love. Our emotions impact what we do, and also impact our life experience. If we are continually in fear of being hurt by people, how will we experience relationships? Contrast that with a person who has learned to trust trustworthy people.

Many believe that feelings simply well up from within us as an expression of our deepest being. While this may sometimes be true, our feelings are related to our beliefs more often than we realize. If you believe I stole your wallet, how will you feel toward me the next time you see me? If you find your misplaced wallet, how will you then feel toward me? Did anything change *about me* to form your feelings? Or do these different feelings reflect your changing beliefs?

Many go through life plagued by problem thoughts or feelings. These people feel themselves to be victims of their mind and heart, as if they are subject to a force beyond their control. But this is not true. Any idea or feeling is there because we are willing to have it there. At some level we have already embraced and affirmed these things, and at some level we must continue to offer our permission for a thought to come before us.

> Affirmation, Attention, and Intention are powers. These exert a vast impact on our lives.

Affirmation, Attention, and *Intention* are powers. These exert a vast impact on our lives. These powers are intended to be tamed, trained, and used constructively. If our control over these is weak, if these powers are like an unruly three-year-old throwing a tantrum in a grocery store, our powers and this child need the same thing: to be disciplined.

It is easy to fall into a trap regarding our embraced beliefs. These ideas form our sense of reality. It is a small step to believe that these ideas define reality. If we see things this way, how do we view conflicting ideas and the people who hold them? These different ideas are not simply *different* ideas; they are wrong ideas. From our perspective these ideas violate reality. Therefore, people who hold and promote these ideas have a flawed view of reality. They lead people astray. It is another small step to believe that such people should be vigorously opposed or even punished. Does this sequence of beliefs explain the acrimony between those with differing views in our culture? The flaw in this thinking is the belief that "our truth" is the definition of truth. This lack of humility erases the basic respect we should have for those who choose to believe and live differently.

For centuries people called philosophers ("lovers of truth") have sought absolute truth. Then, in the eighteenth century, opinion leaders began to focus attention on the fact that people believe many different things to be true. This raised a question that makes sense to a point: If two people believe contradictory things, what right does one have to overrule the other? From this observation comes the conclusion that there is no absolute truth. There is only "my truth" and "your truth," with no meaningful way to decide between them and no reason to do so. We are all welcome to see things in the ways we choose.

I say this makes sense only to a point because this picture only takes into account human choices about what is true. It fails to consider God, who knows the actual answers and has revealed many of these to us in Scripture. Perhaps a better question is why a person would believe his or her perception would reasonably overrule God and His revelation. Are we actually going to be responsible to God for our choices—first and foremost our choice to believe or disbelieve Him?

> Dissenters are wrong. They oppose reality and subvert the truth. They are less than enlightened and perhaps less than human. They are to be punished.

A different level of influence occurs when a group shares a belief. If a *consensus* forms about a belief, this means a particular view of reality is now shared. It is much more difficult to dissent when faced with a group's reality. Groups may take the next step and use their shared reality to form a de facto legal system—either a formal one backed by a police force, or the informal one of a peer group, family, religion, or social movement. Dissenters are wrong. They oppose reality and subvert the truth. They are less than enlightened and perhaps less than human. They are to be punished. Consider public political discussions in our culture, or what happens when a Christian freshman shows up on a college campus. In totalitarian societies thoughts which oppose the government are deemed a crime. Those who spread such ideas have ended up in concentration camps in Russia, China, and other countries. Or they end up on the wrong end of the "cancel culture." Historic freedoms of thought and speech in our country have been, and hopefully will continue to be, in sharp contrast to such totalitarian oppression.

As I studied these phenomena for decades, something stood out. A consensus based on *actual truth* does not create a new legal system, require agreement, and punish outliers. A consensus based on truth may be persuasive, but will not be punitive. Why? Because actual truth stands on its own. Truth invites honest questions. Actual truth is simply a statement of fact or an accurate description of the moral cause-and-effect world we inhabit. God demonstrates a measure of respect toward those who are made in His image. He gives us the power to believe Him or disbelieve Him. As Jesus stood before individuals and conveyed truth to them, He did not chase or coerce those who turned away. There will be consequences for those who persist in turning away from Him and His truth, in this life and in eternity. But those who state *actual truth* respect the humanity of those who believe differently, and the nature of their sometimes-lengthy journey toward belief in God. Coercion plays no constructive role in the journey toward giving one's life to God.

In sharp contrast to such respect, a consensus based on *deception* cannot stand up under honest questioning because it is based on a lie. Therefore, questions are not allowed—they threaten the consensus and are shouted down. Those who refuse to fall into line are rejected in a way that sends a message. Satan rules through deception, intimidation, and fear. We see these elements in full measure as he uses groups to defend and promote his deceptions, from junior high peer groups to cartels to totalitarian governments to the owners of social media platforms. So whenever we see *agreement required,* wherever we see an *alternate reality* and *alternate legal system*—one different from God's—we can be sure these are founded on one or more deceptive ideas. Seeing this pattern in our world explains a great deal.

What we are going to see, however, is the importance of spotting this pattern *within ourselves* and doing something about it.

There is one more impact of embraced truth that is worth noting, for it explains two things we have all encountered. If someone is searching for truth we can provide evidence to help them. If someone is not searching, if this question is already settled in their mind, input is unwelcome and resisted. But there is a deeper effect related to evidence. I wish I still had the reference for a study that was related to us by a professor during my first year of medical school. (If you know the source of this study, contact me so I can attribute this information properly.) Scientists were divided into two groups according to their belief about a scientific question. They were then shown data from a supposed scientific study. Some data supported their position, and an equal weight of data refuted their position. Then these scientists—whose professional life is all about interpreting data—were tested on the data they reviewed. It is not surprising that they more clearly recalled data supporting their position. What is surprising is they often could not recall, even with prompting, data that did not support their position. The conclusion? Our brains are capable of literally screening out data that conflict with embraced beliefs. On one hand, this keeps us from wasting energy reviewing and rethinking issues we believe are settled; on the other hand, this phenomenon may keep reality, truth, and consequences from penetrating our minds and forcing us to question our mistaken beliefs or misdirected way of life. This explains why simply presenting reasons why an idea is wrong often

The conclusion? Our brains are capable of literally screening out data that conflict with embraced beliefs.

does not help. It also explains why people continue to pursue courses that deeply damage themselves and others, and refuse to rethink those courses when it is glaringly obvious to everyone around them that they should do so.

What would happen in our lives if our *embraced truths were actually true*? What if, instead of ongoing waves of negative consequences of our choices, our life was filled with good consequences and blessing? For this to occur, what must happen first? We would need to find a reliable source of actual truth. Then we would need to do what? We would need to go through the process of embracing this truth as our truth. Might this path be part of God's Covenant plan?

"*We must pay the most careful attention, therefore, to what we have heard, so that we do not drift away*" (Hebrews 2:1).

"*Set your minds on things above, not on earthly things*" (Colossians 3:2).

"*Finally, brothers and sisters, whatever is true, whatever is noble, whatever is right, whatever is pure, whatever is lovely, whatever is admirable—if anything is excellent or praiseworthy—think about such things*" (Philippians 4:8).

THE POWER OF ATTENTION

We have the power to direct our attention toward one thing or another. The true impact of this power is often not realized nor its true power utilized. Hold your hand a foot in front of your face with your fingers spread. Focus on your fingers. Can you see what is behind your hand clearly? No, it is out of focus. Now focus on what is behind your hand. This is clearly seen, but your fingers are blurred. You have just used your power of attention at the most basic level, to shift your focus from one thing to another.

This power functions in many ways at many levels. We have more things clamoring for attention and action on a given day than we can possibly respond to. This power sorts out the important things—those that deserve our attention. As we use this more important/less important "sorting power" over time, it forms our value system. Our priorities, ideals and goals, and our vision for our best future are all formed by this power. This power is used to sort the relative importance of things we have already determined are true.

We then use our value system to assess a new idea or opportunity. Does an opportunity offer something important enough for us to redirect our lives, or do we continue to pursue our old agenda? This power oversees our use of time, prioritizes our use of resources, and guides our decisions about the amount of effort we are willing to make toward a given goal.

Another side to this coin is our ability to direct our attention on internal matters. Do we focus on our sadness and loss during adversity, or turn our attention to what God is trying to teach us and the benefits this will bring our lives? Do we allow the rumor we heard about a close friend to create suspicion in us, or do we focus on what we know to be true about this person and our loyalty to them? Do you recall how Eve used her power of attention? What did she decide to put in first place? Was it her *desire* for the "better life" she was offered, or what she knew about God from her own experience?

If we are going to be deceived, a necessary first step is shifting our focus from what we know to be true and right to a *desire*—something we want so badly that we no longer care what is true and right. What we *want* must become more important to us than the consequences of our actions. If we notice ourselves repeatedly imagining the delights of a choice we know is wrong—something not part of God's will for us—we can be sure we are being tempted to embrace a deception.

But life is about more than right and wrong. Much of life is about a proper balance—work and rest, productivity and play, relationships and tasks. There are many good things we might be doing—many more than we can do. How do we bring our goals, values, and priorities into focus to best use our time and effort? Equally important, might we need to review our goals, values, and priorities to make sure these are based on truth? What we are talking about is our *guidance system.* Our guidance system is formed by the combination of what we have embraced as true and the relative value we have assigned to each truth. Whether this system guides us through life toward our best life, or directs us to waste our efforts and our life, is up to us. The difference comes down to whether this system is based on truth. This depends on choices we have made, and perhaps need to remake.

"*I have fought the good fight, I have finished the race, I have kept the faith*" (2 Timothy 4:7)

"*Whatever you do, work at it with all your heart, as working for the Lord, not for human masters*" (Colossians 3:23).

"*Whatever you have learned or received or heard from me, or seen in me—put into practice*" (Philippians 4:9).

"*Whoever looks intently into the perfect law that gives freedom, and continues in it—not forgetting what they have heard, but doing it—they will be blessed in what they do*" (James 1:25).

"*... and teaching them to obey everything I have commanded you*" (Matthew 28:20).

THE POWER OF INTENTION

This is the power that turns ideas into actions. This is the power that follows through, ensuring that we complete important tasks. This is the power that overcomes obstacles and perseveres during times of adversity. This is the power that leaves our stamp on the world. But this power, as with all powers, can be weak or strong. It can be developed or ignored. Therefore, we can also give up when faced with small challenges or be easily diverted. Here is the good news: if this power is weak, we can do something about it.

"Consider it all joy, my brethren, when you encounter various trials, knowing that the testing of your faith produces endurance. And let endurance have its perfect result, so that you may be perfect and complete, lacking in nothing" (James 1:2-4, NASB).

This power has two parts. First, we decide *what to do.* Then we *decide how deeply committed we are* to this objective versus others. Circumstances may alter our agenda depending on our priorities. For example: a woman may be fully committed to her education. Then she becomes pregnant. Does she defer her education and devote herself to raising her young child, or depend on childcare during the child's formative years and make education her first priority? This power expresses into the universe the conclusions we draw by use of our first two powers.

And as with the first two powers, our power of intention at any point may be guided by truth or by "other." We have reasons for everything we do. To build our best relationship with God and our best life we must have reasons that are *sufficient to motivate us.* When faced with adversity we must have reasons that are *sufficient to energize us to overcome obstacles.* For the really important things in life, how important is it for us to make the effort to clarify our reasons? How much effort should we make to ensure that our thinking is founded on truth and reality? I believe we should make any necessary effort. Otherwise we will fall short in days of testing.

"Submit yourselves, then, to God. Resist the devil and he will flee from you" (James 4:7).

INFLUENCE IS WIELDED IN AND OVER OUR LIVES THROUGH THESE POWERS

The choices we make as we use these powers form much of our experience of life and direct much of the course of our life. It is through these same powers that others influence our lives. How? *By influencing the decisions we make* using each power. Think about any time you have been influenced. This effort was always directed at the use of one of these powers. Influence is not always bad. People may love us, and want us to understand and live out truth. But we must beware, for others do not love us—on earth or in the spiritual realm. Everyone who tries to influence us presents themselves as our friend and ally, and their offer as the path to our greatest benefit. Therefore we must grow up, and become wise about who and what we allow to influence us. This is true about which car to buy or where to shop for groceries. But the stakes are far higher when it comes to more fundamental decisions about ourselves and our life.

Influence is not always bad. People may love us, and want us to understand and live out truth. But we must beware, for others do not love us—on earth or in the spiritual realm.

How many ideas have you and I already embraced about who we are and how to live? Where did those ideas come from? Did these sources know all truth and love us perfectly? How many ideas have we embraced and implemented that are one-off, or way off? Do the circumstances of our lives reflect this? If we look carefully and honestly at the key questions about life, we begin to realize how many ideas we have embraced from our world. The same world God says is determined to lead us astray (see 1 John 2). If these ideas are destructive, though, why do we embrace them in the first place? We can certainly be deceived about the real nature of these decisions, but there is something more we must understand about the attraction humans feel toward a life apart from God.

We must realize that something *draws us to ideas and desires* that ultimately damage our lives. Something at the deepest level within us, within our nature, seems to be cooperating with the world to lead us in wrong directions. We do wrong things because we want to. We enjoy these things even though at some level we know they are wrong, and we know they hurt us and others. But we don't care. Why? Because through these things we express part of our nature—the same part Adam and Eve gained through their relationship with Satan. On occasion we do wrong things with the enthusiasm of a salmon swimming over every possible obstacle on its way to its home stream to spawn—it does so because these actions reflect its nature.

> *"For we know that our old self was crucified with Him, so that the body ruled by sin might be done away with, that we should no longer be slaves to sin"* (Romans 6:6).

When we are re-created as new creatures by entering the New Covenant, God deals with the issue of our nature—that irresistible urge to rebel that flows from our old nature. Scripture points out that sin no longer "rules over" us. Yet at this point we don't become totally obedient or perfect human reflections of God. Why? Because of those things that *do not change* at the time we enter Covenant: our character and guidance system.

OUR POWERS EXIST TO BE STRENGTHENED

God does not simply want us to know *about* Him. He does not just want us to know what we are *supposed* to do. Consider a person who learned everything about his or her favorite football team. Everything about the coach, every player, and even every play was committed to memory. If this person suddenly wandered onto the field during a game, was somehow inserted in the lineup and tried to use this knowledge, what would happen? Knowing *about* something and *being able to do it* are different, aren't they? Now imagine that a play is called that this person knows from memory. This person is suddenly in a football uniform and told to carry out the responsibilities of the offensive left tackle. The person knows what to do, but when the ball is snapped …

This person could have spent countless hours in the weight room and on the practice field learning to actually play football. But instead he was content in the stands or on the couch, watching and critiquing. What if this person actually had the innate potential to be a college star and play at the professional level but never developed these inborn powers?

God has given us three amazing powers: to discern and embrace truth, to focus our attention on what is most important, and to complete the most important tasks in life. Yet most people have done little to train themselves to recognize actual truth versus the ever-present sales pitches in our world. Most have done little to refine their sense of priorities or strengthen the capacity to direct efforts where they are most needed. And few have learned to fight through opposition, from within themselves or from the world, to complete essential tasks. Who does not want to be wise, focused, and effective? But to become these things we must work on developing these powers just like we would spend years training to become the athlete we were created to be.

To become faithful to our Covenant, in light of the above do we now understand what is required of us? We must fully develop these powers. There is no way we will consistently make the decisions faithfulness requires unless we have embraced certain truths. There is no way we will make loving our Covenant partner our first priority unless we have a highly developed power of attention. There is no way we will follow through and consistently love in action unless we learn to overcome every obstacle to doing this. One of the most beautiful aspects of God's plan is that we *all* have the ability to strengthen and develop these powers if we make the choice to do so.

HOW ARE OUR GUIDANCE SYSTEM AND CHARACTER FORMED?

Our guidance system is the sum of our decisions about what we want our life to be, want to do, or think we should do. Our character is the sum of our decisions about what we want to be, think we are, or think we should be. These represent our best effort to figure out what is *really true* about ourselves, our life, and life overall.

We embrace some ideas based on what we are told about ourselves or life that we simply accept as true. Some ideas are conclusions we draw from personal experience or observation. Some decisions are about what we aspire to become or the life we want to live. We see role models, live with family expectations, and experience pressure from peers and other sources. Regardless of the sources of our information or the question we are trying to sort out, note the common pattern: we gather all the information we can about an important life question; we decide which information is most reliable; then we render a decision about the way something is. At this point this idea is *affirmed and embraced as true*. This idea becomes part of our view of reality. This is *what I am*; or, *the way life is*; or, *the way other people are*; or, *what I will become*. These embraced ideas descend within us to form feelings, values, viewpoints, goals, preferences, desires, dreams, and many other things. Thus, it is our embraced ideas more than any other factor that form the overall way we express our life and experience our life. Is the relationship now clear between choosing to believe something and living it out?

IN THAT CASE, WHO ARE YOU?

We have a true identity—a "real us"—in the depths of our being. This represents all our fixed attributes: our potential in every respect and the many aspects of our wiring system. These are the things which are unchangeable about us, which are created by God. This includes our conscious awareness. It is a curious reality of life that we cannot look within ourselves and see or know the fullness of our true identity. In fact, we spend our lives trying to figure this out, don't we?

It is a curious reality of life that we cannot look within ourselves and see or know the fullness of our true identity. In fact, we spend our lives trying to figure this out, don't we?

Around this core identity grow other layers of *self*—our character, guidance system, and self-image. These layers are created by us in a way that was just described. If you try to describe yourself, or someone else tries to describe you, almost everything you hear will be about your character, guidance system, or self-image. Other people can't see our true identity any more clearly than we can.

To carry out God's plan of transformation within Covenant we must learn something vital about ourselves. Everything about us which is not part of our fixed identity is an *optional add-on.* Why is this vital to understand? Because when we look at ourselves we cannot perceive the difference between *our true self* and *what we have added via our decisions.* All of these things simply feel like us. All of our embraced ideas simply appear to be statements of truth and reality. So, when God's plan calls on us to act in new ways, ways that are based on actual truth, how will we perceive this call to change? Our initial reaction to some of the things that God instructs us to do will be, "This is simply not based on truth or reality," or, "This is just not *me.*" If we see an injunction from God in this light, are we likely to obey it?

It is vital to make the distinction between what is, and is not, part of our core identity for another reason. When we enter Covenant this core identity *changes*. But our optional add-ons do not. They come forward wrapped around our new nature and identity. Let us think for a moment about the quality of these ideas. We believe these things are true. But are they? From our vantage point the priorities, ideals, emotions, and many other things that are based on these ideas represent not only truth and reality but who we are as a human being. Does God now ask us to be *something we simply are not*?

To correctly answer this question we must first correctly answer some other questions: What is our true identity and what is an optional add-on? And, where do many of our embraced ideas come from? From a world filled with deception and confusion. Is there any chance we bought into some wrong ideas along the way? Even if we were right about ourselves in some ways, what happens when our *self* changes? In light of all of these things, do you think God might reasonably delegate a task to us? The task of shifting our character, guidance system, and self-image from wrong ideas to right ideas? We built these parts of ourselves by use of our Three Powers in the first place. We can change any belief—and all that changes as a result—by use of these same powers.

This is precisely what God directs us to do in Scripture. We are to use these same Three Powers plus the truth of God to build a new character. One that authentically expresses who we are, and one that reflects the Lord who gave us new life in Himself. We are also to build a new guidance system, one that guides us to live out the will of God for our life.

What keeps us from having a character that accurately reflects God once we enter a relationship with Him? The obstacles to accurately reflecting Jesus are all the wrong ideas we have embraced. In order to overcome these obstacles we must first realize where they came from. People often await some act of God to put away these things, but this rarely occurs. Why? Because we built these obstacles by use of our Three Powers, and it is God's plan that we now learn to use these powers for the purpose He originally intended.

To dismantle these obstacles and rebuild on truth we must understand one more thing. We must understand that our perception that an idea is true may be wrong. God gives us a source of absolute truth. We must learn to compare any idea we have embraced with this source of truth. If our beliefs differ from God's Word, what should we do? Cling to our cherished deceptions, or reject them and embrace His truth as the foundation for our character, guidance system, and self-image?

"The Holy Spirit, whom the Father will send in my name, will teach you all things and will remind you of everything I have said to you" (John 14:26).

"All Scripture is inspired by God, and is profitable for teaching, for reproof, for correction, and for training in righteousness" (2 Timothy 3:16).

How, then, do we make sure we are embracing *actual truth*? This can be challenging. Well-intended people—even pastors and loving family and friends—can give incorrect guidance. In our day there is a lot of teaching in the Christian community that does not mirror Scripture. Instead, we see the influence of the world in the lives of Christians and in supposed truths that are proclaimed from pulpits.

Where can we go, and to whom can we turn, to find the truth? This is a real problem, but God has the answer.

Now that we have a better idea of the problems God's Covenant plan needs to solve, we can better appreciate the love and genius of God. All He has ever wanted is to love us and teach us to build the best relationship with Him and the best life. But God's agenda is opposed by a powerful and cunning adversary. This adversary wants to gain our allegiance and lead us away from God, and toward death in his company. Satan has had thousands of years to hone his deceptive skills and perfect his approaches. We must be aware of the reality of this enemy, his agenda and tools, and the remarkably large impact he has already had on our minds and hearts. He poses a threat to our lives that we must take seriously and deal with aggressively. If we ignore him, he will continue to damage and diminish our lives.

Where can we go, and to whom can we turn, to find the truth? This is a real problem, but God has the answer.

For this enemy to exercise any influence over us, though, he must *have our permission*. God tells us that His truth sets us free. From what? From the influence of this enemy that comes at us not only through the world, but also from within our own minds and hearts. It will set us free, that is, if we embrace God's truth and reject the lies of this enemy. It will set us free if we are *transformed by the renewing of our minds* (Romans 12:2). We will soon see how this is done, step by step.

THE TWO PROBLEMS COVENANT MUST SOLVE

God's Covenant plan is designed to solve two essential problems. The first problem is **the sentence of death** that hangs over all of us courtesy of our rebellion against God, and the nature of the author of that rebellion that resides within us. This problem is dealt with by Jesus' offer of the death of our old life and rebirth of a new life that is joined to Him.

The second problem is **our choices**. The new life God gives us and His indwelling Spirit do not solve the problem of our choices. The Scriptures use the term *sin* for choosing to disobey God. When we hear this word we usually think of those things people do that are on the "really bad" list. I hope you now see that sin involves more than wrong in-the-moment decisions. Instead, it is helpful to view sin and obedience as going in opposite directions on the same path. In one direction this path leads toward God and the things of God. Or, we can choose to go in the opposite direction. At a deeper level the problem of our choices extends to all the things our choices have built within us. Some of our choices have built things within us that direct us the wrong way on this path, away from God.

This is why God's Covenant plan involves *repentance*. The Greek word thus translated means literally "to turn and walk in the opposite direction." Note the imagery: wrong direction, turn, go in the right direction. Christian teaching emphasizes our "decision for Christ" and a "prayer of commitment." Repentance is often mentioned, but only in the sense that we acknowledge we are a sinner. But once we enter a relationship with Him, God does not reach down, grab us, turn us around, and give us a push in the opposite direction. Who does the turning? Who chooses to move in the other direction? What does it take to do this? Not one decision, but the array of *decisions which sent us in the wrong direction in the first place* must be remade. These decisions are not remade once, but on a continuing basis. The problems of our old life were largely created by our choices. Our new life will only be correctly built through our choices. Rather than the simplistic view of obedience we often hear in Christian teaching, we must understand that obedience has a larger meaning. To fully obey the Covenant plan of God we must faithfully and consistently guard our hearts and minds against deception. We must root out the deceptions we have already built into our lives. And we must build the new life we were graciously given to maturity. An array of potentials exist within our new life, which we may or may not develop. By following God's plan we will develop each of these. As we do this, we will authentically express the new life we have received, and authentically reflect its author.

God has graciously offered us some very important things we may choose: new life, His truth, a relationship of shared identity and nature with the Creator of the Universe, eternal life in a place where our deepest needs will truly be met, and an opportunity to cooperate with Him here and now in building His kingdom. There is much more. This is but a sampling. Does God love us beyond our wildest dreams? Yes. Would you like to be fully known and fully loved by God? You already are. Would you like to love Him back and know Him fully, at least to the extent that our finiteness allows? This is the offer He extends to each of us. This is the Gospel, an offer made possible by all that Jesus did.

Would you like to love Him back and know Him fully, at least to the extent that our finiteness allows?

CHAPTER THREE

THE NEW COVENANT

JESUS INTRODUCES THE NEW COVENANT

"'The days are coming,' declares the Lord, 'when I will make a new covenant with the people of Israel and the people of Judah ...'"
(Jeremiah 31:31)

Jesus' offer of a New Covenant caught people by surprise, though this offer had been foretold by the prophets. People were surprised by the *specific type* of relationship He offered—a Blood Covenant. People did not understand then, and often do not understand now, why God would offer individuals such a relationship. It is odd how consistently people misconstrue the relationship God desires and requires. This was true in Old Testament Israel. This was true as Jesus unveiled His plan, and it is true today. This is why it is so important to understand *the relationship itself*, as well as its particulars. We must properly understand things like faith, repentance, and obedience.

FIRST, JESUS IDENTIFIED HIMSELF AS GOD

More than once through the years I have heard someone make this statement: "Jesus never claimed to be God." Even a quick reading of the Gospel of John shows He made this claim on multiple occasions, then backed it up. Why is this issue important? Jesus needed to speak with the authority of God to usher in a Covenant different from the one He made with the Israelites. For this Covenant offer to be real His claims had to be proven true. Especially since the sinless life, baptism, outpoured blood, death, and resurrection of God are the heart of this Covenant. Rather than citing all His assertions to be God, here are a few key ones.

First, Jesus commonly referred to Himself as the "Son of Man." This does not, at first glance, sound like a claim to be God—unless one knows the source of the term. In Daniel 7:13 the prophet records a vision of Heaven in which Daniel sees "one like a son of man" who is led into the presence of the Ancient of Days (obviously, the Father). Verse 14 clearly describes this "son of man" also as God. When Jesus used this term every knowledgeable Jew knew its significance. In John 5:23 Jesus says, " … that all may honor the Son just as they honor the Father." He said in John 8:58, "Before Abraham was born, I am." First, had He not been immortal He would not have been alive two thousand years before that moment. Second, the term "I am" is the same term God used to identify Himself to Moses (Exodus 3:14).

But do you wonder how Jesus' hearers understood such claims? In John 10:32 Jesus asked the crowd, which was picking up rocks to execute Him, "I have shown you many good works from the Father. For which of these do you stone me?" Their answer (verse 33): "We are not stoning you for any good work, but for blasphemy, because you, a mere man, claim to be God." Finally, in Matthew 26:64, under questioning by the High Priest, Jesus asserts that He is the One seen by Daniel in his vision: "But I say to all of you: From now on you will see the Son of Man sitting at the right hand of the Mighty One and going on the clouds of heaven." For this claim He was put to death—the claim that He is God. A claim He backed by performing many miracles (John 5:36), then by laying down His life and taking it up again (John 10:18).

JESUS GRADUALLY REVEALED HIS PLAN

Jesus revealed His plan in increments. One bit was told to Nicodemus in John 3. Then another to a synagogue full of followers in

Peter's hometown of Capernaum in John 6. Then more was revealed to the disciples in John 14, and again during their last Passover meal together. Why did Jesus spend three years living around the clock with a small group of followers? Why was this plan unveiled slowly, a piece at a time? And why did His closest followers and confidants still not grasp the heart of His plan while He was being nailed to a Roman cross for execution? Why did Jesus not simply appear on earth, drop off His plan, and head back to Heaven? Because it took years to adjust His disciples' beliefs, viewpoints, expectations, priorities, and a number of other things so they would be prepared to live out God's plan in their lives, then convey this plan to others. In light of our discussion to this point, why do you think it was necessary for Jesus to make these adjustments in the minds and hearts of His disciples? If this lengthy, labor-intensive process was necessary for His disciples, do you think such a process is any less important for you and for me?

We should not be critical of these men or deem them slow learners. God's plan is a *long way* from what anyone expects it to be—and from what any of us want it to be. Throughout history, people have struggled to grasp God's plan and carry it out. But many *have* taken hold of His plan. God in turn has done things in and through these lives that only God can do. May God open our eyes to His plan. May we respond to Him in a way that allows Him to lead us as He desires. May He then build in and through us what He desires. He built the universe; we can trust Him when it comes to building our best life.

We should not be critical of these men or deem them slow learners. God's plan is a *long way* from what anyone expects it to be—and from what any of us want it to be.

What exactly must we do to enter the New Covenant? Scripture, curiously, mentions the elements but does not describe a specific ritual. There is no scripted prayer or specific vow we must say to God. Nor are we provided specific formulas for baptism or the Lord's Supper.

Instead of a ritual, Jesus emphasizes a *particular state of mind and heart* as we come to Him. This state of mind and heart, along with verbally accepting His offer of relationship on His terms, appears to usher us into the New Covenant. This state of mind and heart is termed *faith*, but what exactly is faith? This word has been used in many ways to mean many things. Perhaps we should listen to Jesus as He unveils His offer and outlines the response He expects from us.

> *"For God so loved the world that He gave His one and only Son, that whoever believes in Him should not perish, but have eternal life"* (John 3:16).

Nicodemus, a prominent teacher and political leader, came to Jesus under cover of darkness. (This conversation is recorded in John 3:1-21.) He acknowledged Jesus as a teacher sent from God and waited to hear what Jesus would teach him. Jesus said he must be born again to enter the Kingdom of God. Nicodemus was puzzled. Jesus chided him for not understanding. Then Jesus said that those who believe in Him will have eternal life. This assertion is repeated three times in this passage.

In John 6:28 a question was posed: "What shall we do, that we may work the works of God?" Behind this question was the Jewish belief (and often our belief) that pleasing God is a matter of *doing right things.* Having thus pleased God, we expect Him to make our life better. Remember the contractual thinking we spoke of earlier? Jesus, as He did with Nicodemus, redirects His questioner to the nature of the relationship. Specifically, to *believe Him*—simply to believe the assertion He was making about being the bread that came down from Heaven—and then to *believe in Him.* His hearers struggled with the "came down from Heaven" part because many in the room watched Jesus grow up in Nazareth, a few miles down the road from Capernaum. They grumbled at these words. But the room erupted following His next assertion, then emptied. Why? Because He invited those present to "eat His flesh" and "drink His blood."

Why did people respond this way? Because they understood that Jesus was offering them the opportunity to enter a Blood Covenant with Himself. This was the last offer anyone could imagine based on what they thought they knew about a proper relationship with God. The only people left in the room were His twelve disciples. They were likely shifting uncomfortably in their chairs and mumbling objections under their breath. This offer was news to them as well. Jesus then asked them if they wanted to leave as well. Peter articulated the only reality that could hold these men in their seats: "You have the words of eternal life. … You are the Holy One of God" (John 6:68, 69).

"All Scripture is God-breathed" (2 Timothy 3:16).

"For My Father's will is that everyone who looks to the Son and believes in Him shall have eternal life, and I will raise them up at the last day" (John 6:40).

BELIEVING JESUS AND BELIEVING IN JESUS

What does it mean to believe in Jesus? Obviously we must realize that His words are factually correct. For those who stood before Jesus as He revealed His plan, or those who heard this plan from the first generation of believers, this meant believing a verbal witness that was spoken directly or relayed through those who had been with Jesus. Today this means recognizing that the Scriptures are what Jesus and His disciples asserted they are: words "breathed by God" through human transcribers. We must realize that Jesus speaks as God. He reveals truths to us that we have no way of ascertaining on our own. His perfect character makes it reasonable to believe Him with every fiber of our being, even in the face of our own confusion or internal dissent. This is what it means to believe someone, but what does it mean to *believe in* someone?

"Very truly I tell you, whoever hears my word and believes Him who sent me has eternal life and will not be judged, but has crossed over from death to life" (John 5:24).

"Believe in the Lord Jesus and you will be saved …" (Acts 16:31).

"If you declare with your mouth, 'Jesus is Lord,' and believe in your heart that God raised Him from the dead, you will be saved" (Romans 10:9).

"Yet to all who did receive him, to those who believed in his name, he gave the right to become children of God" (John 1:12).

To *believe in* is to totally trust another person. We trust their loving intentions toward us. We trust their character and integrity that backs up those intentions. We trust that they will take care of us as well as we take care of ourselves, and that they will receive and value our love. This is the heart we have toward another at the altar in our wedding. We think so much of the person that we are willing to totally entrust our lives to them. But any person, no matter how wonderful they are and how much he or she loves us, will fail us and disappoint us because of their imperfections (as we will fail them because of our own). The capacity for this heart response was built into us by God to properly respond to One who loves us perfectly. To One who desires only the best for us, and who has the power and resources to back up His desire for our good. As we come to God to enter Covenant we

The capacity for this heart response was built into us by God to properly respond to One who loves us perfectly. To One who desires only the best for us, and who has the power and resources to back up His desire for our good.

must recognize these things about Him. We must be willing to give everything of ourselves to Him, with nothing held back.

We want a deeper bond than trust with our spouse-to-be. We must feel a profound love for him or her. Part of this feeling of love is a response to who they are, and part arises from our decision to love them. From our love flows the desire to be joined in the deepest possible way. We want to give ourselves to them and receive their life in return. True, honest, and pure love means a total commitment to the other, does it not? This is the essence of our desire as we enter the Covenant of Marriage. But there is more involved in God's Covenant plan than most people perceive or understand. The joining is more profound and powerful, the sharing more extensive, the commitment deeper, and the new life a more radical transformation on a spiritual level than most realize—or make the most of. Some Marriages are characterized by the kind of love for a lifetime that God's plan is designed to build. But is this the case for most? Is the same true for people's relationships with God?

"If you keep My commands, you will remain in My love, just as I have kept My Father's commands and remain in His love" (John 15:10).

"Love the Lord your God with all your heart and with all your soul and with all your mind and with all your strength" (Mark 12:30).

What about a heart of love for God? Where does this fit into the picture as we seek entry into the New Covenant? Where does a heart of love come from to begin with? Think of the deepest love you have ever experienced. This love was certainly expressed in actions. You experienced *consistency*—someone was always there for you in good times or bad. You received love, and your love was received. There was a mutual, growing relationship characterized by blessing each other. The more you did life together, the more you realized who this person is toward you. The more you realized you could trust him or her, the more you felt love toward this person. The more you invested in the relationship, the more your heart grew. The more you came to identify with this person, and the more your lives became intertwined, the more your heart grew. Ultimately, you realized how much this person meant to you.

Now, how about our heart toward God? A heart of love is not kindled by rules, even beneficial ones. Our love is not kindled by benefits, especially if "purchased" by wearisome obedience. Our love is not kindled by admiring someone at a distance, even Someone who is perfect. So how do we build a heart of love for God? In much the same way we would toward another person. If you were invited to spend an hour with the most important person you know, would you spend time beforehand learning as much as possible about this person? You want to have something to talk about. You want to show you are interested in them and knowledgeable about what they have done. Are there shared interests? You want to steer the conversation toward these. How about God? Have you ever thought of spending time with Him—for any reason other than asking Him for something? In Covenant, in fact, are our lives not joined and merged? Are our interests not shared? If we grasp the full nature of our relationship with God, how much might we have to discuss with Him?

A heart of love is not kindled by rules, even beneficial ones. Our love is not kindled by benefits, especially if "purchased" by wearisome obedience.

If you want to build a relationship that may lead to Marriage, you spend a lot of time getting to know someone. If we learn about God in the Scriptures, and His interaction with humanity since the beginning, then see who Jesus is and learn about the offer He makes in the New Covenant, it is hard not to look at God with the deepest admiration, respect, and trust. Then if we consider all the things God has built for us and in us, we realize He has been displaying love toward us our entire lives. He has been waiting for us to notice Him and love

Him back. Then we see how much He wants to love us going forward, and what He wants to do in our lives. All of this is *before* we begin interacting with Him in a daily relationship, before we learn all the ways we can rely on His love in every part of life. This process of learning and interaction is the way a heart of love naturally grows. If we understand Covenant, we come to God realizing the power He wants to unleash in our lives—His life in us, and our lives in Him.

As I began to grasp the realities of Covenant (several years after becoming a Christian), my heart toward Him began to burn like fire. He and I are joined in the most intimate bond. *I* am literally *within Jesus* at this moment as He sits on His throne. Over the last forty years He has built things in me and through me I never would have believed. And this is just the beginning of His outpoured love for all eternity! How does my heart feel toward Him in light of all this? I have decades of experience with this One. Part of such a heart is based on experience. But part is also based on the same logic that Peter spoke about. "You are God, therefore ..." "God invites me into this relationship. Though I do not understand it all, *still* ... " We can begin with what we do know. This is sufficient.

I am literally *within Jesus* at this moment as He sits on His throne. Over the last forty years He has built things in me and through me I never would have believed.

"Whoever eats My flesh and drinks My blood has eternal life, and I will raise them up at the last day. ... Whoever eats My flesh and drinks My blood remains in Me and I in them" (John 6:54, 56).

RECEIVING THE LIFE OF JESUS

While on earth Jesus illustrated the life-exchanges of Covenant by taking on myriad elements of our lives. He invites us to join Him in this pattern of exchange: to take on the life of God. He invites us to enter the Kingdom of God *here and now*, not just in eternity. He offers us the opportunity to enter a family relationship with the living God—to become a child of the Father, a brother or sister of Christ, and brother/sister to all in Covenant with Him. An opportunity to have an inheritance in this Kingdom that is ours alone! An opportunity to enter the will of the Father, to join Him as He works in our world, and to be rewarded for doing so.

"*... there is a friend who sticks closer than a brother*" (Proverbs 18:24).

"*Jonathan became one in spirit with David, and he loved him as himself*" (1 Samuel 18:1).

Thus we trust the offer He makes: to enter the New Covenant. We trust that when we offer up our life into His hands—to be put to death in its current form—that He will also raise us to new life, one with a new identity and new nature. But along with an intellectual belief in these realities there must be a heart response. Historically, it has always been assumed that two in Covenant would have a stronger affinity toward each other than toward anyone else in their lives. This is true for Marriage and also assumed for Blood Covenants. Two enter the strongest form of friendship possible. See the relationship between Jonathan and David referenced above, which was undoubtedly a Blood Covenant. Covenants are not just about trust or having confidence in the other. God desires our entry into Covenant to dramatically impact the way we live and the way we love.

'THE MESSAGE OF TRUTH, THE GOSPEL OF YOUR SALVATION' (EPHESIANS 1:13)

First, we must recognize we are *hearing* a real offer of relationship from a reliable source—and that source can only be Scripture (John 5:24; Romans 10:14). Second, we must learn enough about *God's love for us and the perfection of His character*—proven by His interactions with humanity throughout history—so we can reasonably believe Him and believe in Him (John 3:16; 1 John 4:19). Third, we must *recognize that we cannot live successfully* now or in eternity following our own path (Romans 3:23, 6:23). We have been led astray by our heart and mind, and by others. Realizing this, we are willing to repent—to turn from our own path, about face, and commit ourselves to God's path (Acts 2:38). We therefore *receive* Jesus' offer of new life in the New Covenant by offering ourselves to God on His terms. We do this by praying to Him (John 1:12). At this point we become a new creature (2 Corinthians 5:17) by the death of our old being and being raised to new life just as Jesus was (Romans 6:3-11). The Spirit of God inhabits this new creation in the pattern of Covenant life-exchange (Ephesians 1:13; Romans 8:9-11) just as we now inhabit Christ (John 6:56). When this occurs we are now in a New Covenant relationship with God. We are to give public testimony to this by baptism in water, also following the pattern of Jesus (Matthew 3:15), a baptism that signifies our death, burial, and resurrection as new creatures (Colossians 2:2; Acts 2:38).

There is another baptism that occurred on the Day of Pentecost (Acts 2:1-4), ten days after Jesus ascended to Heaven and fifty days after the Passover, on which eve He was crucified. This "baptism of fire" and special filling by the Holy Spirit came to those who had already received the Spirit of God on the evening of Jesus' resurrection (John 20:22). These disciples were already Christians, but they were now filled with God's Spirit in a way that conveyed special power for ministry. Paul discusses these gifts and their proper use in detail in 1 Corinthians Chapter 14. Much has been written and discussed in our day about this second filling of the Spirit, the one occurring in Acts 2. Often it is said that this phenomenon occurred only in the early church. Others bear witness to such a second "baptism of the Holy Spirit" occurring in individuals and groups throughout history. Godly people differ on this point. One point I do want to stress is that this second filling is often in association with an expressed desire that the Spirit of God fully inhabit one's life, and with a desire that God fully have His way in this life. There is no suggestion anywhere in Scripture that God placed a time limit on a filling by the Spirit, or on these gifts.

At any point it is appropriate to ask God's spirit to fill our lives. It is appropriate to ask God to have His way in every part of our lives. What He does next is up to Him.

And how we build our new relationship with God is up to us. There is a clear analogy to Marriage here. One may be in a Marriage Covenant yet not acknowledge or live out the realities God created within and between the parties. This Covenant is in full effect. But the realities this Covenant is intended to produce will not grow until people acknowledge the realities of Covenant and choose to live them out. As we enter the New Covenant we may say the words "Jesus is Lord." Yet our choices may prove that we are still lord of what we think of as our life. In this case, will the blessings of Heaven be showered upon us?

Even if we want to submit ourselves to God's leadership, this is a process. We must prove to ourselves beyond any doubt that God will do a better job directing our lives than we can. In fact, immeasurably better. At this point we may be willing to finally pry our fingers off the steering wheel and actually follow His directions.

"Enter through the narrow gate. For wide is the gate and broad is the road that leads to destruction, and many enter through it. But small is the gate and narrow the road that leads to life, and only a few find it" (Matthew 7:13, 14).

"Not everyone who says to me, 'Lord, Lord,' will enter the Kingdom of Heaven, but only the one who does the will of my Father who is in Heaven. Many will say to Me on that day, 'Lord, Lord, did we not prophesy in your name and in your name drive out demons and in your name perform many miracles?' Then I will tell them plainly, 'I never knew you. Away from me, you evildoers'"
(Matthew 7:21-23).

THE COMMON MISCONCEPTION

This is the entry point to God's Covenant plan. Why is grasping this plan and entering this relationship such a problem for so many people?

Do we worship His perfection and accept a relationship with Him on His terms, or do we just want His benefits?

And once in this relationship, why is building a relationship with God to its potential such an infrequent outcome? It is extraordinarily helpful to understand the hurdles we all face as we try to understand and follow God. This understanding will help us overcome the things that hold us back.

"Very truly I tell you, you are looking for me, not because you saw the signs I performed but because you ate the loaves and had your fill" (John 6:26).

First, we must come to God because we realize He is God! But why does this matter to us? For one of two reasons. One, we realize *who God is* and who He wants to be toward us. In this case we willingly offer Him our lives to do with as He pleases. Or, second, we see power and resources in God that can add value to *our* lives. Do we worship His perfection and accept a relationship with Him on His terms, or do we just want His benefits?

"'For My thoughts are not your thoughts, and My ways are not your ways,' declares the Lord" (Isaiah 55:8).

FOUNDATIONS FOR MISUNDERSTANDING

We often look at people who are mistaken with an overly critical eye—as if we have never been wrong. Perhaps it is better to feel some sympathy, especially when it comes to the things of God. Even when we are trying to understand and follow God we may not put things together correctly in the moment. Perhaps this is why earthly life typically lasts many decades. It will help us to learn from the mistakes of others.

Three factors, in some combination, are the foundation for misunderstanding the heart God desires as we approach Him. The first is one of our strongest human drives: self-preservation. The second is our perception of self-interest. The third is not understanding the change and merger of identity God accomplishes in Covenant—and the essential role these changes play in building the things God intends Covenant to build in our lives.

"Whoever wants to save their life will lose it, but whoever loses their life for Me will find it" (Matthew 16:25).

MISUNDERSTANDING SELF-PRESERVATION

We will vigorously protect and defend our lives against any lethal threat. People voluntarily lay down their lives only in very special circumstances. People who come to God have in mind *improving* their life. They usually do not envision ending their life as they know it.

People who come to God have in mind *improving* their life. They usually do not envision ending their life as they know it.

"My life is my own" is a primary human misconception. Is this *our life*? Did we create our life? Can we sustain it on our own? If God wants our lives back at any point, do we have the power to stop Him? Or does His creation belong to Him, to do with as He pleases—including us? If we embrace the view that our life belongs solely to us, we are in charge of protecting our life. We spoke earlier of what we view as our life. Thus, defending our life means we must also protect our beliefs—at times, even from God.

If we remain confused about who owns our life, God intends to resolve this once and for all by inviting us to enter Covenant. He offers us an entirely new level of connection in the New Covenant. What an offer, in fact: to exchange lives with God! Would it make more sense to hold tightly to things in the life of a perfect and all-powerful God instead of the imperfect things we bring to the table?

> *"There is a way that seems right to a man,*
> *but its end is the way of death"* (Proverbs 14:12).

> *"As many as I love, I rebuke and chasten;*
> *be zealous therefore and repent"* (Revelation 3:19).

MISUNDERSTANDING SELF-INTEREST

We have spent our lives honing our sense of self-interest, trying to understand what most benefits us. Though many of these ideas are wrong, we approach God with our set of expectations. How much time did Jesus spend confronting and adjusting the expectations and beliefs of His disciples? Many things had to be rebuilt within them before they were ready for leadership in Jesus' kingdom.

The drive to make the most of the life God has given us is completely appropriate. But healthy self-interest can be distorted by the influence of Satan. Our guidance system can point us toward beneficial things in one moment. Then, in the next minute, toward something that is counterproductive or dangerous. One of the most common distortions is the belief that our self-interest can be advanced by weakening or damaging others. We try to climb to the top on the backs of others. And there are myriad other ways our lives can point in the wrong direction.

A problem arises when God challenges our embraced beliefs. We think: *I've got this, with a little adjustment.* God sees us like small children playing in the middle of a busy street or as someone headed over a waterfall who cannot quite yet see what is ahead of him. When God warns us of grievous dangers in the spiritual realm, do we believe Him? Or ourselves? Whose reality do we accept and act upon?

If we believe God, and believe in Him, we expect to experience His love. But we already have in mind the form this love should take: "my life, made better." Then, we define "better." However, God's plan does not square with nearly anyone's expectations. We want peace and joy while God may offer chastening and adversity to teach us vital lessons. God's goal for us is not comfort and ease. It is maturity, good character, and learning to love in action. In order for depth and strength to be built in us we must go through many challenges. There are certainly many good things in this life. No one raises questions about these. It is the hard things we question. The real question is whether such things could possibly be in our best interest. The answer, to our surprise, is yes. But we are only confident of this after years of walking with God. Also, when people look at the lives of Christians and see adversity, this life does not appear attractive. It is only later that the benefits of a life refined by God's training process become obvious.

While God was making a Covenant with Abram (later called Abraham), he was probably considering all the blessings that would flow from a Covenant with the Creator of the universe. What was Abraham's first experience in this Covenant? Circumcision. This was probably not at the top of his list of expectations. There will be a significant mismatch between our expectations and what our lives in Christ hold for us. Because of this we may question God's love, or perhaps His existence. The further we walk down God's path, the more we recognize the blessings He has poured into our lives all along, even through challenges and adversity. He does love us, and He shows this in a myriad of ways. The life He designed for us before the foundation of the world is truly the best we can live. But His leadership takes a little getting used to! The Jews confronted this same dilemma when they faced the question of obeying God or turning to the gods of surrounding nations.

"*... having a form of godliness but denying its power*"
(2 Timothy 3:5).

MISUNDERSTANDING THE TRANSFORMATION OF COVENANT

No one saw this kind of relationship coming. Marriage is analogous to this in many ways. At the time of Jesus' first coming people had thousands of years of experience with Marriage. But the nature of the joining of Marriage was unclear to most people. In Matthew 19:3-6, in response to the Pharisees' question about Marriage, Jesus pointed back to its original *one flesh* nature. He said, "Therefore, what God has joined together, let no one separate." The power of God had joined them to their wives in a way—if they had understood it—that was the key to building the Marriage of their dreams. But they did not understand what God had done or His plan to build the relationship. They built this relationship *their* way. The result? They wanted out. They wanted the freedom to go find the "right person." Jesus pointed out that God prohibited them from doing so, and they did not like this limitation. Was the real problem the limitation God placed on their freedom to make their next mistake? Or was the problem that they did not understand the power of God and His plan?

THE JEWISH FOUNDATION FOR MISUNDERSTANDING

Jews who were trying to understand Jesus had additional hurdles based on misinterpreting centuries of interaction between the Jewish people and God. God delivered the children of Israel from Egypt, then delivered His Law through Moses. This was God's leadership for His people, a path intended to build the best character for them as well as their best society. This was to be a nation dedicated to the worship of God. The Israelites were instructed to love God. And some did. There were always some among the Hebrews who were faithful to Him and evidenced the fruit of His plans in their lives.

> The gods of surrounding countries, whose identities and agenda we earlier discussed, led people to engage in the very destructive behaviors God said to avoid.

Due to the intricate system of rules God conveyed, obedience to these rules was seen as *the* condition for a right relationship with Him. The idea of an intimate, personal relationship with God was not part of most people's thinking. This first and most important of these rules was to worship only God and avoid worship of the gods of surrounding nations. God wanted to build a society in which people displayed good character and did no harm to their neighbors.

The gods of surrounding countries, whose identities and agenda we earlier discussed, led people to engage in the very destructive behaviors God said to avoid. If people disobeyed God's first rule, worshipping and following these gods, it would lead them to violate many other rules. The predatory way of life in these nations differed sharply from God's intent, celebrating dishonesty, violence, and child sacrifice among other things.

WHAT IS A 'GOD' AND WHY DO WE NEED ONE?

Let's think for a moment about the role played by a god—or the real God—in people's lives. Are we not self-sufficient, especially if educated, well-funded, and reasonably intelligent? If we think we are, we have not lived long enough. Life has always been uncertain and randomly devastating. There were many more imminent physical risks in the ancient world than ours today. Still, our lives today easily can be turned upside down by any number of adversities. Over time we recognize our limitations. We do not see things coming. We do not fully understand life—ever, if we're truthful about it. Our resources are limited. Even if we draw from the resources of an entire nation as its leader, our success is not assured. No human can be self-sufficient in this life. Our deepest needs are always at risk, even life itself. Perhaps our most glaring deficiency is not being able to see into the future.

"For our struggle is not against flesh and blood, but against the rulers, against the authorities, against the powers of this dark world and against the spiritual forces of evil in the heavenly realms" (Ephesians 6:12).

In a day when many deny any spiritual reality, including the existence of God or gods, we still have concerns about our present and our future. We need help from a source of power beyond our own. Oddly, one of the most popular entertainment genres is superheroes. The idea of superhuman powers is very attractive. And where, in our "modern" culture, do we look for answers? Do we not entrust our future to scientists, educators, and technology? If one questions our willingness to bow before these "leaders"—well, consider the response to the Covid-19 outbreak. Vast amounts of *actual* data-based science were ignored; certain scientists, in tandem with politicians, told the populace what *we must do* to ensure our future. Yet this course of action did far more damage to the fabric of our nation than yet another in a long history of flu epidemics. We were not led by true science but by a new priestly class: "recognized experts" who were ordained as such by the media and politicians. Dissenting voices were censored, even if they came from actual experts analyzing real data.[13] This is not a commentary about science itself. As a doctor, I understand the essential nature of science and the imperative of correctly approaching a pandemic. It is about our *willingness as a culture to follow voices defined as "scientific,"* even when this leadership was nonsensical and wildly and widely destructive. What do you think is behind all of this ?

A god (a fallen angel) is a supernatural being, but is still a *created* one. These beings have perceptions and powers beyond our own. But the human concept of a god goes beyond the reality of these beings. Humans have believed for millennia that gods know and control the future, created something about our world and played a role in fashioning us. People have believed these things because fallen angels have claimed these things as they interacted with humanity. While this type of angel has supernatural power and understanding, and is smarter than we are, it is also devoted to deceiving us. We can be forgiven for overestimating them based on the claims they made to the Sumerians, and ever since. (These *Annunaki*, or "beings from above," claimed they created the Sumerians to be their miners, laborers, and worshippers.[14] It should be noted that some modern scholars, in light of the seemingly impossible technologic advances in the earliest civilization, believe these beings are aliens visitors from an advanced civilization. The author of the cited reference holds this view. While this author does not share this view, Sitchin has published much compelling evidence that non-humans guided this nascent culture. My personal belief is that evidence from multiple sources, including Scripture and para-Biblical writings, makes it far more likely that these beings were fallen angels. Regardless of what any of us believe, the Sumerians were utterly convinced that these beings were gods—because they said so.) Believing these gods were real and had great power, people throughout the ancient world sought to appease them and follow their guidance to ensure their own prosperity and future.

"'In that day,' declares the Lord, 'you will call me "my husband"; you will no longer call me "my master"'" (Hosea 2:16).

The real God created all things and has power over them. His presence is seen throughout His creation. He knows all things and has total control over outcomes now and for all eternity. The terms used for these realities are *omniscient* (all knowing), *omnipresent* (everywhere present), and *omnipotent* (all powerful). He also created us in *His* image to *love us*. His love takes the form of teaching us to build the *best* life by obeying Him. God does not invite us to an easy life but to the best life. His heart and plan have always been that this life would be fully shared with Him.

It is worth considering why the Israelites would turn from this God, who delivered them from Egypt with great power and many miracles. People then, as now, want the best for themselves and their families. Their focus was generally on material things and protection. These surrounding gods, if appeased, promised power over circumstances and material blessings. In other words, these beings offered a quick fix for life's problems while promoting enticing behaviors forbidden by God—sex without boundaries and other immoral behaviors. The sales pitch is: "You can have what you think you need and have what you desire if you simply bow before us."

"God disciplines us for our good, in order that we may share in His holiness. No discipline seems pleasant at the time, but painful.

> *Later on, however, it produces a harvest of righteousness and peace for those who have been trained by it"* (Hebrews 12:10, 11).

In stark contrast, the real God required restraint. It is vital to understand why. Working through adversity in a virtuous way, hand in hand with God, builds character and maturity. This is always the path to a better life going forward. Thus God's involvement in our lives often *does not* involve deliverance from our adversities. He wants to use these adversities for our long-term benefit, as any loving parent would.

From our vantage point, though, wouldn't we rather have the easy answer? The quick fix? Wouldn't we rather simply get what we want in life without having to put that much effort in?

From our vantage point, though, wouldn't we rather have the easy answer? The quick fix? Wouldn't we rather simply get what we want in life without having to put that much effort in? God's approach limited behaviors that some found beneficial or pleasurable. Although the very adversities people wanted easy deliverance from were often the consequences of their disobedience, people wanted to continue making the same choices and yet have positive outcomes. They had no interest in turning from these things. When people examined the offer of God, versus their surrounding gods, who offered a better deal if the goal was: "My life, made better"? Many sold their souls to what they thought was the higher bidder.

We see a consistent pattern in ancient Israel, in the Garden of Eden, and in our lives today. Satan's representatives are master salesmen and manipulators. They recognize or create a desire, then offer us what we want—for a price. The deal is deceptive—always. If we follow their lead we are now following God's enemies. Their path ultimately damages and destroys, but this only becomes apparent later. "Deception" means you haven't figured out the real deal yet. Sin may produce benefits in the short run. Though people left God to worship these beings, over and over many of those people came back to God. Why? Because the damage caused by Satan's ways eventually became evident. God remained their only hope.

"Then the king called together all the elders of Judah and Jerusalem. He went up to the temple of the Lord with the men of Judah, the people of Jerusalem, the priests and the prophets—all the people from the least to the greatest. He read in their hearing all the words of the Book of the Covenant, which had been found in the temple of the Lord. ... Then all the people pledged themselves to the covenant. The King ordered Hilkiah the high priest, the priests next in rank, and the doorkeepers to remove from the temple of the Lord all the articles made for Ba'al and Asherah and all the starry host. He burned them outside Jerusalem. ... He did away with the pagan priests appointed by the kings of Judah. ... He took the Asherah pole from the temple of the Lord to the Kidron Valley outside Jerusalem and burned it there. He also took down the quarters of the male shrine prostitutes which were in the temple of the Lord" (2 Kings 23:1-8).

Despite periodically returning to God, the overall trajectory of Israel across the centuries was one of turning further from Him. God sent prophets to warn people, to remind them of the consequences of turning from Him. These warnings were rarely heeded, and when they were, never for long. Therefore, in 722 BC the Assyrians invaded the Northern Kingdom (Israel). Most Israelites were carried into slavery in foreign lands—never to return. The Southern Kingdom of Judah did not heed even this warning. It was invaded by the Babylonians for a final time, and for good, in 587 BC. (The Babylonians first invaded Judah with some success in 605 BC.) Jerusalem was reduced to rubble, the Temple of Solomon destroyed, and the inhabitants taken as slaves to Babylon.

It was very sobering to me to walk through the Ancient Israel section of the Israel Museum in Jerusalem in 2019. Scores of small clay figures were on display, often with exaggerated genitalia or pregnant bellies, and there were better rendered figurines of Ba'al and other gods of the surrounding countries. These were the household gods worshipped in public and private by the Israelites before the Babylonian captivity. It was sad beyond words to stand in front of the means through which average people continued to reach for the very enemies of God. By this they ensured the destruction of their nation.

A group returned from Babylon seventy years later to rebuild Jerusalem, but Israel as a nation never recovered from God's judgment. From 500 BC until Christ's first coming, the nation was ruled by, or oppressed by, a series of other nations. So, burned into the psyche of Israel was the association between disobedience to God and destruction. The path to national survival was thus deemed to be *obedience*. Deuteronomy 6:5 instructed Israel to *love God* and pursue a *relationship with Him*. But this relationship was now firmly focused on only one imperative: obey. If one "does the works of God," in other words, one is secure. "If we all do this, the nation is secure." Their relationship with God was reduced to a simple contract. As this concept came to rule religious thought, a group of teachers emerged who were committed to teaching and *enforcing* obedience (as they defined it). This group, the Pharisees, comprised the most respected of the teachers. In addition, they controlled the Sanhedrin, the seat of Jewish political power. They, along with the Sadducees, the historic line of high priests, controlled the nation.

Their relationship with God was reduced to a simple contract. As this concept came to rule religious thought, a group of teachers emerged who were committed to teaching and *enforcing* obedience.

If obedience *is* important, how did this go so wrong? When Jesus appeared and offered His plan, why was it not merely misunderstood, but instead opposed with murderous rage by the nation's leaders? First, these leaders were thoroughly convinced they had it right based on their assumptions about the nature of a relationship with God. In addition, in their place of power they found many benefits. These temporal benefits began to outweigh an actual relationship with God in most (but not all) of these leaders. Jesus—God, who stood before them interpreting the very Scriptures they held so dear, showing them the error of their ways—was not the path to a better life in their view. Instead, He was a *threat* to the life they had built according to the things they had come to cherish. The people of Israel were caught between these two sides. Jesus clearly spoke with the authority of God, yet everyone's assumptions about the nature of a relationship with God were also challenged. In their minds, as noted earlier, Jesus appeared to challenge the bedrock reality of their existence. How could they reconcile these different realities? One day they would wave palm branches and shout, "Hosannah to the One who comes in the Name of the Lord!" Just a few days later, these same people shouted at Pilate to release Bar-Abbas and crucify Jesus. Is it not remarkable that the most magnificent offer every heard by human ears, straight from the mouth and heart of a loving God, should provoke this response?

There is some indication in Scripture that before Satan began this rebellion he led the worship of God in Heaven. In Israel, the Pharisees controlled the worship of God by teaching the Law and also through controlling civil law. Both were tempted to shift this worship to themselves in an effort to *replace God.* Both elevated their interests above the interests of the Almighty. Then they joined forces to assassinate Him on a Roman cross. Two thoughts led to this attempt: *my life, made better;* and *you shall be as God.* This is certainly the motivation for human disobedience. But we must also understand that this can fuel human obedience (though for the wrong reasons). This is the contractual mind-set: trading our effort for God's blessing. God's real plan also requires our efforts, so what is the difference? Everything comes back to the key question: Whose life is it? It also comes back to recognizing the power of God and what He has done in our lives. His plan to transform our lives and lead us to our best life rests firmly on these two foundation stones.

Do you realize where this misconception—*my life, to do with as I please*—comes from? Not the Pharisees, and not even Adam and Eve. This idea originated in the first being who rebelled against God. With this idea in Satan's mind, rebellion was necessary to try to remove the authority of the One who would judge him. This adversary bought into the most fundamental lie. His life is not his own any more than ours is. His rebellion has a shelf life. It will end, and the punishment to be meted out is already recorded in The Revelation of John and other prophesies. This original lie will be shown as the lie it is. Is this a lie we ever want to speak or think?

> *"For we know that our old self was crucified with Him so that the body ruled by sin might be done away with, that we should no longer be slaves to sin—because anyone who has died has been set free from sin"* (Romans 6:6, 7).

I want to make this next point very carefully. People may be uncomfortable juxtaposing a relationship with God with sexuality (as if God did not create sexual intercourse). God created intercourse, and He did so for a purpose: to enter the Covenant of Marriage and to celebrate that Covenant, as well as to perpetuate humanity. Let's compare a person's heart and mind when approaching God with the heart and mind with which one approaches a romantic relationship. God built all the circuitry for romantic love within us—mental, emotional, and physical approaches—for the purpose of creating a Covenant relationship that is a lifelong love affair. But people approach these relationships with different motivations, don't they? Just like they approach God with different motivations.

One couple may build a relationship with the goal of giving their lives to each other in Marriage. Another couple may want some of the blessings of Marriage, like a sex partner, but not embrace the realities and responsibilities that come with a Covenant (even though by having intercourse they establish one). What is the difference in the mind-set of these two couples? One has in mind the giving and receiving of each other's lives, and joining for a lifetime. The other has in mind "my life, made better," which includes limiting undesired responsibilities. I merely want to point out that anyone who wants to enter a relationship with God, but believes this relationship will be about my life, made better, is not actually offering himself or herself to God on His terms. This is akin to trying to live with God instead of marrying Him. This is trying to gain His blessings, but failing to fulfill our initial responsibility as we enter this Covenant: offering our current life up to God to be put to death so we can receive a new life joined to Him. If the basis of a previous commitment we made to God is unclear, I would simply invite each of us to affirm that we are truly offering our lives to God on His terms, with nothing held back.

"They claim to know God, but by their actions they deny Him" (Titus 1:16).

"Then I will tell them plainly, 'I never knew you. Away from me, you evildoers'" (Matthew 7:23).

"Search me, God, and know my heart; test me and know my anxious thoughts. See if there is any offensive way in me, and lead me in the way everlasting" (Psalms 139:23).

WHAT IS OUR NEW LIFE?

"Therefore, if anyone is in Christ, he is a new creature; the old things passed away; behold new things have come" (2 Corinthians 5:17, NASB).

"This is the One who came by water and blood—Jesus Christ. He did not come by water only, but by water and blood" (1 John 5:6).

Everyone who enters Covenant with God will notice something different about themselves. A deep sense of peace. A new joy, a sense of being loved, a new desire to read Scripture and a new understanding as he or she reads. There may be a new desire to pray or to do other things. We notice some things, but do we notice everything that changed? Can we accurately perceive what within us *has* and *has not* changed? No, we cannot fully perceive these things. We must look to God's revelation and understand the nature of the Covenant we entered to make sense of our new life.

The Spirit of God is within us. We are in Christ and He is in us. We are joined to God by a bond of nature and identity. But we may not perceive much, or any, of this. Though the identity of God is within us, we do not *become* God any more than a man becomes female by marrying his wife, or vice versa. Our old identity joined to the nature of God's enemy ceases to exist. Our new bond of shared nature and identity means our life is conjoined with the life of God in the strongest possible bond. How, then, would we describe the new being we have become? What is the relationship between everything we were up to the point we entered Covenant and what we are going forward?

Have you ever wondered who you really are? We all have. This is because our true identity and nature are definite things, but not things we can pull out and examine. Figuring out who we are is somewhat like a detective story as we go through life. We see clues and try to put them together. Some clues point in the right direction. Some we misread. What is our true potential in any area? We do not know until we explore our potential. Can we be an elite guitarist, or must we be content entertaining ourselves? Our true identity consists of all our potential and hardwiring. What is our IQ or our physical potential? Are we an auditory or visual learner; an introvert or extrovert? Our identity also includes our deepest emotional needs. People's core needs are different. We all need love, but we each need to receive love in particular ways. This reality is explored in Gary Chapman's book series on the five love languages. These different languages reflect hardwiring and apply to all our key relationships. In sum, our identity is all the things about us that are created by God and unchangeable.

We have discussed other layers of who we perceive ourselves to be—our character and guidance system—which represent choices we have made through life. It is these things that form much of our *experience of life,* including our emotions. Our preferences, desires, and appetites are a product of our choices, as are our values, goals, and priorities. These *optional add-ons do not change* when our identity shifts. Only our identity changes.

Our new identity is fully and immediately present in one sense. Once our DNA comes together in a fertilized egg, this being now contains all the potential a person will ever have. All that is needed is time to grow and mature. But something else is needed. Our inherent potential can be developed—or not. Many people do not feel they are living "authentically." They sense that they are not expressing *who they really are* with their life. And they are likely correct. Because potential is just that—something that awaits development. We must choose to develop it. Or, we can allow others to influence the course of our lives. We may be coerced into a life that reflects little of who we are. We may come to believe we should be certain things instead of discovering and living out our true identity. There is a hard sell coming from our culture: "You can be whatever you want to be!" Really? No, you cannot. You can develop your inherent potential and enjoy expressing your strengths, or you can devote your time chasing someone else's great ideas about how your life should look and end up with that inauthentic feeling in spite of any success you do achieve.

Potential is just that—something that awaits development. We must choose to develop it.

"Like newborn babies, crave pure spiritual milk, so that by it you may grow up in your salvation" (1 Peter 2:2).

"Whoever will not receive the Kingdom of God like a little child will never enter it" (Luke 18:17).

Now we are a new creature. The nature of Satan was removed, and the nature of God becomes part of us. And, linked to God, His resources are now committed to us (according to His loving will for us, not to simply fulfill our desires). This new potential includes spiritual gifts—new capacities for relationship and ministry (Romans 12:6-21). The 2011 New International Version Bible places a heading over Romans Chapter 12: "Love in Action." This is the goal of Covenant, to learn to love others with action. God created our initial identity as well as our new one. The fact that our new one is "completely new" does not mean it will be altogether different from the old one. Our physical or mental abilities usually do not change.

At the point of entry into Covenant we become, in a sense, infants. An infant needs the care of others to learn, to grow, to be nourished, and to be protected. As a child grows, she or he must learn much about life. How to behave, what to do, what not to do. We are to imprint God's Word as our new guidance system. This is a decision, and also a lengthy process of ongoing commitment and action. We must learn how to function successfully in our family and our world based on an entirely new set of beliefs, values, priorities, and relationships. As we grow to maturity, the first time or the second time, two things exert the most powerful effect on the course of our growth. First, who we *actually are*. Second, who we *think we are*. We may recognize our potential and build it, or live out someone else's observation that we are stupid, ugly, or a loser. If we are to develop our new creation to its potential we must realize who we are in Christ. The more we live out our true identity and the more we develop the potential of our bond with Christ, the more we will become what God created us to be, then *re-created* us to be, at massive personal cost to Himself.

I hoped my new creature would be better looking and smarter. Neither happened. But something much more important did happen. My relationship to *sin* (rebellion, disobedience, walking away from God, tearing down) changed.

As the being that shares a nature with Satan died, and the being that shares a nature with God was born, I no longer had the same relationship to disobedience. I was a good, responsible, and generally constructive guy on the outside at the time I became a Christian. I was in medical school, not in rehab or jail. Yet down inside there were all kinds of thoughts and feelings flying around. And on occasion there was an urge to damage something or someone simply for the sake of doing so. This urge is common to humanity apart from Covenant with God. Also, there has been a worldwide education program throughout history that instructs me to live *my life,* and build it, if necessary, at the expense of others. These two—our nature and education—explain the harsh world we inhabit. The unity of all people works only on bumper stickers. The reality we live in is a world of people *not joined* in any real way, people whose interests compete and collide. This is a world devoted to domination. "Me first" is the endpoint. There is no "us"—just me versus everyone else. This is the nature of Satan lived out through human lives.

The unity of all people works only on bumper stickers.

In Covenant we are restored to our original, right relationship with God. However, we can still choose to do wrong. Eve and Adam did, even though they did not yet have a "sin nature" driving them to rebellion. They disobeyed God for the same reason we do. They embraced deception and acted on it; we too embrace and are guided by deception. Fortunately, God has a plan to deal with deception. He offers us truth, in the form of His Word, to which we can compare any idea. And He offers us a plan of transformation within Covenant to strip from us the deceptions we have already embraced. Once in Covenant we will inevitably make mistakes. It is through the process of repentance, plus God's forgiveness, *plus embracing God's truth* that we progressively shift our guidance system into alignment with God's Word. Through a similar process we progressively shift our character into alignment with His character. We will cover this part of God's plan in detail farther down.

"For the flesh desires what is contrary to the Spirit, and the Spirit what is contrary to the flesh. They are in conflict with each other" (Galatians 5:17).

When we look at God, do we see ourselves within Him? When we look in the mirror, do we realize God lives within us? How would these realizations change the way you look at God or yourself? What is most important to know about our new identity? First, we cannot fully perceive it. Second, our perception of who we are must shift from our observations and beliefs to God's revelation. Third, the choices we make and our character are not made new by God. We built our guidance system and character initially through our choices; we must now remake them in God's plan by being "transformed by the renewing of our mind" (Romans 12:2). Some desires, values, and beliefs may change immediately. Most will not. God largely delegates the task of transforming these things to us. Therefore we must learn to exercise our power of Assent and Dissent in a new way—matching everything we currently believe, and every decision we make about *what is best for us* against God's Word. If we understand Covenant and God's plan for our transformation, growth, and maturity, this understanding will guide us to correct choices. This is how we build a life that authentically reflects who we now are.

THE BOND OF NATURE AND IDENTITY

You roll over in bed the morning after your wedding and look at the person next to you, your new husband or wife. Who is this person? And who are *you* now? Whatever the answers to these questions, you know you just signed on for an amazing journey of adventure and discovery. You envision a wonderful future together. Now you just have to … well, you'll get around to breakfast later, then start building the rest of your wonderful life together.

If we have any sense of who God is, the reality that we have just entered a relationship analogous to Marriage with Him is awesome beyond words. The possibilities of this joining are endless. I bear witness after forty-plus years of this relationship that God has done things, built things, and taken me places—geographically, and within myself—beyond my wildest dreams. I had plenty of plans for my life. I would trade all of my plans for a fraction of His. I feel loved by God in the deepest possible way on a regular basis. I get up most mornings excited about what God is going to do today. I live in the same world we all do, and this together-life with God is not without trouble, to say the least. Yet even in trials, struggles, and reversals I have learned to *learn from Him*. Instead of being devastated by loss, I know He is trying to teach me things needed for the next chapter of life. Failure is the pathway to victory—*if* we follow His plan for understanding and dealing with painful things. And follow His plan for dealing with successes and delightful things. *And* His plan for resting before Him and delighting in His presence. Our relationship with God is intended to be like the best Marriage imaginable—but one with the Creator of the universe. But, like any Marriage, this one must be built carefully and with great effort. Covenant, remember, is an all-in thing.

Yet even in trials, struggles, and reversals I have learned to *learn from Him*. Instead of being devastated by loss, I know He is trying to teach me things needed for the next chapter of life.

"I pray also for those who will believe in me through their message, that all of them may be one, Father, just as You are in Me and I am in You. May they also be in Us so the world may believe that You have sent Me" (John 17:20, 21).

ONENESS WITH GOD

The word *one* is often used in relation to Covenant. Several times in John Chapter 17 this term is used to describe the relationship between the Father and Son, between the Son and believers, and between believers. This word in the original language does not refer to a singular thing, but to multiple things that share a nature or identity. This perfectly describes the relationship created by Covenant, and it also describes the relationship among the authors of this Covenant, the Trinity. Three beings, each fully God and together fully God, all joined by a bond of nature and identity. This is a spiritual reality that defies full description or understanding. But as we contemplate this reality and what it means for us, will our hearts ignite with passion for the One who has done all of this for us?

What does it mean to be *made in the image of God* (Genesis 1:26) in the first place? Parts of us are different from any other animal. We have a sense of justice, a moral sense, and a capacity for creativity that built our current civilization. We appreciate beauty, seek meaning and purpose for our lives, and determine whether something is true or false. All of these reflect our Maker, and all are intended to come into play as we interact with Him. When we are made new, now joined to Him, a much stronger bond is forged. We are never alone, for He is literally within us. We can now become an accurate representation of Him to the extent our finiteness allows. "Christian" means "little Christ." His mind, His heart—these are within us. We can hold an extensive description of Him, the Scriptures, in our hands. Thus, we have full access to God and His presence in our lives. Now we must learn how to live in this reality.

"I have given them the glory that You gave Me,
that they may be one as we are one" (John 17:22).

"He has given us new birth into a living hope …
and into an inheritance that can never perish, spoil, or fade.
This inheritance is kept in heaven for you" (1 Peter 1:3, 4).

NO MORE 'MINE' AND 'YOURS'—ONLY 'OURS'

If two selves are joined in this way at the deepest level, it is only logical that two lives are joined and shared in the same way. One of the most important and powerful truths of Covenant is this: There is no more "my life." My life independent from all others has *ceased to exist*. My life is now conjoined with another. With two humans this involves sharing families, resources, friends, enemies, debts, and assets, among other things. The other in Covenant now assumes first place in one's priorities. Their honor is our honor, their benefits are shared, and so are their trials and struggles. This is the closest possible alliance and friendship.

How does this work with God? There is no "my life" independent of God any more, only *a life conjoined with His*. This joining is spoken of in some Scriptures as a family relationship—though these terms do not capture the fullness of this reality. We are called Christ's brothers and sisters. We are given an inheritance, something reserved for family. We are invited into the "family business," which is building the Kingdom of God. We will judge angels (1 Corinthians 6:3). In stark contrast to a world divided by diverse and conflicting interests, beliefs, and agendas, the Kingdom of God is characterized by unity. Our conjoined life is best described by the Scriptural term: "We are one" (see John 17, the entire chapter). Under God's loving lordship we are united by our love for one another, by the agenda of God, and by the truth of God. All of these flow from being joined to the life of God. This is God's plan and intent now and for eternity. But this is also a plan we must learn to follow. Our character and guidance system must be transformed if we are to follow this plan faithfully. If these continue to be laced with deception, forces within us will continue to pull against God's agenda.

"Make every effort to keep the unity of the Spirit through the bond of peace" (Ephesians 4:3).

" … so that the Body of Christ may be built up until we all reach unity in the faith and in the knowledge of the Son of God and

become mature, attaining to the whole measure of the fullness of Christ" (Ephesians 4:12, 13).

Imagine for a moment growing up in the perfect family. A big and loving family, one without a hint of strife or discord. A family in which you were seen and known. Where your needs were met. Where your potential was recognized and developed. Where you were taught how to live successfully in the family and the world. Much of the New Testament was written to guide believers away from the challenged, conflicted, and conflicting lives they were living toward the life of fulfillment, harmony, and peace that God intends for them. To build this kind of family requires maturity, and maturity must be developed. This is a process we must choose to engage in. It is God's plan and intent that we do so, not only for our own sake, but for everyone's. One of the most important elements of God's plan to grasp is the importance of the building process within Covenant. We must envision the plan of God in the same way we view the process by which a surgeon is trained, or a professional athlete. This process of development requires total commitment, much time, considerable effort, and no small amount of pain along the way. But we count these sacrifices a price worth paying to become what we want to become. How much commitment should we have toward becoming what God wants us to become?

Our new *self* comes mainly in the form of potential, and this must be properly developed for best results. Our new *relationship* comes mainly in the form of opportunity, which must also be recognized and developed.

Or people can continue living what they believe is *their life* to do with as they please. Do you wish people would choose God's path more consistently in the Body of Christ? So does God, and He will bless those who do.

EXCHANGE OF LIFE AND WHAT IT MEANS

Have you ever wondered why God had to die? Yes, He died "for us." But why? Why did He become human in the first place? I have heard it said this was necessary because, if we want to communicate with worms, we would communicate most effectively if we *became* a worm. Besides the unflattering analogy, the problem with this reasoning is that Jesus had already been seen by Daniel in a vision of Heaven in appearance *"like a son of man."* This was before He actually became one. Also, Jesus spoke with Abraham and wrestled with Jacob, as God, *in the form of a man.* So the issue is not one of a disarming appearance for better communication. In addition, as fully man and fully God, why did Jesus endure so many indignities and insults? This brutality was actually not necessary to forgive sins. And Jesus told several people their sins were forgiven. Bystanders noted correctly that "only God has the power to forgive sins." Jesus does have the power to simply do this (Luke 5:24). So, beyond being executed, why the added pain and suffering?

Not only did He become human, He was rejected by those He came to love, serve, and save. His own Word was thrown in His face by Satan and the religious leaders of His special people. As He hung naked on a Roman cross He could have incinerated His tormenters with a word—but did not. Consider further: why was He tormented in the first place? The thing that has struck me most of all was that Jesus, so weak from a prolonged beating, could not even carry the tool of His execution to Golgotha. A stranger passing by was pressed into service to carry His cross. God … so very, very weak. Why did Jesus do all of this, or any of this? Because of Covenant. And why does Jesus ask us to do all the things He asks of us? Because of Covenant. Jesus leads the way in all things, including the most costly displays of faithfulness. What does He ask in return?

COVENANT EXCHANGES

"He is the faithful God, keeping His covenant of love to a thousand generations of those who love Him and keep His commandments" (Deuteronomy 7:9).

In Covenant, flowing from the exchange and merger of identity, other things are exchanged between the parties. In the New Covenant these are particularly exciting things. These exchanges are a big part of God's plan to address every need of heart, mind, and body for each of us. The principles of Covenant lived out are a very strong functional definition of love. Covenant is the vehicle and structure through which God pours out His love toward us.

We know God loves us in a general sense, but what can we trust God for *specifically*? There are two things we can trust God for. First, we can rely on God keeping specific promises in Scripture. This is familiar ground for mature Christians. We can easily recognize these promises. They are always phrased in this general way: "If you do this, I will do that." One such promise is in Philippians 4:6, 7. Numerous promises are scattered throughout Scripture. If *we* do what God says, we can be assured He will do what He says. Second, we can rely on God to fulfill the principles of Covenant. God authored this relationship and set these principles in place. This is the vehicle through which He shows love to us and through which He requires our love in return. Therefore, God will always provide, protect, defend, and honor. We can count on Him to be faithful in every aspect of Covenant. God is perfectly faithful. We will be less perfect in our faithfulness. He leads the way, and He wants us to follow.

First, let's look at some specific things that are exchanged between God and us. Then let's look at how we can interact with Him in regard to these things. For the sake of not over-lengthening this book, I will not cite all the scriptural examples of Jesus taking on elements of our humanity or offering the things of God to us. I will leave that search to you. But see how many of the following things you are already aware of. And with your new understanding of Covenant, see if you can identify additional exchanges.

Jesus' perfection exchanged for our imperfection.

Jesus' righteousness exchanged for our sin.

Jesus' strength exchanged for our weakness.

Jesus' wisdom exchanged for our foolishness.

Jesus' power exchanged for our powerlessness.

Jesus' wealth exchanged for our poverty (and not only in regard to material things).

Jesus' glory exchanged for our humiliation.

Jesus' love exchanged for our hatred, bitterness, strife, and selfishness.

Jesus' joy exchanged for our emptiness, disillusionment, and discouragement.

Jesus' peace exchanged for our internal state of conflict and confusion.

Jesus' kindness exchanged for our harshness and lack of caring.

Jesus' gentleness exchanged for our brutality, coercion, and desire to dominate.

Jesus' holiness exchanged for our uncleanness and shame.

Jesus' family relationships exchanged for our alienation within Satan's household.

Jesus' inheritance exchanged for a destiny of eternal separation and pain.

Jesus' indestructible, eternal life exchanged for our present frailty and future death.

At first our attention goes to all the "human" things Jesus became, did, and endured. But, make sure to look at the second part of each statement. For each aspect of our lives, look at what the life of Jesus offers in exchange. This exchange is *not* "see it, want it, get it." There is a process by which each of these exchanges is made real in our lives. But be assured that God will honor this exchange and make it real if we play our assigned role. In order to receive the fullness of most of these items, new things must be built within us. Many of our current problems flow from wrong ideas we embraced that show up in our lives. These determine the ways we think, feel, and act. For these ex-

Now we simply await an easy and luxurious life in God's Kingdom. Right? No, it is nothing like this!

changes to be completed in our new life we must first *put off* parts of our old life.

All of these things are now within us in the form of potential, waiting to be lavished upon us. Now we simply await an easy and luxurious life in God's Kingdom. Right? No, it is nothing like this! We may have a new peace that passes understanding. We may experience the love of God in the depth of our hearts. We may experience acceptance and feel the glow of His smile and many other good things. All of us probably enter a relationship with God equating an outpouring of God's love with a delightful life. As we enter the Kingdom of God we expect this outpouring to greet us. But God's infinite and perfect love takes a different form and has a different motivation. While we are thinking *blessing and delight,* God is thinking about the *blessings of maturity*, and how to get us there.

We live in a troublesome world; our lives are challenged in many ways. It seems God could make it easier on us at points. But this is often not His plan. Instead of eternal vacation, think football practice or training to be an Olympic athlete. God does not always deliver us out of difficulty, but He does always grant us the resources to live in and work through difficulties—and grow in the process. His goal for us is to develop godly character, a guidance system based on His truth, and a loving heart. These do not arise from a life of ease and indulgence, but through learning how to live and love in a world awash in challenges, heartache, pain, and loss. Jesus did not shrink back from these challenges, nor does He expect us to. He will lead and empower us along our way.

As we walk through these things, we do so arm in arm with the Lord of all creation and the lover of our souls. He will never leave or forsake us. On rare occasions God may strip away everything from our lives we have relied upon and cherished—other than Himself. In this He proves He is totally sufficient for us. He may literally be all that we have. I met a man in Ukraine who had encountered this, living for years in a Siberian gulag camp because he dared to be a pastor in a Communist country. The presence of God was so powerful in this man that, as he entered the room, everyone simply turned and looked at him in silence. As He walked through the room he hugged everyone. In his eyes, as he hugged me, was the deepest love and compassion I have ever seen on a human face. God's ultimate goal is for the relationship between Him and us to grow deep, broad, and strong. He wants our relationship with Him to become a wellspring of life and love flowing into a lost and dying world. Certainly new life in God is a delight and joy, with many pleasures and much beauty. God obviously delights in blessing us in incredibly meaningful ways throughout our lives. But it is unfair and incorrect to portray our new life as one divorced from the problems of life. If God intended to simply separate us from this world when we come to Him, we would all drop dead physically as we enter Covenant and arise in Heaven. Instead, He has plans for us here.

As He walked through the room he hugged everyone. In his eyes, as he hugged me, was the deepest love and compassion I have ever seen on a human face.

"Therefore, just as sin entered the world through one man, and death through sin, and in this way death came to all people, because all sinned … " (Romans 5:12).

"Now, if I do what I do not want to do, it is no longer I who do it, but it is sin living in me that does it" (Romans 7:20).

SIN AND THE NEW COVENANT OF DEATH AND LIFE

Jesus died. All humans die as a result of the original curse: " … for when you eat of it you will certainly die" (Genesis 3:17). The sentence of death for disobedience was one consequence of this act. But our understanding of Covenant offers a more complex picture. Scripture speaks not only of the above consequence but also of two exchanges. The nature of Satan became part of the first humans, and the dominion over the earth that was given by God to Adam and Eve passed to Satan. There is no mechanism other than entry into covenant with Satan by Adam and Eve—via their trusting, trusting in, and following Satan—to account for these exchanges. In addition to the sentence of death from God, their covenantal relationship with God ended even as a new one with Satan began. Their problem was now threefold: a sentence of death, separation from God, and the incorporated nature of their new master.

> *"I lay down My life—only to take it up again. No one takes it from me, but I lay it down of my own accord. I have authority to lay it down and authority to take it up again. This command I received from My Father"* (John 10:17, 18).

Jesus became human by the union of the Spirit of God with Mary. Inasmuch as He did not have a human mother *and* father, He did not fall under the curse of death. Inasmuch as He was God, He had an indestructible and eternal life. A life that created everything we find in our universe (John 1:3). If Jesus had not died on a Roman cross, would He have died as every other human dies—of natural causes, injury, or disease? No, His earthly life would have been just as Adam and Eve's were intended to be—unending. As they were made in God's image, they bore His image (which also could not be a more clear depiction of their original Covenant-joining). As Eve was created, she came to life already in Covenant with Adam, being flesh of his flesh (one flesh). And as Adam and Eve were created, they were fully joined to their Creator. Thus Jesus shared in humanity in its *pre-curse form,* just as God originally intended humanity to be. Then He joined humanity in its *post-curse form* through death. The Scriptures are clear that Jesus laid down His life and took it up again; it was not taken from Him.

"I have come that they may have life, and have it abundantly" (John 10:10, NASB).

JESUS TOOK ON DEATH FOR US

Much has been written about why Jesus offered Himself up for execution by the Romans, and this at the instigation of the Jewish leaders. He was the sacrificial lamb and the perfect offering. His sinless life is highlighted to explain why His unjust and unwarranted death could pay the penalty for the sinful lives of the rest of us. In most teaching the *sacrificial* aspect of Jesus' death is the sole focus. His death *paid the penalty* we owed for sin, both expressing God's love and satisfying His righteousness. In this rendering, we are *just forgiven*. And it is because we are forgiven that we can enter a relationship with God.

But do you notice missing elements in this picture? Does the focus of this picture *only on sin*—behavior—and *the penalty for sin* remind you of anything? How about a contract, one which focuses solely on behavior and the reward or penalty for various behaviors? Instead, the focus of a Covenant is *new life* and *joined life*. The point of a contract is *new behavior*: "not sinning." The point of a Covenant is to build our new life and our new relationship. With this in mind, let's see what else should be in the picture.

"In Him we have redemption through His blood, the forgiveness of sins" (Ephesians 1:7).

"Unless you eat the flesh of the Son of Man and drink His blood, you have no life in you" (John 6:53).

"One who has died has been set free from sin" (Romans 6:7).

"Who will set me free from this body of sin and death?" (Romans 7:24, NASB).

> *"No one who is born of God will continue to sin, because God's seed remains in them; they cannot go on sinning because they have been born of God"* (1 John 3:9).

The offering of blood to enter Covenant has always been understood to be the offer of one's life (see Trumbull). Certainly, in this case there is also a sacrificial aspect that was prefigured in the Old Covenant sacrificial system. This system ended once the perfect sacrifice was made. It clearly states at many points in Scripture that our sins—past, present, and future—are forgiven because of this perfect sacrifice (if we are in Covenant with Him). Much of current Christian teaching puts a period here, as if this sacrifice is the sum of what Jesus did for us. However, if we were merely forgiven, but kept our old life, the issue of our sin nature would remain. Many Scriptures speak of our changed relationship with sin after we enter the New Covenant. Sin no longer has the same power over us because our nature no longer shares the nature of Satan. This is not due to forgiveness but because our old self died and we received a new life joined to God—a new identity and nature.

> *"He is also head of the body, the church; and he is the beginning, the firstborn from the dead, so that He Himself will come to have first place in everything"* (Colossians 1:18).

JESUS LEADS THE WAY IN THE EXCHANGE OF DEATH AND LIFE

In laying down His life, Jesus also joined humanity in another Covenant exchange, the act of voluntarily laying down one's life. We will all die as humans, and we'll do so in a way we cannot control. But if we desire to enter the New Covenant with God we must choose to lay down life as we have always known it, in a very real sense voluntarily offering this old self up for death. Covenant is a life-for-life exchange, but it is also a death-for-death exchange. Two deaths, two new lives, now joined by identity and nature. Thus, Jesus in every sense leads the way in this Covenant relationship, laying down His life and taking it up again as the "firstborn from the dead" (Colossians 1:18). He joined Himself to humanity then offers us the opportunity to join ourselves to divinity by laying down, then taking up, His human but sinless life. The only difference is that Jesus' life was at His command. We must await a gift of new life from God that we have no role in acquiring except by believing in God, believing His offer, and offering up our own lives.

> Covenant is a life-for-life exchange, but it is also a death-for-death exchange. Two deaths, two new lives, now joined by identity and nature.

"I have come that they may have life, and have it to the full" (John 10:10).

" ... that you may believe that Jesus is the Messiah, the Son of God, and that by believing you may have life in His name" (John 20:31).

MORE THAN ABOUT GOING TO HEAVEN

I hope we can now see that Jesus' death on the cross represented a much more expansive, far-reaching, and powerful offer to us than merely forgiveness of sins and a promised place in Heaven. His life—laid down and taken back up—was offered to us. In fact, He offers us "life to the full." This plan has never emerged from the imagination of any human in history. Satan asserts that he offers humanity a better and more fulfilling plan than God does. Even Satan has not counterfeited such a plan in his myriad religious and worldly offerings. This plan stands as unique in all of history, in all of creation. Only from the mind and heart of God could such a thing come. Only a God who loves those made in His image would devise such an offer. He loves those who have turned from Him, scorned Him, ignored Him, rebelled against Him, and even willingly joined the efforts of His enemy.

And yet *still* He extends His love and His life to us. He is not willing that any should perish. In fact, the only way we will spend eternity apart from God is by rejecting His second-chance offer. People will only be separated from God eternally if this is what they choose.

"Therefore, anyone who chooses to be a friend of the world becomes an enemy of God" (James 4:4).

"Even Satan disguises himself as an angel of light" (2 Corinthians 11:14).

"Some have in fact already turned away to follow Satan" (1 Timothy 5:14).

ANOTHER NOTABLE COVENANT EXCHANGE

There is another exchange we should carefully consider. We take on not only the relatives and friends of our Covenant partner, but also the enemies. God has a mortal enemy. This being led one-third of the angels in Heaven in rebellion against the Creator. This being has passed himself off from the beginning as the friend and benefactor of the human race. His first success was deceiving Eve and Adam, and in turn every human. Every person has in some way rebelled against the rule of God. Instead of benefactor, Satan hated every one of us from the beginning. We are made in the image of the One he seeks to overthrow and destroy. Yet we are somehow useful to him, at least for now. As long as people remain in his kingdom he continues to seduce them with enough benefits to keep them alive … barely … most of the time.

"Put on the full armor of God, so that you can take your stand against the devil's schemes. For our struggle is not against flesh and blood, but against the rulers, against the authorities, against the powers of this dark world and against the spiritual forces of evil in the heavenly realms" (Ephesians 6:11, 12).

What happens when we exit his kingdom and join ourselves to God? Though now under the protection of God, receiving His love and provision, we are also on the front lines of a heavenly war. This enemy is real. He deceives and wounds us. We are more vulnerable if we are not aware of his activities. His influence in individuals and groups creates the sum of all problems of the human race, individually and corporately, from the very beginning until today's evening news. Specifically, if we do not recognize Satan's primary weapon—deception—and defend ourselves against this weapon as it comes at us, from the world and from within ourselves, we place our lives at far more risk.

This enemy is real. He deceives and wounds us. We are more vulnerable if we are not aware of his activities. His influence in individuals and groups creates the sum of all problems of the human race.

Interestingly, God has not yet laid this foe to rest. He will one day, but not yet. We still face the same foe who worked in Judas to betray Jesus. Who through the Sanhedrin and Jewish religious leaders put Jesus to death. Who incited the crowds that stoned Paul and crucified Peter and killed other apostles. God seems to work powerfully in and through us even as this foe continues to damage us, our families, and the rest of humanity. Several Scriptures warn believers not to be surprised or dismayed when attacks and adversity come. Instead, we are to expect these things. Why does God allow this? As James says, "Consider it pure joy, my brothers and sisters, whenever you face trials of many kinds, because you know that *the testing of your faith* produces perseverance. Let perseverance finish its work so that *you may be mature and complete, not* lacking anything" (James 1:2-4).

This is God's desire for us: maturity; our sanctification; and that we learn to love Him and each other wholeheartedly. But how do we do all of this? As always, God has a plan.

THE PRIORITY OF OUR COVENANT AND OUR COVENANT PARTNER

Our lives are buried under a pile of conflicting priorities and urgent matters. Productivity seminars stress learning how to focus on the most important things, then making sure these important things happen. God gave us the power to sort through things and determine those which are most important. But how can we be sure we are not missing something of vital importance?

By entering Covenant we make our Covenant partner and our relationship the most important thing in our life. In *The Blood Covenant,* author Trumbull notes that many ancient cultures had stories of the lengths to which people would go to fulfill Covenant obligations. This was counted as the height of heroism, and such people were greatly honored. It was deemed the height of dishonor to ignore these responsibilities. Since deities were called upon to enforce this arrangement, it was considered the height of stupidity to create a divine enemy in this way.

God clearly states that He, and our relationship with Him, are to be our top priorities. This relationship is more important than a Covenant with our spouse and certainly more important than any other consideration. Imagine what it would be like if people actually made Him first priority. What kind of world would this build? Have you made Him the highest priority in your life? If not, how would doing so change your life?

In our world many priorities compete with Marriage, family, and God for first place. Why? Why do we assign a certain priority to one thing or another? This goes back to our power of Assent and Dissent and our power of Attention. What is true about a thing, and what is its true importance? Based on what we believe, we determine where an item fits on our list of priorities. We have been taught by our culture that many things are vital for our best life. Certainly, many things are more important than our relationship with God. But how much of this is true? If we are deceived about the true value of a thing, where will we put it on our list of priorities? How important is it to pay our taxes or our mortgage or a credit card bill—or to pay for that new bass boat? Well, it depends on how much you like to fish.

God uses an interesting term for things we put ahead of Him on our list: *idols*. In the Old Testament this term primarily referred to the gods of surrounding countries. Is there any correlation between the false gods the Israelites chose to worship in preference to Jehovah and the things we place ahead of our relationship with God?

Any time we embrace a belief that *something other than God* will lead us to our best life, or secure our future, what are we doing? Are we worshipping a false god? Now let's think back to the spiritual war we inhabit and Satan's principle weapon: deception. How did Satan approach Eve? "Here is something God does not offer you that *I will* offer, that is *essential* for your best life." When we brush past God reaching for something He does not offer us, are we reaching out to an idol to provide something essential for us? Eve sought a better life apart from God. She was deceived. Could this be said of us?

In Covenant our partner has first claim on our time, resources, effort, talents, and potential. Think about what this would mean in my life and your life for our relationship with God. What would this look like if He truly becomes our first priority? Is there anything more important than God that would go missing? Things would go missing to be sure! We only have so much time and energy; more spent here, therefore less there. Priorities will need to be adjusted in order to build what God wants us to build within our Covenant.

Priorities will need to be adjusted in order to build what God wants us to build within our Covenant.

Adjusting such beliefs requires soul-searching and involves pain. We may need to say goodbye to cherished things, but only so we can replace them with more important and valuable things. God never tells us to sacrifice to simply deprive us, or purely for the purpose of pain. When He calls us to give up something, it is always to make room for better things—like Himself. Over time we will discover through our obedience that He loves us more than we love ourselves.

"The rulers of the gentiles lord it over them. ... Not so with you. Instead, whoever wants to become great among you must be your servant, and whoever wants to be first must be your slave—just as the Son of Man did not come to be served, but to serve" (Matthew 20:25-28).

Jesus spent three years living with twelve men, and spent considerable time with His larger entourage. Why? So He could adjust their beliefs, values, priorities, goals, vision of the good life, and many other things. Why did this take so long? You will learn why if you walk closely with Jesus. There is a lot within us that needs revision. We must stay close to Him over a long period of time to discover these things. God's ultimate goal within Covenant—to teach us to how to love and transform us so we are able to love—can be fulfilled only in the context of relationship. If we are not in a close relationship, no one sees us clearly enough to spot the contradictions within us. It is these contradictions, based again upon embraced deceptions, which lead us to *not love.* From our perspective we are just being real. From God's perspective and the perspective of those close to us we are being unloving and disobedient to God. We often think: *I've got this, because I've already thought through it. I know what is going on here.* It takes time for us to trust Jesus when He tells us, "No, you have not 'got this.'" And it takes even more time to realize that Jesus is the One who does understand it all—because He created it all. This would seem an easy concept to grasp and apply, but it is not. This is a reality we can only grasp through experience. This is why our journey of transformation will last lifelong.

"My sheep hear my voice; I know them, and they follow me" (John 10:27).

" ... and teaching them to obey everything I have commanded you" (Matthew 28:20).

We often believe we can synthesize other approaches with God's and somehow do better. We are used to choosing what we think is true, beneficial, and important. Thus we often approach God's Word like a buffet line. We take what we want, we leave the rest. Jesus is adamant, however, that we cannot mix His approach with any others. Why? Because of the source of these other approaches. What is the source of any idea that does not square with God's approach? Why not follow other approaches along with God's if we don't see anything wrong with them?

Thus we often approach God's Word like a buffet line. We take what we want, we leave the rest. Jesus is adamant, however, that we cannot mix His approach with any others.

My view of this question has changed completely after seeing decades of outcomes in many lives. We do not see the risk of our choices clearly on the front end. Let's do an exercise: define *deception*. Jesus refuses to allow synthesis between His injunctions and any other source of guidance because of the origin of this not-God guidance. When we strip away the veneer, these ideas are designed to lead us away from God and down an alternate path. Every path other than God's will ultimately lead to the same place. You do not want to go there.

> *"This, then, is how you ought to regard us: as servants of Christ and as those entrusted with the mysteries God has revealed. … Now it is required that those who have been given a trust must prove faithful"* (1 Corinthians 4:1, 2).

FAITHFULNESS IN COVENANT

With all this in mind, God designed the centerpiece of our response within Covenant to be faithfulness. Faithfulness means we are to *recognize and embrace everything we are called on to do in this relationship*, and then do it. Since this relationship is our most important priority, we must let nothing get in the way of doing these things. But faithfulness has other shades of meaning. It speaks of loyalty, consistency, and correct execution in the service of another. In Covenant there is yet another layer of meaning. To do the things God calls us to do and live the life God calls us to live, we must go through a lengthy process of growth and development. Scripture uses terms like "putting off" the old person and "putting on" the new. We are called to grow from infants in Christ to mature men and women of God. So faithfulness involves more than "in the moment" decisions to do the right thing according to Covenant. It also involves a commitment to build a character and guidance system based firmly on God's truth. Only then can we do all that God instructs us to do.

FAITH AND FAITHFULNESS

Another way of viewing the word faithfulness is in light of the word *faith*. Faith is something we are told we should want more of, yet most do not understand exactly what faith is. What do we want more of? Is it a feeling of confidence that things will turn out as we want? Is it a feeling of confidence that God loves us enough to give us what we need, which we often define as what we most want? Scripture tells us that if we have "enough faith" we can tell a mountain to move itself into the sea and it will obey us (Mark 11:23). This is qualified by Jesus' words, "If you ask anything *in My name*, I will do it (John 14:14)." The phrase "in my name" suggests we are to explore this power *only* by asking for exactly what Jesus would ask for. And this suggests we know the answer to this question because we know Him well, from learning His Word and working side by side with Him. If we are "full of faith," can we also term this "faith-full"—or "faithful"? I believe *faith* and *faithfulness* are two sides of a coin. It is impossible to have one without the other. Another picture of faith is to believe in something we cannot see: God's revelation. Then to act as if this revelation is true. We cannot "see" into the spiritual realm or "see" God's cause-

and-effect system of consequences. We can only test God's spiritual assertions in hindsight. We can accept them, though, because they come from a trustworthy source. A source we believe in because we know His character and His heart toward us.

A more complete definition of faith begins to sound like Covenant terminology! If faith is what we can be sure God will do, what in fact are we sure of? He will be faithful to His end of our Covenant relationship, period. He is perfectly faithful. We can count on this. We can pray that God will honor His Covenant with full confidence. This requires, of course, that we understand our Covenant with God. So what does it mean for us to be faithful to Covenant? It means that God can be confident *in us*—that we will hold up our end of this relationship. Let's take a closer look at what that means.

OUR COVENANT OBLIGATIONS

THE DUTIES, RESPONSIBILITIES, AND OBLIGATIONS OF COVENANT

What is the central imperative of Covenant? To love our Covenant partner in action consistently across the spectrum of life. This is what builds the best Marriage. This is what builds the best relationship with God. But this requires a bit more than merely saying, "I'm going to love you … perfectly." There is a process by which we learn to love in action, instead of just with good intentions. We go through this just like any other learning process: one step at a time. This is God's Covenant school of love.

Love in action involves, well, action. We have specific duties, responsibilities, and obligations to our Covenant partner. This concept has become confused or gone missing altogether in Christian teaching when it comes to our relationship with God or Marriage. In Scripture we see what we are *to be* and *do*. From an understanding of Covenant we learn not only what we are supposed to do, but why we are to do it and how we become able to be and do what is necessary.

Let's be clear: this way of approaching a relationship is a radical departure from everything our culture tells us about relationships. We have spent our lives in relationships doing what we want to do. We only give what we want to offer. All of our relationships have been contracts: trading something of ourselves to get something for ourselves. In Covenant God invites us to shift to an entirely new way of thinking. In Covenant we are to do what is necessary to build the best relationship, to love our Covenant partner in action, and to build (and rebuild) our own character and guidance system in the process. We are to do what we have committed to do by entering Covenant, not what we feel like doing.

First, what are our actual responsibilities according to Covenant? For those who want to be guided by Scripture (which should be all of us), where are the responsibilities of Covenant in Scripture? The specifics are scattered throughout Scripture. In the first book of this series, *What Is a Covenant?*, we correlated the duties of Covenant with specific Scriptures. Then in *The Covenant of Marriage*, the second in this series, we did the same for Scriptures specifically related to Marriage. I have quoted many verses that relate to Covenant already in this text. For the sake of time and space these will not be collated into a list for the New Covenant. Frankly, though, once we understand Covenant, most verses have some relation to this relationship in both Old and New Testaments. As I began to write this series, I started reading through the New Testament to collect pertinent verses. It soon became obvious that it would be easier to list the verses that had *no connection* to Covenant. So I invite you to read this material with a Bible in one hand and some good study aids in the other. You would benefit most from your own Scripture study on this topic alongside the verses referenced throughout the text.

Let's review Trumbull's list of Covenant responsibilities (drawn from *The Blood Covenant: An Ancient Rite and Its Bearing on Scripture*).

ASPECTS AND RESPONSIBILITIES OF COVENANT

- Two parties agree to enter a lifelong bond of mutual benefit and mutual responsibility.
- A public ceremony is arranged for this purpose.
- The two make vows to each other and to deity, vows to honor, protect, defend, provide for, and generally promote the best interests of the other party in every way possible. They vow to pay any price and make any sacrifice to fulfill these vows. Their lives and futures are to be inextricably joined.
- Blood is taken from each and taken in by the other via several possible techniques. The blood of each is understood to contain the identity of that person, and the offering of it to represent the offer of one's life to the other.
- A mark is generally made on the body, one that is a visible, permanent token of these vows. Alternately, an amulet or other ornament becomes the symbol of this joining, and it is to be worn henceforth.
- Clothing is exchanged to signify the exchange of identity.
- Armor and weapons are exchanged to signify the obligation of mutual defense.
- A meal is eaten by the parties and assembled witnesses to signify the obligation of mutual provision.
- Gifts are exchanged to signify the obligation of mutual blessing. The two parties often compete to give the most extravagant offering.
- Now that identity is altered and joined, relatives are shared. Full familial obligations are now in force toward the other's extended family.
- Friends and enemies become mutual, as do obligations of friendship or vengeance.
- Debts, assets, obligations, and resources are shared.

- Basically, any asset, resource, capability, or potential of one is at the other's disposal as needed.
- The honor of each is at stake in fulfilling these vows. The highest honor is found in upholding the honor of the other party.
- Temporal and supernatural consequences for unfaithfulness are assumed. For thieves or others whose character could not be trusted in any other circumstance, these bonds are held most sacred and almost never violated. It is counted the height of foolishness to incur a divine enemy in such a way.

Consider how these items translate to a relationship with God. We are used to thinking of all the things God does for us in our relationship. Unfortunately, we are often taught that God does it all. He does *all* of *some* things, but He also delegates some things to us and requires certain things of us in this relationship. Look again at this list and see if you can identify things you can do or be toward God in keeping with the reciprocal nature of Covenant. This is an all-in relationship on the part of both parties. How can we be all-in for God?

HONORING GOD

Our first and highest Covenant duty is to honor our Covenant partner. They are in us; we are in them. We are to regard them and their interests as we regard ourselves and our interests. We are to make every resource and everything of ourselves available to our Covenant partner. Covenant is the ultimate blank check: whatever you need, whatever I have, whatever I am or can become. Beyond every obligation listed just above, we are to love them in ways that are reflected beautifully in historic wedding vows.

"Husbands, love your wives, just as Christ loves the church" (Ephesians 5:25).

"Love the Lord your God with all your heart and with all your soul and with all your strength and with all your mind" (Luke 10:27).

LOVING GOD WHOLEHEARTEDLY

How does God enable us to love Him with our whole heart and mind, as well as with the entirety of our strength? By taking us through His school of love. In several passages in the Old and New Testaments, God likens His relationship with His people to a Marriage, a *one-flesh* relationship. There are four parts to love: what we *believe*, what we *choose*, how we *feel*, and how we *act*. There is a striking similarity between the ever-deeper love God's plan produces in Marriage and the heart He intends us to have toward Him in Covenant. Both could be described as pure and perfect love. If our heart of love for God is analogous to our love for our spouse, how do we develop this kind of love for a husband or wife?

We often think of romantic love as something we fall into, a random and mysterious force that simply overtakes us. This is not true. True love is far different from random attraction. People have a flickering of attraction at many points that they could pursue if they decided to. This goes back to what we believe about the person and the situation, and the decision we make based on these beliefs. There may be a strong attraction one decides to move away from, or a weakest flicker that, if pursued, turns into a Marriage. Love is something we decide to pursue and build—even within our hearts. Love is also something we choose how we will display. We may feel an attraction early in a relationship. But true love—and the feelings that go with it—only grows in the ground of deep investment and total commitment. All of love is founded upon our choices. This is why God can reasonably require love from us.

We often think of romantic love as something we fall into, a random and mysterious force that simply overtakes us. This is not true. True love is far different from random attraction.

If you are Married, what did you first notice about your beloved that sparked your interest? What other things did you find out about this person that continued to fuel your interest? Now consider God. Who is He? What is His character? Does He notice you? Has He reached out to you, revealing His heart toward you and His intentions for you? Our heart toward God is not romantic. But consider how one would feel as an orphan on the street who encounters the love of a perfect father, one who wants to invite him into His family. On the other hand, Scripture also refers to us as the "bride of Christ" (2 Corinthians 11:2). How then do we display and experience this love? The plan with the Covenant of Marriage is to first love the other as we love ourselves. However, do we love ourselves perfectly? We do not. So God's next step is to teach us His much broader and deeper definition of love. Then, He holds us accountable for loving in this way (as Christ loves the Church). For this to be possible our hearts must grow and be transformed. Everything that urges us toward not-love must be subtracted, and the life of God in us must grow. Marriage is the same form of one-flesh Covenant as the New Covenant. Do you think God might have a similar process within this Covenant to grow our capacity to love Him?

HISTORIC WEDDING VOWS

Let's look at a part of God's design for Marriage to see if we can find things we can apply in our relationship with God. Start with this: what do we vow to be toward each other in Marriage? Let's look at a sampling of traditional wedding vows obtained from *Wedding Paper Divas*[15].

1. Leave family of origin, friends, and everything of the past behind to join together with another person to become two new creatures in a new entity, a new family.
2. This joining is a lifetime commitment, a permanent joining.
3. The other party and you are now *us*—with no part of life held back. There is no protected personal space in which the other has no right to be.

4. Love and friendship in their fullest possible definition are pledged.
5. To honor
6. To cherish
7. To be faithful
8. To be devoted
9. Protect and defend
10. Provide and nourish
11. Trust in the other party, and be trustworthy.
12. Persevere
13. Purity
14. Honesty
15. Charity
16. Kindness
17. Patience
18. Gentleness
19. Self-control
20. To prefer one's Covenant partner before all others.

"Where you treasure is, there will your heart be also" (Matthew 6:21).

A more full definition of these terms was provided in *The Covenant of Marriage.* This helps us better understand what is being asked of us by terms like "persevere." Again, review this list with this question in mind: How can I be faithful to God in the ways described by this list? Many important principles are involved in building love. Feelings *follow* decision, investment, and commitment. Loving feelings are based on respect and trust. True love is the experience of oneness with another, and a life of oneness with another. In light of this, how is Covenant created to grow such love?

We have a natural affinity for family members. Why? Because we *identify* with them. People we are related to are a part of us. Now consider the bond of shared identity created by Covenant. This is the ultimate in "identifying with," for we are *within* the other. When we look at the other, we literally see an extension of ourselves, and when we look in the mirror, we literally see them as well. This is the foundation for the deepest loyalty and fiercest devotion of which humans are capable. Every other thing we are called on to do is a direct result of this sharing of identity.

Above all, we are called to honor our Covenant partner. We are to promote and defend our partner's honor at every point. We are to add to their lives in any way that enhances their honor. With God, we can make Him no more perfect than He is, but we can defend His reputation. And, called by His Name as we are, we can avoid doing anything that would dishonor His Name.

HOW CAN LOVE GROW FROM LIMITING OUR BEHAVIOR CHOICES?

Look at the Covenant responsibilities and wedding vows one more time. Realize that we vow *always, without fail* to treat our partner in these ways. What would this mean for each item in relationship with God? Now let's go back to Scripture for additional guidance about loving God in action. Jesus says obedience to Him equals love for Him (John 14:21, 23, 24); disobedience to anything He taught therefore represents a lack of love for Him. Covenant is all about loving our Covenant partner, not about checking off items on a "to-do list" of obedience. Think hard about these next statements. If we are to love Jesus because we are *in Him,* among other reasons, how do you think Jesus wants us to *treat someone who also contains Him within themselves?* Does Jesus enjoy being mistreated? Instead of simply requiring obedience, Jesus is inviting us to love ourselves as we love Him. He is inviting us to love Him and ourselves by loving those in the Body of

Christ. By conducting ourselves in this way we create the best consequences and build the best lives for ourselves. That is, Jesus tells us to do things so we will build, grow, enjoy, and be blessed. When we look at all the things Jesus said to do, does it help us if we understand why we are doing these things?

IS LOVE ABOUT FREEDOM, OR SOMETHING ELSE?

In past generations people took vows, duties, obligations, and responsibilities more seriously than most do today. These define and constrain our behavior—in constructive ways. In our culture today we have been sold the idea that having the freedom to make whatever decision we choose is somehow the path to the best life. When people can do what they want to do, what do they do? Sometimes they do good and beautiful things, and sometimes things that are puzzling, horrifying, or terrifying. We have embraced the (deceptive) idea that the path to freedom is lack of constraint. This is perhaps Satan's most fundamental lie. As if gaining the freedom to do things that damage self and others is doing us a favor! Oddly, the converse is true. We find true freedom through limiting our choices to beneficial things.

As if gaining the freedom to do things that damage self and others is doing us a favor! Oddly, the converse is true. We find true freedom through limiting our choices to beneficial things.

In our unbounded culture people are choosing to do a vast number of destructive things, and these have even more negative consequences than the damage we are seeing. Character and relationships are damaged. Addictions form. Mental health is damaged. The "freedom" to choose wrong or stupid things does not lead to true freedom. Instead, this leads to bondage. The antidote to this poison? Learning the right thing to do and confining ourselves to these things. God limits us because He loves us.

LOVE IS A SKILL WE MUST LEARN

In any realm of life where creativity and innovation are valued, like music, art, sports, or surgery, before one can effectively create one must first be extensively trained. Trained to do what? To confine ourselves to the rules of a particular discipline (note carefully the term we use for these important realms—a *discipline*). To create great music one must first master an instrument, then various forms of music. Only then can the elements be combined into a transcendent piece of music. A gifted athlete can only be successful by learning and applying the rules of physical development, team play, and the game. Those who play outside the rules never have long-term success. True freedom requires a high level of discipline and a significant degree of training if we are attempting to do anything that really matters. Building a relationship with God is perhaps the highest-skill job on the planet. Or we can do what we feel like and figure it out as we go. Suppose a person decides to become a brain surgeon—because "we can become anything we want to be." He'll get your brain tumor out of there, but he'll need to figure out how once he gets your skull opened up. The good news? His fees are the lowest in town. Who would you rather have, the highly skilled and disciplined one, or the one who is expressing his freedom?

Loving others is the most multifaceted task we face as humans. Love follows certain principles—first do no harm, for instance. But loving others means understanding them and their needs. Loving means understanding what you have to offer in the moment that can bless. Love means commitment, devotion, and loyalty. As we go through this book many aspects of love are discussed. God has many things to say about what it means to love others in Scripture. God first tells us to love others as we love ourselves. This more or less represents a choice on our part. If we are loving ourselves in particular ways, we need only choose to extend this treatment to another. Understanding our relationship to other believers provides motivation to actually do this. God's rightful role in our lives, as Lord, gives Him authority to direct us. This provides additional motivation.

God's school of love has four parts: transforming us, informing us, conforming us, and again transforming us. He first changes us and joins us in a way that makes loving others make sense, and creates in us the potential to do so. Next, He tells us to love others as ourselves. But this does not reflect the fullness of the loving behaviors He desires. So He shares with us His view of love and instructs us to love each other with the love of Christ. We are not there yet, even if we want to be. We may have the intention to love others, but what else is needed? In addition to a more clear understanding of what it means to love, we also need proper motivation to make these behaviors our first priority. Even if highly motivated, though, there are things within us that will oppose loving, and oppose obeying the One who instructs us to love. The next part of God's plan is to use the problems and conflicts that inevitably crop up in relationships to direct us to the things within ourselves which oppose love—beliefs we have embraced, and what has been built within us as a result. We are to be transformed by the renewing of our minds, which means identifying the lies we embraced and built upon, rejecting these, and embracing new beliefs which support love and obedience. This is the second transformation we speak of, and it is a lifelong process.

There is a parallel process we follow to learn to love God. The things about us which invite transformation will be seen, not through interpersonal issues, but by our unwillingness to obey God and follow His path. He equates obedience to Him with love for Him. When we experience the inevitable urges to not obey, we must do more than dig in our heels, grit our teeth, and try harder to do what God says. Or play games with God's leadership and pretend it is OK to not scrupulously follow His Word. We must look within ourselves and identify the root causes of our disobedience. This will always be a life benefit we expect to occur if we follow other guidance. We are to examine these beliefs carefully, for these ideas are always a deception. We are to be transformed by the renewing of our minds and embrace the truth about what is truly best for us.

Once we see the entire plan, the sequence we must follow to truly follow God and be faithful in our Covenant, it becomes clear that this relationship is more than a relationship. It is a rigorous training process that demands considerable time and effort for the rest of our lives. This training process is far more involved and lengthy than the process of getting accepted to medical school and going through its rigors, then completing a surgery residency (which is a 14-year process overall). Why is this process necessary?

To obey orders in the middle of a battlefield is far more difficult than obeying orders on a military drill field, and far more important. To consistently make a basketball shot from 10 feet away takes practice. To make this same shot consistently with someone guarding you takes much more practice. To make this shot under pressure in the last two seconds of an important game, with someone in your face, takes vastly more prep work. We are training to build our best life in the middle of a battlefield. We must do things far more difficult than ringing a basketball goal. Consider the list of vows of Marriage in this section. We sign up for all of these, and far more. The process looks like it does because this is what it takes for us to build what God wants us to build.

> *"The Lord disciplines the one He loves, and He chastens everyone He accepts as his son"* (Hebrews 12:6).

Beyond loving God, many other things are required of us in a Covenant relationship from the above lists. The purpose of these goes far beyond building a heart of love. But ultimately, all are about growing our relationship with God. These require a vast amount of time, energy, focus, commitment, and sweat. How much should we be willing to be disciplined and constrained for the sake of building the most important things in our lives?

IS OUR NEW COVENANT RELATIONSHIP ONLY WITH GOD?

We can only be in one Covenant of Marriage. Creating another Covenant through adultery severs the original Covenant. But a person can be in Blood Covenants with multiple people. Christ can also be in multiple New Covenant relationships (obviously). But what happens between two people who are in Covenant with Christ? Each is in Christ. Christ is in each. Does a bond of nature and identity now join these two who did not enter a Covenant with each other? Are their identities comingled? Yes, they are mingled within Christ! Is there a common element of identity within each person? Yes, the Holy Spirit is now in both. Thus, these two are in a full Covenant relationship. How can we be certain of this? Because God says so in John 17:20-23.

Consider what this means. What kind of bond actually exists among Christians? What kind of shared life are we to live? What duties, responsibilities, and obligations have we assumed toward each other by entering the New Covenant? What does it mean to have the obligation to love each of these people in action? What would it mean for us to be loved back in the same way?

This reality is a wonderful foundation upon which to build the Kingdom of God. Covenant is about total commitment, love in action, and growth and transformation. Why? So we learn to love each other as God loves us. What would happen if people understood they were in this kind of relationship with fellow Christians? Can you think of some things that might be different if this were so? Of course, the same can be said of our Covenant with God. Many things would look different in the Body of Christ if this relationship was better understood.

This assertion is founded on understanding the nature of Covenant joining. Is there anything in Scripture that supports this view? Let's look at a few other Scriptures; see if you spot any Covenant elements in God's description of the relationship among believers.

"So we, who are many, are one body in Christ, and individually members one of another" (Romans 12:5, NASB).

"Just as a body, though one, has many parts, but all its many parts form one body, so it is with Christ. For we were all baptized by one Spirit so as to form one body" (1 Corinthians 12:12, 13).

"If one part suffers, every part suffers with it; if one part is honored, every part rejoices with it" (1 Corinthians 12:26).

"I pray also for those who will believe in Me through their message, that all of them may be one, Father, just as you are in Me and I am in You" (John 17:20, 21).

"I have given them the glory that You gave Me that they may be one as we are one—I in them and You in Me—so that they may be brought to complete unity" (John 17:22, 23).

"A new command I give you: love one another. As I have loved you, so you must love one another" (John 13:34).

God's "new commandment" corresponded to His New Covenant: "Love as I have loved you." Is this not the guiding purpose of Covenant? Love in action, then learning to love more and more deeply across the spectrum of life? In *The Covenant of Marriage* we looked at the processes of growth and transformation that are required if our capacity to love is to grow. Which it must if we are to obey God's command. The most clear description of the relationship among the Trinity, between the Trinity and individual believers, and among believers is Jesus' prayer in the Garden of Gethsemane (John 17). Our relationship with God and our relationship with other believers is intended to reflect the Trinity. Is there any evidence that the first generation of Christians understood this?

"All the believers were together and had everything in common. They sold property and possessions to give to anyone who had need" (Acts 2:38).

Consider for a moment what this means. (For the sake of space we will not repeat the principles of Covenant or our responsibilities in this relationship, but it would help to turn back and review these.) We have the general sense that we are to be on our best behavior toward others in a church environment. But this often translates into merely being a bit nicer toward one another…most of the time. We read or hear of God's injunctions to love one another, but often file these along with all His other sort-of-followed commands. Most feel no serious sense of obligation on this point, nor any real sense of what it would mean to "love each other as I have loved you." This is another benefit of understanding Covenant. We now have a very clear starting point for loving others in action. We can simply follow the lists of behaviors we saw earlier. (You can review the expanded definitions of these things in *The Covenant of Marriage*.)

There is no question that all in the body of believers are in a mutual Covenant, one shared with Christ. He is the firstborn, we are brothers and sisters.

"By this everyone will know that you are my disciples, if you love one another" (John 13:35).

There is no question that all in the body of believers are in a mutual Covenant, one shared with Christ. He is the firstborn, we are brothers and sisters. There is no question we are under the most serious possible obligation to conform our lives to this reality. But how do we do this? How do we become willing, or even able, to do this? For this we turn to God's overall Covenant plan: inform, conform, transform.

CHAPTER FOUR

LIFE IN THE NEW COVENANT

You are confronting a situation common in modern life. In front of you is a large box, now opened, and an array of parts. In your hand are sheets of paper stapled together, the proud work of an English-as-a-second-language student. On the front page is a picture of your new barbecue grill. This is what it is supposed to look like. But your instruction manual has only four pages—this picture, a list of parts, and how you are supposed to use (and not misuse) your new grill. There are no instructions about how to build this thing so it actually works! Fortunately, for grill-building we have a backup: YouTube.

What about the instructions for building a working Christian life? In Scripture we see a picture of what our life is supposed to look like. We have do's and don'ts. The parts are right in front of us: in the mirror and in the truths of God. Are we really left to just figure out on our own how all these parts fit and work together? Where is *the plan*?

AN OVERVIEW OF GOD'S PLAN

We are now going to shift from learning about this relationship to *building it.* God has a plan, but we must choose to follow it, and we must build. What is a blueprint? If you want to build a house, you must have one. The first page of a blueprint is always a picture of the finished product. (Until this point, that is what this book has provided.) Next there are details of each part to be built, pictured in enough detail to actually construct them. A blueprint allows one to see at a glance the relationship between these parts—how they fit together into a seamless whole. But God wants us to construct not just a building; He wants us to build a factory. This factory has parts that work together to produce new and important things for our lives and the lives of others. Are our lives what God desires? One cannot enjoy the things made by a factory until one builds the factory to produce them.

One of the most frustrating experiences of my life was listening to Dr. Frank Barker paint a glowing picture of the glories of the mature Christian life—one aspect after another, week by week. Why? Because once I saw the big picture clearly, I wanted this life to be *my life*. But I had no idea how this life was actually built. I had the general sense that effort was needed on my part, but I did not know what effort. I had the vague sense that God's transformation was crucial if I am to have a new and different life. But I did not understand how or when such transformation occurred—or what *transformation* even meant. I was trying to do right things with mixed success. But overall it felt like I was stuck in one place, turning in circles. On a hundred-mile journey, it seemed I had managed to move about ten feet.

I was doing all the "Christian things." I was going to church and listening to a wonderful teacher. I was surrounded by mature Christians, people whose lives reflected many things I wanted to see in my life. I was in a high-commitment Bible study with a former Marine who would not allow the busyness of medical school to overshadow a more important teaching process: learning the Word of God. But my life was not changing much. In some ways, yes, I saw new things. But I was not closing the gap very fast between my life and life as it could and should be.

There was a point when God began to answer my prayers. He started to show me the path to a new, different, and much better life. People began to come alongside and mentor me, teaching me how to change my life using the truths I was learning from God. Soon I began to teach and mentor others. This taught me many new things about the various ways people grow and change. Then I learned about

Covenant. This put the individual parts of this plan I had learned into proper position and showed me how these parts worked together to allow change in deeper parts of our being. All of these are parts of God's plan. This is His path of growth and transformation. This path leads to enthusiastic obedience. We are not only to live this life; God's intent is that we enjoy it. This is the path I want to share with each person reading this book. The painful frustration I experienced that first year provided a lifetime of motivation for me. I was motivated to do whatever it takes to know God better and to make the most of the life He has given me. My prayer for you is not just to learn about this plan. My prayer is that you will be sufficiently motivated to follow it.

From now on, think of what is in front of you as the plan for your life with God. There will be specific things to build in specific ways. There are tools you must learn to use. And there is a definite sequence of building. You cannot tile the bathroom before you complete the house foundation. You may already be far down the path of building your relationship with God. You may have built many good things in your relationship with God. But we all benefit from seeing the overall plan. One of the powerful benefits of understanding Covenant is putting every aspect of Christian life in its proper place. All of these things—very good as isolated items—are intended to function in an integrated way to produce certain outcomes. If any part is weak or missing, important outcomes are impacted.

God's plan has three general parts: Inform, Conform, and Transform. Let's look at one part of His plan for us—loving others—and get a sense for how His plan works.

"Love your neighbor as yourself" (Mark 12:33).

"We love because He first loved us" (1 John 4:19).

"May the Lord lead your hearts into a full understanding and expression of the love of God and the patient endurance that comes from Christ" (2 Thessalonians 3:5).

INFORMING US ABOUT LOVE: THE HEART OF COVENANT

First, God instructs us to love others with whom we are in Covenant as we love ourselves. He makes this easier by making these "others" literally an extension of ourselves. Then God instructs us to extend this same love to our neighbors. But do you see a problem? We do not always love ourselves perfectly, do we? If we love others this imperfectly, sometimes we do them no favor. God's next step is to enlarge our understanding of love. Scripture is full of instruction about the many aspects and dimensions of love. Jesus said the entirety of the Law and Prophets (the Old Testament) could be summed up as, "Love the Lord your God … and love your neighbor as yourself" (Matthew 22:37-40). Every commandment about our relationship with God, or how we are to treat other people, is in some way about love.

> *"Therefore, as God's chosen people, holy and dearly loved, clothe yourselves with compassion, kindness, humility, gentleness, and patience. Bear with each other and forgive one another if any of you has a grievance against someone. Forgive as the Lord forgave you. And over all these virtues put on love, which binds them all together in perfect unity"* (Colossians 3:12-14).

MOVING TOWARD GOD'S UNDERSTANDING OF LOVE

God starts with the command to love as best we know how. This means we all start at different places. The best way to really learn about love is to experience it. If we interact with God often as we go through our day, we will see His love displayed toward us in many ways. It is vital that we learn to see and appreciate His love. Only then will we actually experience His love. We will *feel* loved. We start out *trusting in* God because we know He is perfect—in an abstract sense. That is like looking across the room and seeing that person we "just *know* is the one." This is before we know almost anything about him or her. Yet we are already envisioning picking out the forever-home in which we will live together happily ever after. Sometimes we are right, and sometimes ... well, sometimes reality does not match our expectations, does it? Fortunately, God's perfection means His love will be exactly what is needed in any circumstance of life. But His love is not always shown toward us in the way we expect. Therefore, understanding God's love and learning to trust Him from experience are more of a process than we expect.

"My goal is that they may be encouraged in heart and united in love, so that they may have the full riches of complete understanding, in order the they may know the mystery of God, namely Christ, in whom are hidden all the treasures of wisdom and knowledge" (Colossians 2:2-4).

CONFORMING TO GOD'S DEFINITION OF LOVE

The further we travel down God's path, the more we will learn to trust Him with every fiber of our being from our own experience. From Him we learn what acting in the best interests of another actually looks like. This does not mean saying yes to every request. As our hearts settle deeply into this relationship we are nourished in every way that really matters (just like the "living water" Jesus offered to the Samaritan woman that would allow her to never thirst again; John 4:10-13). If we learn to see, appreciate, and become nourished by God's love, this creates an abundance of love in our hearts that overflows to others. "We love because He first loved us" (1 John 4:19).

God defines many aspects of love in Scripture. The responsibilities, duties, and obligations of Covenant mirror God's Scriptural commands. God equates love for Him with obeying Him. Also, when we do the things God says to do in relationships, we begin to see the wisdom of His approach and the rewards that come with it. If we are to make the effort to learn God's definition of love, then apply this definition to our behaviors, we must be highly motivated. God's plan includes every motivation we need. All we need now is a willing mind and heart.

REASONS TO CONFORM TO GOD'S PLAN

God is the master motivator. His plan contains every reason we need to carry out His plan. As we consider whether to embrace His overall plan, and as we confront the daily decisions to faithfully follow His plan—or not—we should keep the following reasons in mind.

First, God created us, then re-created us in His image. As our Creator and the Lord of all things He has every right to command us in every detail of life, and has the power to compel obedience. Instead, He chooses not to force us to obey. He allows us the freedom to choose. But these choices have consequences now and for eternity. We do well to keep in mind that God will fully enforce His words to humanity at a point, and that we will all reap the consequences of what we have sown, for better or worse. Those in Covenant with God will spend eternity with Him but will experience the presence or absence of rewards based on our degree of faithfulness and obedience.

The next reason to be faithful to God is that we have committed ourselves to this. As we entered this relationship we proclaimed Him Lord of our lives. The requirement to enter Covenant is to *believe in* Jesus. This means that we entrust ourselves to Him and His Lordship over our life. If we enter a relationship with Him with this state of mind and heart, for what reason would we turn around and be *unfaithful* to Him? If God has created not only this relationship, but the world we inhabit to reflect His requirements through the consequences of our actions, why would we choose less than the best for our lives, much less to actively damage ourselves? This is precisely what occurs when we are unfaithful or we disobey Him. God offers us the opportunity to build an intimate and powerful relationship with the Lord of Heaven and Earth. Would we make little or nothing of this opportunity? God offers to love us perfectly, and teach us to love as He does. Is this an opportunity worth pursuing? He offers us the opportunity to participate with Him in building an eternal Kingdom that we will inhabit. Is this an offer that might interest us?

Yet there are things within us which argue against faithfulness and obedience. We have a curious wiring system as humans, and can become convinced that we, and those who lead us away from God and

His plan, know best how to live. God has given us the ability to observe, analyze, and reason. He has given us a power of discernment. If well-trained, this can spot lies and deception. We have the power to identify truth, and the inner equipment to respond to truth as God desires. We have all that is needed in Covenant to become increasingly faithful and obedient. The question literally comes down to our choices. Do we choose truth, faithfulness, obedience, and love; or do we follow those who rebel and sell deception? We have every possible reason and every possible motivation to follow God and be faithful to Him. We have every possible reason to love Him with every fiber of our being. But we have a choice to make, in whole and in every detail. We should make these choices as if our lives depend on them, for they do.

The first step toward doing anything is knowing that we really need to do it. Then comes embracing the task, making it a priority, and doing our best. This will get us a long way. But when it comes to loving others—or God—perfectly with every fiber of our being, none of us are quite there yet. Yet this is what God requires from us. Is He unreasonable? No. He has a plan.

THE CHALLENGE OF LOVE IN ACTION

If we seriously attempt to love God and others, we will discover an important reality. There are things within us that oppose love. God tells a man to love his wife as Christ loves the church. But there are times we simply will not feel like doing this. Instead we do something very unloving. Why? Sometimes we believe we have a good reason to do other things. This is a matter of adjusting our beliefs. But sometimes the urge to do wrong things comes from deeper within. We have patterns of life that do not reflect in-the-moment decisions. Some say this is due to the continued presence of our sin nature. If this is so, we can do nothing about this problem. Yet this is something God commands us to do something about. Will God command us to do something that is impossible? No. We cannot be judged for falling short if something is literally impossible.

TRANSFORMATION: WHAT, WHEN, AND WHY

Something changes at the time we enter Covenant: our nature and identity. Scripture also mentions at several points elements of ourselves that we are to choose to change. We are to choose to put off the "old self," put on the "new self," and "be transformed by the renewing of our minds." As Christians, a simple reading of Scripture leaves us confused about what *has changed,* what *needs to change*, and how either of these changes impact our life. We remain confused about what God has already transformed and about what we are responsible for transforming. If we understand Covenant, this confusion disappears. Let's take a few moments and develop more clarity about the parts of us, how these parts fit together, and how God's plan of transformation is carried out.

NATURE AND IDENTITY VERSUS CHARACTER

What is our character? From our vantage point it feels like the very center of who we are as a human being. Our character creates much of the life we show to the outside world. Are we optimistic, powerful, lazy, or often discouraged? Almost any adjective used to describe you or me is describing our character. We have a true identity, and this also manifests through the way we live. We often confuse these two. We often think the way we feel flows from the core of our being (or our true nature). Instead, almost all emotions arise from our character and are based on our beliefs.

The difference between our *nature* and our *character* is this: our nature and identity are fixed things, created by God; our character is built by our decisions, and is thus subject to change at any point by our decisions—if we know which decisions to make. We *cannot* change our nature. We can change our character by changing what we believe. We can change our emotions by changing what we believe. Our character was formed by decisions we may no longer recall, decisions that were made very early in life. We are so used to living based on these decisions that they no longer feel like decisions. Instead, these things feel like what is real and true about us. Our character also reflects what we believe is real and true about life and other people. I paint this detailed picture to convey an important reality. There is as much resistance to changing the decisions which formed our character as there is to amputating our arm. However, if we made these decisions the first time, we can *un-make* these decisions and *remake* new ones if we are sufficiently motivated. This is not an easy thing to do, but it can be done if we have a good enough reason and know how to do so.

Why would we want to do so? In Covenant, we are called to love perfectly. If we take this seriously and commit ourselves to faithfully following God's plan, the parts of our character built on Satan's deceptions will stand in our way. We are instructed to be faithful to our Covenant. What stands in our way as we try to be faithful? The parts of us which are built upon deception. Jesus instructs us to obey everything He commanded us. Yet, we struggle with this overall, and find some of these things beyond our reach. Why? Because there are parts of us which oppose obedience. Where did these elements of ourselves come from? Are we beginning to see a pattern here? This kind of personal transformation is a necessary step in many aspects of love, faithfulness, and obedience. We ultimately have only two choices: compromising our faithfulness or accomplishing the transformation that God assigns to us.

Why have I gone to such lengths to stress the importance of character and guidance system transformation? Because much current Christian teaching infers or teaches that God is the one who transforms us. This is in part true, as we have seen. But many people sit for decades in church pews awaiting the transformation that would lead to better lives. And waiting … Why? Because they are waiting for God to do something that He has assigned to us in His Covenant plan. God certainly can transform anything about us at any point. He has the power and the right to do so. He is God. But He rarely engages in such special acts of transformation, especially if we believe this is necessary only because we have neglected our Covenant responsibilities.

A NEW LIFE, NEW CONNECTION TO GOD, AND NEW FAMILY

"*… not abandoning our own meeting together,*
as is the habit of some, but encouraging one another"
(Hebrews 10:25, NASB).

"*… having a form of godliness, but denying its power. Have nothing to do with such people*" (2 Timothy 3:5).

ENTERING THE CHRISTIAN COMMUNITY

When a person becomes a Christian he or she typically has a relationship with at least one Christian (often the person who led them to enter this relationship). We typically begin going to church and thus enter the visible world of Christianity. The part of this world we encounter at any place and time may beautifully reflect the realities of a relationship with God. Or … it can be something else. I vividly remember going to a church service with a roomful of scowling people. It was really amazing; the room was filled with this attitude. There was perfunctory singing of hymns that were absolutely glorious as one read the words. The musical performance was beautiful, as was the room in which we sat. Then the pastor stepped to the pulpit and delivered a message that drew virtually nothing from the Word of God. To the extent he referenced God's Word, it was to disdain it. This is all to say, when the word "Christian" is used to describe something, it does not always mean God is accurately represented. In fact, He may be grievously *mis*represented. Jesus warned us that this would be the case. Therefore, the first lesson we must learn is the importance of associating with people and groups who are sincerely trying to build relationships with God and are basing those efforts on His revelation to us.

"For they received the message with great eagerness and examined the Scriptures every day to see if what Paul said was true" (Acts 17:11).

As I have moved through the Christian community for more than forty years, several things have deeply impressed me. First, we must always remember that our relationship is first and foremost *with God.* Second, we must always remember that we can only know the reality of anything—ourselves, God, life, relationships—from God's truth revealed to us. It is absolutely amazing how much deception fills our world. Unfortunately, quite a bit has found its way into all of our lives and into our churches. Therefore, the word or example of a person or group can only be properly evaluated in light of the one true standard for truth! We must be open to learn from mature brothers and sisters in Christ. But we must also be on guard—always. No human (including this author, to be sure) gets everything right. We are called to love imperfect people, including spiritual leaders and teachers. But we are to follow God only. He is our Head, our Lord, our King, and our God. We worship and serve Him only. Spiritual leaders exist to help us relate properly with God. If they do not do this, we are not to regard them as leaders or accept their leadership. Farther down we will see why it is vital to embrace only God's truth—but first we must consider what this truth is and how to recognize it.

> But none of these things follows us into eternity. *Nor do these things determine our quality of life now.*

OUR NEW LIFE IN GOD AND CONNECTION WITH GOD

Since God is a spiritual being we cannot see or touch, and the realities of a relationship with Him are beyond testing in our physical universe, how are we to understand this relationship? Let's start with some basics.

WHAT IS REALITY?

The answer to this question seems obvious at first glance, but look again. Often our minds go to what *we think* about the way things are. But are anyone's beliefs a reliable guide to understand reality? Reality includes our physical universe. The chair you sit in as you read this book is real. Then there are forces in play in our material universe, the ones we employ as a child on a swing, or the ones studied in laboratories by scientists. There is a spiritual aspect of reality as well. This includes a realm that is distinct from our physical realm. We enter this other realm at the point of physical death, so we will all have first-hand experience with it at some point. This realm contains beings, including God and angels—those loyal to God and those who are not. Another aspect of spiritual reality is the impact of things from that realm on our physical realm. Its beings have regularly interacted with humanity throughout history. God's moral system of cause-and-effect is woven into the fabric of our universe, and it impacts all of our lives.

"Do not be deceived: God cannot be mocked. A man reaps what he sows" (Galatians 6:7).

Our decisions whether (or not) to lie, steal, or do drugs sets in motion one group of consequences or another. The certainty of these consequences is as real as the sun in the sky above us. So which realm is more substantial? The physical world we can see at this moment, or the spiritual world we cannot see (at least for now)? Oddly, it is the spiritual realm. This place and its beings are eternal. Our lives here and every physical thing we see will have an endpoint (2 Peter 3:10; Revelation 21:1). Spiritual realities will prove to be far more important in the end. But these realities are also more important right now.

"So do not worry, saying, 'What shall we eat?' or 'What shall we drink?' or 'What shall we wear?' For the pagans run after all these

things, and your heavenly father knows you need them. But seek first His Kingdom and His righteousness, and all these things will be given to you as well" (Matthew 6:31-33).

The way we interact with these spiritual realities has more impact on our quality of life than any material thing. We need food, water, shelter, clothing, and other things to survive. Other material things add to our life in different ways. But none of these things follows us into eternity. *Nor do these things determine our quality of life now.* Think of people you know who have everything they want, like children of the rich and famous. Are these the happiest people you know? Or the head of a street gang or a cartel? No material pleasure is withheld from them. Yet …

What material object has made your life deeply meaningful? Is acquiring material things our true purpose? Or is how we interact with others—in relation to these spiritual realities—more important? Is it the spiritual things—love, Marriage, family, integrity, honesty—that lead to the deepest satisfaction? In reality, the spiritual and physical realms cannot be separated. Spiritual realities impact literally everything we experience in our world, including this temporary physical reality that was spoken into existence by an eternal God.

> That there is death in our world, we owe to him. That we are fractured and fragmented from each other, and within *ourselves*, we also owe to him.

THE RELATIONSHIP BETWEEN TRUTH AND REALITY

What is the relationship between truth and reality? Actual truth is a correct description of reality, both physical and spiritual. It is an accurate description of the cause-and-effect spiritual nature of our world and of the identity and nature of the beings who inhabit the spiritual realm. It is also a correct description of the world we can see. Where do we find *actual truth*? From the embraced ideas of one human or another in a world awash in deception? Or can this kind of truth only be revealed to us by the God who created both realms and all the creatures therein?

"Love does not delight in evil, but rejoices with the truth" (1 Corinthians 13:6).

"Now that you have purified yourselves by obeying the truth, so that you have sincere love for each other, love one another deeply from the heart" (1 Peter 1:22).

THE RELATIONSHIP BETWEEN TRUTH AND LOVE

What, then, is the relationship between truth and love? Love and truth both originate in God and are conveyed to us by Him. He is the example and the teacher for both. We can have a relationship without truth. We can have feelings for each other, an intense connection, and share benefits between us. But without truth and honesty a relationship is just manipulation. The relationship is not *real*. It is not love. Love is the ultimate expression of truth: wholehearted commitment and wholehearted desire for the best for another backed by the determination to display love in action.

THE RELATIONSHIP BETWEEN REALITY AND LOVE

God's highest stated priority for us is that we love—Him and other people. Why? Is this some sappy bumper sticker slogan—nice words but completely out of sync with real life? Consider the bigger picture. God created Adam and Eve in a state of perfect love with Himself and each other. Now He invites us to enter a newly restored relationship, one characterized by ... what? By wholehearted love for Him and for other people. The love God calls for reflects the foundational reality of Covenant, a bond of shared identity and nature.

What is the source of the opposite of love? If God totally rules us, there is only love. In eternity with God our reality will consist only of love. We will fully know truth. Let's call the opposite of love *not-love.* This not-love was introduced by a being who seeks to elevate himself to the throne of the universe. Not-love is the essence of his rebellion. This being has no love for God or His creation. He comes to kill, steal, and destroy. And to dominate. His tool is *not-truth*—deception. His goal, should his plan succeed, is to revise reality so that the moral cause-and-effect universe is turned upside down. Good is evil; evil is good. We see the opening act of this revolution all around us. Its end will find expression in the worldwide rule of a person empowered directly by Satan, one termed the *Anti*christ. His reign will be brief and end painfully, as his master's rebellion is put down.

The master of this rebellion has been tutoring us about life, as he has been doing with every human society throughout history. The challenged, frustrating, and painful parts of our lives we owe to him. That there is death in our world, we owe to him. That we are fractured and fragmented from each other, and within *ourselves*, we also owe to him. We owe to him the reality that we are often not loved, and do not know how to love perfectly. Prior to entering Covenant with God, we shared in his not-love nature. Before and after entering the New Covenant, his guidance is still firmly lodged in many parts of our being.

Our desire to seek a relationship with God ultimately comes down to recognizing that Satan's plan has damaged us deeply. But this reality is often obscured from our view. Our lives and our world are not merely painful, they are also familiar. They may be challenged, but we have made peace with the realities of our challenged existence. We often resist exchanging a difficult present for an unknown and untried future—thus, we resist the changed life that we may, at some level, also desire. Why? Because the world we have become accustomed to, distorted by the enemy of God—loveless, deceptive, surreal—is the only world we have ever

Even Satan quoted Scripture to tempt Jesus. He accurately quoted the verses, but his intent was to mislead.

known. The absence of these things is difficult to conceive. Yet God tells us His truth will set us free. From what? From the delusional system of His enemy. From the deceptions we still cling to because we agreed that these things are "true." Satan has done a masterful job convincing all of us that not-love is the path to our greatest benefit, that *untruth* is a useful tool, and that reality necessarily includes these things. After all, that's just the way things are in his kingdom.

If we are to enter the Kingdom of God, one condition is that we repent. This does not mean just to be sorry for serious mistakes we have made. It literally means that we are to turn around. That is, *turn from the way we are going*—the path we are following—and move in the other direction. Let this picture sink in. We are to now follow guidance that takes us directly away from everything we were moving toward. This is not just away from things we view as bad. We are also to turn away from our goals, aspirations, and values—if these are founded on Satan's deception. So if we can have no reasonable confidence in virtually anything we have come to believe is true, where can we find actual truth? What new guidance replaces these old ways? What is the new path we are to walk under the guidance of God?

"Sanctify them by the truth; your word is truth" (John 17:17).

THE SEARCH FOR ACTUAL TRUTH

In Deuteronomy 17:6 God lays out the criterion for establishing an important truth. A person cannot be put to death on the testimony of one witness only. Two or three witnesses are required to establish such an important truth. This standard was generalized thereafter to establish important matters. Jesus was initially revealed as the Messiah at His baptism by John the Baptist (John 1:29-34; Matthew 3:13-17). Who was John? He was sent before Jesus as a witness to the fact that Jesus is the Son of God. The second witness came as Jesus came up from the water of His baptism. The Spirit of God descended on Him "like a dove, alighting on Him." The third witness was God Himself:

"And a voice from heaven said, 'This is my Son, whom I love; with Him I am well pleased.'"

Some assert the Bible is the standard for truth against which everything is to be matched. This is true, but it's also an incomplete statement. Pastor Allen Jackson of World Outreach Church, Murfreesboro, Tennessee, made an important observation in a sermon ("Experience God's Deliverance," November 1, 2020); the witness of God's truth is threefold: the written Word of God (the Bible), the life of Christ, and the Holy Spirit within us.

Why is this important? The Christians in Berea were commended by Paul for cross-checking everything the apostle said with the Scriptures. They did this to ensure Paul's words were true (Acts 17:11). But we must remember that simply citing words from Scripture does not ensure that we are properly directed. The words may be misinterpreted or misused. A passage may only represent one aspect of the full counsel of God. A single statement may be taken to an unwarranted extreme. Even Satan quoted Scripture to tempt Jesus. He accurately quoted the verses, but his intent was to mislead. Jesus rebutted him with Scriptural truth spoken accurately. The Pharisees could recite the entire Old Testament and were anxious to direct others in its application. But they misdirected people overall. The hearts of many Pharisees were set on assassinating the God they pretended to serve. To ensure that our understanding of God's direction for our life is heard correctly, we are to corroborate *everything* using these three sources.

To follow God's guidance for our lives we must do more than hear truth and make proper in-the-moment decisions. God has a much more extensive plan for us, one designed to produce a life that is radically transformed and remarkably better. To truly obey, to follow God's path faithfully, we must understand and follow the other part of God's plan. For our life to change in significant ways, the way we direct our life must change.

In the genius of Covenant, we are to bring our guidance system and character into harmony with who we became at the deepest levels of our being as we entered Covenant. We became joined to God by a bond of identity and nature (by His indwelling Spirit, and by now being in Christ). Yet we must recognize, embrace, and live out these realities. One can be married but choose to continue to live much of one's old single life. Or one can choose to be all-in to his or her Marriage. Results vary accordingly. So it is in our relationship with God. We can continue to pursue our old life, or we can live out our together-life with God. Let's say we want to do this: obey and be transformed in our outer life as we have been in the depths of our being. What is this truth we are now to base everything in life upon? How will we know God's truth when we see it?

THE THREEFOLD WITNESS TO DETERMINE TRUTH

John's Gospel begins with curious imagery. "In the beginning was the Word, and the Word was with God, and the Word was God (1:1). … The Word became flesh and made His dwelling among us. We have seen His glory, the glory of the one and only Son who came from the Father, full of grace and truth" (1:14). John calls Jesus the Logos, the Living Word. Jesus' very life is the definition of truth! Some describe this as a sinless life, one which we typically interpret to mean He did nothing wrong. But a much more important reality is that He did the will of His Father at every point. His life perfectly illustrated every truth He taught. He leads the way in the obedience He requires from us.

Therefore, the first point of reference to understand the truth of God is the life of Christ.

"All Scripture is God-breathed and is useful for teaching, rebuking, correcting, and training in righteousness" (2 Timothy 3:16).

THE SCRIPTURES ARE THE REFERENCE POINT FOR ABSOLUTE TRUTH

The second reference point is the written Scriptures, both Old and New Testaments. Time and space will not allow us to fully explore the reasons for viewing this source as entirely credible—in fact, one more credible than any other source, human or nonhuman. Or to rebut the assertions that it is not. There are many references we can consult on this point. *Evidence That Demands a Verdict*,[16] a wonderful little book by Josh McDowell, is an excellent one.

Briefly, in the Scriptures we have an unbroken written record beginning at least 3,500 years ago—the time of Moses—of the interaction of God with humanity. Yet this record also includes an account of the previous 2,500 years as well—back to Adam and Eve. It has been alleged that the Hebrew account was actually written much later, that it was all oral tradition until after the Babylonian captivity because the Israelites did not have writing until that point. However, God wrote the Ten Commandments for Moses to give to the people. Prior to Moses, the Israelites spent four hundred years in Egypt, a civilization with a written language. Based on the belief of earlier illiteracy, and translations of accounts from other cultures that are variations on biblical stories, it has been asserted that the Israelites merely borrowed and co-opted earlier Babylonian myths of a catastrophic flood and other important events. But it has also been discovered that cultures had written languages in the area where biblical figures such as Abraham lived, in Mesopotamia, not only in 2000 BC (while Abraham was alive), but for the previous fifteen hundred years.

Some Hebrew writings were believed from the beginning to represent direct revelation from God. These were termed "Scripture," and were viewed as the definition of truth. These writings were preserved with remarkable fidelity, unlike any other literature in the ancient world. McDowell's book details the complicated system of cross-checks used by Hebrew scribes to ensure that the lengthy texts were transcribed with 100 percent accuracy—letter for letter—through the centuries.

Throughout the Scriptures we find historical references: people, cities, battles, civilizations, dates. These also serve as a cross-check on textual accuracy. If the text had been corrupted, this history would have been altered. While many assertions have been made that "Scripture does not correspond to history," subsequent archaeological findings have consistently confirmed the Scriptural accounts. To be sure, everything mentioned in Scripture does not have artifact confirmation. But where this is available, and dates are confirmed (not the product of conjecture), the Scriptural narrative is proven correct. This speaks to the integrity of the text, though not necessarily its divine authorship.

As I confronted the issue of bowing my knee to a truth beyond the ones in my own head and heart (this took place in my first year of medical school), I first approached the Scriptures with skepticism. My university was liberal, and my education loaded me with reasons to not believe that the Bible was a unique communication from God. Instead, I thought these writings represented the religious yearnings of people. Of course, this means I had never actually read the Bible, but this was my frame of reference as I started to read to learn about God and a relationship with Him.

One thing convinced me of God's authorship beyond any doubt: fulfilled prophesy. There are hundreds of specific predictions in Scripture. Most can be clearly documented to have been written well before the event in question. And when the history is matched with the prophesy, they correspond exactly. The real God actually does know the future, which He holds in His hands. People have been predicting things throughout history, sometimes accurately. But there is no other writing from the ancient or modern world with anything close to 100 percent accuracy in foretelling the future. In addition, there are more than three hundred prophesies fulfilled by Jesus in His first coming. These were precisely fulfilled, including the year and location of His birth. To me, these fulfilled prophesies proved to be an unquestionable stamp of Divine authorship. This allowed me to trust in these writings and in the God who revealed them to us. If these Scriptures were truly authored by God, what should I do if my views differed from what was written in them? Logic demands that my views are incorrect if they differ from God's revelation. He is right. It is my responsibility to adjust my beliefs.

We only have two options as we engage with the revelation of God. We either sit in judgment of these words—pulling out the editor's pen or eraser to make them suit our preferences and biases—or we are judged by them. God's Word invites us to make adjustments. God intends the Word of God to be the second reference point for truth in our lives.

"The Holy Spirit, whom the Father will send in My name, will teach you all things and remind you of everything I have said to you" (John 14:26).

THE SPIRIT OF GOD, WHO "WILL TEACH YOU ALL THINGS"

The third reference point exists within us if we are in Covenant with God. But this is not our own beliefs, ideas, and preferences. It is the Spirit of God who now lives within us. As we engage with God in real-time dialogue, and as we walk hand in hand with Him through life, He will lead and guide us in specific situations. As we read Scripture, He will direct us to certain truths and open our eyes to new understandings. He comforts, corrects, encourages, and strengthens. Beyond a conscience, we now have the Spirit of God within resisting sin in our lives. This is why one in Covenant with God can certainly be deceived. A person can make a mistake or even commit a grievous wrong. But this will lead, under God's plan, to repentance, correction, and a new conviction—not a lifestyle of ongoing rebellion.

THE LIFE OF JESUS

A few years back many Christians wore a bracelet with the letters *WWJD*. "What would Jesus do?" This is an excellent question. In order to answer this, though, we need to carefully study everything He did and said as recorded in Scripture. But truly understanding what He did and said is no easier for us than it was for His disciples. Only as we mature and draw into a closer relationship with God will we begin to understand some of these things. It is vital for our growth and transformation that we spend our lives searching out the life of Christ.

After all, *this is now our life*. It is to become our expression of life. As we watch the love and wisdom of Jesus handling everything from a woman who was thrown at His feet to be stoned by the crowd to the Pharisees repeatedly trying to entrap Him, we see the perfection of God. We need to devote serious time toward understanding His heart and mind so we can better appreciate who He really is.

I love how Pastor Jackson described the way these three crucial ingredients work together. If we are seeking to find our way from one point to another, we can get written directions. Such directions offer a one-dimensional view. Or we can get a map. Now we have a two-dimensional view. We see not only the path, we see a much more clear picture of the journey. However, the most clear view of what is required comes from a three-dimensional view. The full truth of our journey includes hills and valleys and many other details which can only be seen in a three-dimensional rendering. What was it like for Jesus to live out some of these truths? What does God want me to be doing today on my journey? God's Spirit knows, and He is delighted to guide me if I consult Him. What does integrity really mean in this situation? God knows, and He wants us to know.

These three sources always agree. On occasion we may hear an interpretation of something in Scripture that conflicts with the life of Jesus. Worship of Mary, his mother, was rebutted by Jesus (Luke 11:27, 28), yet it is promoted by some. The assertion that enough "faith" or "giving" will always lead to material prosperity is another example. This is rebutted by the life and words of Christ. Or someone may claim, "God told me to … " In essence, they are claiming a direct communication from God's Spirit. Yet what this person says conflicts with the clear teaching of God's Word. If a truth is from God, all three will agree: the life of Christ, the Word of God, and the Spirit of God. Upon *this* truth we can stake our lives.

NOW, LET'S GO TO CHURCH …

Now we know *who we are in Christ*. We know how we are connected to God. We are also connected to Him *by His revelation of truth*, for this is the only way we know anything about Him or anything else with certainly. Now we are prepared to enter the visible Christian community.

BE BAPTIZED (ACTS 2:38)

We discussed the visible ceremony that is to accompany our entry into the New Covenant. We are to be baptized. Throughout the New Testament this was done as soon as possible following the initiation of this Covenant. Baptism is a public proclamation of our Covenant. It symbolizes many aspects of Covenant, and is one of our most profound acts of worship. It is to be our first major act of obedience, one to "fulfill all righteousness," as Jesus said (Matthew 3:15).

COMMUNION (LUKE 22:19)

This ceremony is observed in various ways and at various intervals in most churches. It is generally viewed as a symbolic ritual. People will usually say something about the blood of Christ shed for us, almost always in terms of His sacrifice for our sins. I vividly recall the flood of new meaning this act assumed when I learned about Covenant. This repetitive celebration of our entry into Covenant plays the same role as intercourse in Marriage (or, at least one of the roles). It is to *remember and celebrate* our Covenant. We physically take something into our bodies that symbolizes the blood of Christ and body of Christ (John 6:53-56). As I consider all this means, and all it has meant to me each time I participate in this ritual, I feel overwhelming emotion and gratitude for what God has done.

THE PICTURE OF A LIFE DEVOTED TO GOD

I like a picture the Navigator ministry used to depict a balanced life in Christ. Envision a cross with yourself in the middle. Pointing upward, above you, is personal communication with God. Looking downward we see the foundation of the Word of God. Looking to our right are our brothers and sisters in Christ and everything entailed in our relationships with them. Looking to our left we see those not in Covenant with God, and we view our relationships with them.

PRAYER

The part that goes upward depicts our reaching toward God and interacting with Him. God is not a distant figure whose attention we must gain. He is in as intimate a relationship with us as a husband or wife. A "oneness" exists between us and God that mirrors the relationship among the Trinity. We do life together with a perfect and all-powerful Partner. Thus our prayers are to be a wide-ranging discussion that will clarify many things for us as well as offer us a chance to ask for what we want. More importantly, such time in God's presence offers us an opportunity to refine what we want. We begin to merge what *we* want with what *He* wants. Our love and care for others includes the privilege of bringing their needs before God. As we learn to bring our deeper problems before God, to wrestle with these issues in His presence, He has opportunities to reach more deeply into our lives. As we open ourselves before Him more and more, His healing can reach more deeply into our heart and mind. His power and love are real. As we see these poured out in our life in various ways, we come to *know* our Covenant Partner.

God in turn reaches into our minds and hearts through His Spirit. If we are listening for Him we will soon recognize His voice within. It is a bit hard to explain this, but within my mind there is a "location" from which He communicates. This is in the form of ideas that enter my mind. Extremely rarely, this seems to be almost an audible voice. Jesus says, "His sheep … know his voice" (John 10:4). Then other ideas can pop into our minds—some of our own making, some not. This is part of the spiritual reality we inhabit. I can usually sense when I am hearing from the other side. The things we hear within our mind must also be cross-checked with God's truth.

This leads us to the part of the upright that points downward.

THE WORD

This is our foundation: the Word of God and truth of God. In order for this to actually become our foundation we must devote our lives to learning it just like a musician devotes his or her life to mastering an instrument and a form of music, or just like a physician continues learning about the body and how to rectify its problems. To grow in our relationship with God it is vital that we devote ourselves to reading, studying, and applying the Word of God in our lives.

We do well to pursue a systematic study of God's Word. This can take many forms, and it can be a combination of personal and group study. Basically, we want to always be doing two things with God's truth. First, we need to become broadly educated in it. We do this by reading through all of Scripture. Then we engage in focused study of key books. This study can also take many forms. The first goal is a strong overall understanding of the major truths revealed by God. Then we want to deepen understanding of every truth that impacts our life. This involves more intensive study of individual chapters, memorization of key passages, and meditation on important truths. Through the years a consistent habit of study can produce a remarkably broad and deep understanding of God's revelation. But the most important part of this effort is translating these truths into flesh and blood in our own lives.

> We are to become an integral part of the body and play our assigned roles in it. We are to discover our gifts and use them.

The second thing we should do on an ongoing basis is study Scripture related to our life issues. If we are grappling with something we need to become adept at finding all that God has revealed related to this topic. Then we need to follow the five-step pattern we will outline to plant God's truth in these areas deeply into our mind, heart, will, and life. Growth and transformation are aided if we have an accountability partner. It is exceedingly helpful to have someone pray for us and check on our progress, and to return this favor for them. Having a more mature Christian in this role adds the possibility of mentoring. This can be even more beneficial.

FELLOWSHIP: BECOME INVOLVED IN A LOCAL CHURCH BODY

Next is the crosspiece. To our right is the body of Christ. Some question the need to be part of a local church body; they believe their "relationship with God" is all that is needed. Three realities speak against this position. First, this is no longer *my life* to live as I choose—it is *our life*. Our communal life includes God, and this also includes those in the body of Christ. These are to be actual relationships, not metaphorical ones. Second, the ultimate point of Covenant is love in action. In order to develop this life we must be in real relationships. Third we must learn to love, and this involves both growth and transformation. We may believe we have a heart of perfect love when we are alone, but as we work together in a group it doesn't take long to realize we still have much to learn about love. It is only by trying to learn these lessons that we encounter our need for transformation.

> We can be led to new heights or betrayed. Our needs can be served or someone may steal from us. Why did God throw us in the midst of this? To teach us how to love across the spectrum of life.

Fellowship. This term is often associated with relationships in a church. Most do not realize that this term is associated directly with Covenant. This term describes the overall *together-life* in Covenant. We are in a Covenant relationship with every member of the Body of Christ, and every requirement of Covenant is in full force. However, almost no one today is aware of this fact. Nor could most people describe what this means. People in Covenant have a remarkably large claim on each other's lives. A blank check, in fact. The answer of Covenant is: "Whatever it takes, whatever I have, am, or can become." There is literally no limit to our obligation to one another. Have you seen this in action lately in a local church? My prayer is that God uses those who read this book to open the body of Christ to God's heart and lead them to His Covenant plan.

"As I have loved you, so you must love one another" (John 13:4).

Therefore, joining with a local group of believers is about far more than teaching, music, and socializing. We are to become an integral part of the body and play our assigned roles in it. We are to discover our gifts and use them. We are to grow and mature and lead others toward maturity. We are to learn many things. Most importantly, we are to learn to love our brothers and sisters as Christ loves us.

Therefore, we are to become friends in the deepest sense: as brothers and sisters *in Covenant*. We are to become involved in each other's lives and serve one another (Matthew 23:11). We are to encourage one another, strengthen one another, mentor one another, teach one another, and be there for one another in every way. We should take a much greater interest in the lives of our brothers and sisters and be ready to stand beside them in whatever way is needed. God's heart is that we truly learn to love each other. This is a command He repeats frequently.

Churches have historically been places of teaching and corporate worship. Both play a vital role in our spiritual lives. What does it mean to "worship" God? If a person walks into most churches, "worship" seems to be equated with listening to and/or singing spiritual songs. If instead we realize that this is the time to thank God for everything He has done in our lives through the previous week, we can lift our hearts to Him in soaring gratitude. We can contemplate who He is and glorify Him for one perfection or another that we have encountered the previous week.

This, of course, presumes He is doing things in our lives we are aware of and that we are learning things about Him to celebrate. Many view church as their only point of real contact with God. They view a church service as the only place to hear about the things of God or commune with God. For the rest of their lives, it is business as usual. Or people offer to God what they want to offer from their life during the week. Might our scanty investment in this relationship equate with a meager return? If not much goes on during the week between us and God, what is there to celebrate? Well, maybe the music will be good …

> God's heart is that we learn to love those made in His image—whether in Christ or not.

Many greatly desire to find a church filled with people who treat them with perfect love. This is what God intends, but some assembly is required. This is what God's training process is designed to produce. But are the people who seek this willing to fully engage in God's school of love so *they* can be a source of this kind of love toward others?

Instead, must of us walk into groups only partly refined by this process—if at all. The up-close involvement of Covenant with even one imperfect person, much less a roomful, will raise an entirely new set of issues in our lives. Our "together-life" with imperfect people can be funny, inspiring, touching, or infuriating. We can be strengthened or criticized inappropriately. We can be led to new heights or betrayed. Our needs can be served or someone may steal from us. Why did God throw us in the midst of this? To teach us how to love across the spectrum of life. But not just for our benefit. We are to go to God's school of love to learn how to build up the Kingdom of God and lead others toward it. And to reflect Him in every way in the process. This is what it means to be faithful to our Covenant.

While many consider the church hour to be their (only) time with God, what does Covenant say? What role does our Covenant partner play in our lives? What role are we to play in His life? Let's do the math. Do we offer our Covenant partner 1/168th of our life (0.6 percent)? Or one hundred percent? According to God's plan, what are we to do with the rest of our week?

OUTREACH

To our left are those in the world. We are to love them also and be sustained in this by the love we receive from God. We are to love in action, to get involved. We are to reach out in word and deed, to display the love of God before a lost and dying world.

"Always be prepared to give an answer to everyone who asks you to give the reason for the hope that you have. But do so with gentleness and respect" (1 Peter 3:15).

This love can take many forms, from feeding hungry people to leading an evangelistic program. Many believe that simply serving is witness enough of God's love. Many think telling other people about God or sharing His gospel is a job for trained professionals. If this were the case Christianity would have died in its cradle. Early Christians, with rare exceptions, did not have theological training. In fact, the group with the most theological training were the ones who put Jesus to death. Each person in the Body of Christ understands enough to put their trust in Jesus and receive Him as Lord. Each person in the Body of Christ has a personal story of their life in Christ that others can relate to. It takes only a little preparation and practice to walk someone through eight or ten verses that illustrate how to enter Covenant with God.

God's heart is that we learn to love those made in His image—whether in Christ or not. And that we reach out to them as He does, knowing that only a few *will* respond. But a few will respond. I have heard many accounts of people whom a Christian friend thought was a "lost cause." The Christian therefore refused to share this part of his or her life. When someone eventually led this lost cause to Christ, their cry was, "Why didn't someone tell me sooner!" You can't tell by looking at someone whether (or not) they are dying to know about Jesus. If you would offer a drowning person a rope to pull them to safety, would you offer a word that can save them from spending eternity with Satan and his angels? And if they refuse this way of escape, and even answer harshly, you can still feed them.

ENGAGING WITH GOD

Many books have been written on spiritual growth and the path to Christian maturity. God's love of diversity is shown by the variety of ways people draw close to Him. We have different spiritual gifts and different natural gifting. We play different roles in the body of Christ (Romans 12:4-8). Therefore, God has different paths of preparation for us. There is no one-size-fits-all plan for everyone. There is, however, an overall plan with definite principles and realities within our Covenant relationship. Within this framework we will find our individual path. Let's look at some key aspects of relationship-building with God.

> It is very important to learn to *feed ourselves* from Scripture. That is, to pick up the book and learn how to draw deeply from it.

We do well to approach relationship-building with God as we would with someone we intend to marry. Or, in this case, *have* married. Now we want to build love for a lifetime. If we are truly interested in someone, we want to know all about him or her. We want to spend time with this person—every spare minute, in fact. We want to build something together and see where our together-life leads. The goal of our relationship with God is an actual relationship, versus learning facts about someone—like George Washington—whom we never actually get to know. Covenant is about love and relationship, not simply knowledge.

I was amazed while I was building a love relationship with Holley how much energy I had for relationship-building. I was a surgeon with a busy practice and four preteen children. For the first several months we met to walk early in the morning, met for lunch, and talked many nights until late in the night—all while we were working full schedules and caring for children. I often got less than four hours sleep, but I never felt fatigued during this time. In fact, I had more energy than I have ever experienced. All of us are busy. But to build a relationship this important I found all the time I needed. In fact, I also had to fit Holley in around the other love in my life—God—and the time I was spending with Him. The point? We all need to fall in love with God. If we seek this, I assure you God will provide all the time and energy you need, even in the busiest life. So how do we do this? Let's explore some ways.

LEARNING ABOUT HIM

The best way to learn about God is to spend as much time as you can reading His love letter to us: the Scriptures. First, as we discussed above, we must realize what we hold in our hands: God's revelation of absolute truth. We read to know and understand, not to select or critique. There are several levels at which we read, and thus several ways to study Scripture. It is important to sample many of these and find the approach that impacts us most powerfully.

First we simply read through the text. It is extremely important to read the entire letter, beginning to end, as early as possible in our journey. From this we get an overview and context. We get a better overall sense of who God is. Some "prefer" the God they read about in the New Testament (as if we get to vote on what God is supposed to be; we do not). Once we see the overall picture of God, the details begin to make more sense. These details make even more sense when we understand the people—and the spiritual forces behind these people—whom God had to deal with.

It is very important to learn to *feed ourselves* from Scripture. That is, to pick up the book and learn how to draw deeply from it. This involves word studies, topic studies, and expositional studies. A word study is simply reading a chapter and looking up any word with an unclear definition, in English and in the original language. There are many aids to draw from for this. A topical study takes this same chapter and lists the topics covered, then examines what is said about each topic. An expositional study combines these two, taking apart each sentence, and it also examines the historical and cultural context behind each sentence. From this more in-depth study we get as clear a view as possible of what was intended as these words were initially spoken or written. For instance, you can now offer an in-depth definition of the word Covenant. And you can identify Scriptures that reference this relationship even if the word Covenant is not used, because you understand this relationship and what it involves.

From reading through and studying the Word we learn much about God. And we also learn what He expects of us. In a human love relationship we want to know what we can do to please our beloved. The more we love them in action, and the more he or she responds to our love, the more our heart grows toward them. In the Scriptures there are many injunctions—things God says to do or not do. When we find one that is an issue in our life, it is important to memorize the Scripture so we know exactly what God requires. We also do not want to over-limit ourselves by misquoting God, as Eve did. Obedience is correctly understanding and following.

Once we recognize this spiritual cause-and-effect operating in our daily lives, it cuts through all the confusion we see around us.

The next step in personal application is *meditating on God's Word.* (I will save this full discussion for a later section.) For the moment, know that this will prove to be one of the most powerful tools we have for life transformation. But we need to understand a few more things before we will fully understand its power.

How do we spend time with people to build a relationship? We go on dates. We schedule time to be together. We talk on the phone and send messages to each other. So it is with God. We benefit greatly from putting specific times on our schedule to read and study His Word. As we read for information we learn about Him, but as we read and compare with our own life, we begin to *engage with Him.* God's Spirit will start to show us things we did not see the last time we read the same material, things that pertain to us (Ephesians 1:17). God is bringing these things to our attention to urge us to understanding more deeply, or because we need to adjust something. How much time do we schedule with God per day or week? How much time would you devote to someone you were falling in love with? That is a good starting point. In reality, start where you can. Once you see the benefit of this time, your desire to spend time in this way will grow. But you will not experience this benefit if you are not really willing to commit significant time and heart to God. If this is the case, perhaps taking a closer look at what we believe is important will help us.

PRAYER

> Over a few days, as I decreased the interval between short prayers, something unexpected began to happen. I began an ongoing conversation with God that has continued for decades.

Most begin to pray with a list of things they want for themselves or others. This is not a bad thing, but it largely misses the point of spending time with God. Prayer is a way to get to know Him better. My wife and I have spent hundreds of hours through the years talking over the issues in our lives, trying to understand things at deeper levels, and trying to find the best approach to many situations. Holley and I do not just recite to each other a list of things we would like to see in our lives then move on. We talk things out. I have had this kind of conversation with God on hundreds of occasions: working over issues, trying to understand what is going on in myself and others, trying to get to the essence of a matter, trying to determine the best solution. This often involves trying to figure out how Scripture applies in a given situation. And it often involves asking for specific guidance when there is no specific guidance in Scripture. This is what it means to do life-together with God.

It is good to spend regular times in prayer. It is good to record prayer requests and insights gained so we can see what happens going forward. God does love us, and in the same way you delight in doing something special for your beloved, He delights in doing special things for you.

"Therefore, holy brothers and sisters, who share in the heavenly calling, fix your thoughts on Jesus" (Hebrews 3:1)

When we pray we are aware of the spiritual realm, for we are speaking to Someone who is there. But how often during the rest of our day are we aware of anything beyond the world we live in? We noted that the spiritual realm is ultimately more important than this one, and its principles and realities impact everything in our realm. Once we recognize this spiritual cause-and-effect operating in our daily lives, it cuts through all the confusion we see around us. The physical realm frequently does not make sense if we just look around. But if we factor in what is going on behind the scenes in the spiritual realm, suddenly everything begins to make sense. We are on a battleground in the "fog of war." The problem, again, is that we often lose sight of a realm we cannot see.

But we can develop our power of attention in a way that keeps the spiritual realm always in mind. In *Practicing the Presence of God*,[17] written by Brother Lawrence more than three hundred years ago, an exercise was suggested that I tried while in medical school. At this time I was in class many hours each day. Lawrence suggested turning our hearts to God in a short prayer at increasingly short intervals: every three hours, then every two hours, then hourly, then every thirty minutes, then every ten minutes, and finally briefly every minute. Since there was a clock in front of me on the wall, this was easy to do. Over a few days, as I decreased the interval between short prayers, something unexpected began to happen. I began an ongoing conversation with God that has continued for decades. Rather than having to turn my attention to Him, I was no longer *unaware* of Him. It was like knowing someone is nearby, in another room. You cannot see them, but they are still within earshot and always available to talk. After a couple of weeks of shifting my focus back to God on a regular basis while in and out of the classroom, this conversation became a permanent part of my life. Going forward I began to "see" both the natural realm and the spiritual ream simultaneously. The realities of each realm are palpable.

One key aspect of an intimate relationship is paying attention to each other frequently. Do you think this new pattern was a game-changer for my relationship with God?

DOING SPECIAL THINGS FOR EACH OTHER

What does God like? That we honor Him, sing praise to Him, do good things for His children, tell others about Him, and many other things. See the Scriptures for details. Do you know the joy of doing something really special for your beloved? Try doing special things for God to say "I love you." Then watch what happens next. You literally cannot out-give God, but it is fun to try! Or we can look at all the things we are told to do in Scripture as a burden and sacrifice we do only under duress because "God says so." Which approach will build a heart of love for God?

There is another place to find the things God likes: the principles of Covenant. If we simply look through all the elements of Covenant we are sure to find things we can do to show our love. Consider the list of Marriage vows. If we choose one per week and try to do and become what is vowed, how might this impact our relationship with God?

Many things that are done as mechanical rituals in many churches are actually full of meaning, including gathering together. We worship together, pray together, study, sing, and commune. We remember our Covenant by taking Communion (also often called the Lord's Supper). We witness a baptism or encourage a missionary. We offer part of the resources God has entrusted to us back to Him. Once we understand Covenant we see that everything we do as Christians is because of the nature and realities of this relationship. We do things to celebrate and worship God and our new together-life with Him. Or to renew our minds, to change our lives in accordance with the new life within us and the God to whom we are joined. Or to acknowledge our Covenant with each other in the Body of Christ and our obligation to love and serve each other. If we begin to see our relationship with God as a journey of discovery, as a wonderland filled with the delights of love, as the greatest opportunity we will ever be offered, then our hearts will be open to building the relationship God desires—and the relationship we desperately need.

CULTIVATING A HEART OF APPRECIATION

The more we understand about good people and good things, the more we appreciate them. The more we understand the challenges people face and the price they pay to be and do good things, the more we love them for simply being who they are. And the more someone has given to our lives in important ways, the more we love them—if we recognize what they have done. Appreciation, or the lack thereof, is a huge variable in our quality of life, and a variable that is totally under our control.

> We are continually bombarded with the deceptions of the world. It is imperative that we immerse ourselves in truth so we are continually aware when we are not hearing truth.

Pastor Ray McCollum at Bethel World Outreach Center in Brentwood, Tennessee used an illustration in the mid-1990s that impacted me deeply. He spoke of a person running. This person crossed one line of chalk on the grass, then another. People were beginning to get out of their seats and shift around. Another line was crossed, then another. People began to yell. Another line, and they yelled louder. Some began jumping around. Then the person shifted a brown leather bag he was carrying from one hand to the other. One more line was crossed, and people were screaming at the top of their lungs. The pastor's question: "What has this person actually done for anyone in the stands by scoring a touchdown?" Then, two more questions: "What has Jesus done for you and me? For which of these should we be more excited?" One way to fuel a heart of love for Jesus is to really consider what He has done for us and why He has done these things.

OUR PRIVATE LIFE: THE FRUITFUL TREE AND ITS ROOT SYSTEM

BUILDING OUR ROOT SYSTEM

Have you ever been around a deeply mature Christian? Some have not. In such people we can feel the presence of God. We see the character of Christ in their face and their actions. We see a life truly worth living. We see God doing things through his or her life that only God can do. The Scriptures refer to these visible outcomes of a godly life as "fruit" (Luke 3:8). Envision a mature Christian as a large tree from which is hanging delicious, ripe fruit. Everyone who sees this life wants this same fruit in his or her life. But there is another part of the tree, an unseen part, that is vital if such fruit is to be produced: the root system. For a tree to grow and be productive it must first develop an extensive root system. It is from this root system that the tree receives the nourishment necessary for growth. But only the smallest part of this root system is seen by others. Most of it is underground, out of sight. In the Christian life this root system consists of all the things people do in private to build their relationship with God.

One can grow to a certain point in his or her Christian life by taking part in the public activities. But this is not the same as developing one's own root system. This time is like the "together time" of a married couple, the intimacy that builds the relationship in special ways. The most intimate activities are the ones most carefully hidden from the view of others. Can you imagine the relationship of a married couple if they only spent time together in public? Anyone who builds a deep relationship with God devotes significant time to this relationship on a daily and weekly basis. The goal is to learn to feed yourself the truths of God. While we can often access good teaching, at times we cannot. Unless we have a solid foundation in Scripture, we cannot determine what is good teaching and what is not.

Mature Christians have a devotional life. This is regular time devoted to God for Scripture reading, study, memorization, meditation, and prayer. Over a couple of years of regular reading and study one can become quite familiar with the major truths of Scripture. Over a decade of regular reading and study one can become deeply versed in a wide array of God's truths. Over several decades one will have spent far more time studying the Word than any seminary education would require. Also, while Scripture should remain our main focus, reading good biographies and other works by gifted teachers is of benefit. We are continually bombarded with the deceptions of the world. It is imperative that we immerse ourselves in truth so we are continually aware when we are not hearing truth. Our discernment must be honed to a razor's edge by a deep understanding of truth if we are to guard our hearts and minds properly.

> An intimate relationship is like a mirror held up in front of us. Unfortunately, when dealing with another human, this mirror is distorted by their issues and compromises.

MENTORING

How do we learn to do these things? By definition, these root-system activities are done away from public view. We can only see this part of a person's life if he or she chooses to reveal it to us. In the body of Christ there exist *mentoring* relationships. A less mature Christian meets on a regular basis with a more mature Christian to learn more about this life. It is only through this kind of friendship that one can reveal this root system to another. The two do these things together for a time. This kind of one-on-one transmission of key life habits has always been the path to deepest maturity in the Body of Christ. These friendships become very close, and deep trust develops. Therefore these types of relationships offer an opportunity to explore deeper life issues, things that may not be "group discussion" material. These very issues, when resolved, will lead to the most important growth and transformation. The Christian life was never intended to be a solo mission. We need God every moment. And we need each other.

The next kind of outreach is to those not in Covenant with God. God has delegated to us the role of reaching out to a lost and dying world in His Name, one person at a time. It's imperative that we learn to lead another person through the Scriptures and show them God's plan to enter Covenant. Mentoring is simply a more experienced person sharing something important with another person. Each of us can relate his or her own journey of understanding, commitment, and life change, hopefully illustrated with Scripture. It is a truth that people do not care what you know until they know you care. We naturally want to share important things with our friends, and we hear these things best from our friends. The easiest way to become comfortable in the role of sharing Christ with others is to walk beside someone who is already doing this in the course of his or her life.

WE ONLY LEARN TO LOVE WHEN WE ARE IN RELATIONSHIP

It is significant that God's plan for our growth, development, and transformation is a relationship. If we are not functioning in an intimate relationship, it is easy to imagine that we are all things good and pure. We have a curious capacity to imagine ourselves to be different from what we are—usually in a better way. We only find out what is actually inside of us in a close relationship. Then we can see our ability to follow through versus our intentions. We see attitudes, priorities, values, habits, and character qualities that interfere with loving another in action. We all make compromises with truth along the way. We have made peace with such compromises. We make them because we are persuaded they serve a greater good. They advanced our best interests in some way (so we thought). But other people, or God, are not OK with these compromises, nor should they be. An intimate relationship is like a mirror held up in front of us. Unfortunately, when dealing with another human, this mirror is distorted by their issues and compromises. This is why we must seek God's vantage point on truth, and on who and what we are, as well as listening with a discerning ear to feedback from other people.

God invites us to enter the most intimate of relationships with Himself. And in this relationship He includes every other Christian. We are to be in a deep relationship with everyone. Not all in the Body of Christ are mature; not all are transformed in deep ways. As we engage in relationships with our brothers and sisters, some will lead the way to deeper maturity. The immaturity of others will present us with challenges. These relationships often provide our agenda for growth and transformation by highlighting our own issues.

FAITHFULNESS TO COVENANT

THE ROLE OF OUR DECISIONS

The intent of Covenant is a radically changed life. Is this happening in your life?

The most fundamental response required by Covenant is *faithfulness.* This is to simply do all that we vowed to do as we entered a Marriage or the New Covenant, or to obey God perfectly as He instructs us to do in Scripture. Faithfulness involves a single decision: to *buy in and embrace* the role God assigns us in Covenant. Then faithfulness involves myriad daily decisions to back up and live out this overall decision

We spoke of the importance of our choices. The most fundamental and powerful of all decisions are the ones we make about what is true and what is false. Everything we build in life flows directly from one or another of these decisions. We follow and live out what we determine to be true. We have talked about many truths of Covenant. Are these now your truths?

We have talked about what Covenant is—its realities and principles. We have talked about the mechanisms God placed within us that allow us to function properly in this relationship—our three powers. We have talked about the way these powers can be misdirected through deception. Our guidance system can be corrupted; our character can be misformed. We spoke of the moral fabric of our universe, how mis-guidance and misbehavior produces all the problems in our lives and our world. We spoke of the spiritual war in which we live. God loves us and wants a restored relationship, then wants this relationship to function as designed to build the most beneficial lives and the best relationships. On the other side are beings posing as our friends and benefactors. Instead, they are intent on destroying both those made in God's image and every blessing God intends for us. But due to the nature of deception we often do not recognize their evil intentions for us, and we follow their guidance.

We have spoken of obedience as more than a checklist of behaviors that appease God or buy His favor. Instead, God invites us to build a transformed life in intimate communion with Him. We are in a relationship with Him when we enter Covenant. But this relationship turns out in many different ways, just like Marriages, and for the same reasons. We said that the New Covenant is a plan, not just a relationship. For the intended results to become real, we must play our part in this plan. Therefore, we must be faithful to our Covenant and our Covenant partner. We have laid the pieces on the table. We have talked about the reality of our transformation in Covenant, and the second transformation that must take place to fully live out this relationship. We have spoken of obedience to Scripture and the reasons this is always best for us. Everyone is equally married, but all Marriages are not equal. So it is with relationships with God. What is the variable? God is the same, and we all enter the same relationship. The variables are *our faithfulness, our decisions, and what we choose to believe is true.*

OUR THREE POWERS IN ACTION

Remember our three powers: to determine what is true; then, if something is true, to determine how much it matters; then, to determine what, if anything, we are going to do about it. If our decisions are this important, perhaps we need to consider more carefully what goes into making our decisions and what happens *after* we make our decisions. Let's look not only at our decision about what to wear today, but about the ideas that form and guide our lives. We are always looking for our best move. And we are always faced with choices. What goes into making our decisions about something we might do or say or choose? We quickly dial though our sources of information. We have a vast reservoir of experience. We "know" that some things work and some do not. We look around and see how others handle similar questions and how things turn out for them. If we are a Christian devoted to following God, we check this decision against our understanding of Scripture. If we understand Covenant, this adds another level of understanding that can guide us.

If our decisions are this important, perhaps we need to consider more carefully what goes into making our decisions.

The bottom line, though, is we do what we do *for reasons.* We line up our reasons and make the choice based on the *most compelling* reason. And why do we deem a reason most compelling? Because of other ideas we have embraced. Should we really be not very different from our culture so we won't get blowback from our friends? Or should we really be all-in to our Covenant? Again, the bottom line is always going to come back to our understanding of our self-interest. And our understanding of self-interest will come from one of two sources.

If we make a wrong choice, get off track with God, and our conscience raises a red flag, what should we do? Rather than just struggling to do the "better" or "more right" thing the next time, should we not take a serious look at our reasons? We have a huge reservoir of ideas that we have embraced as true. We had good reasons for believing these things at the time we made these decisions. But in our troubled and deception-filled world we have inevitably bought into a vast number of ideas that are not of God. Some of these do not drag us off a cliff, they just impair our lives in more subtle ways. But always these pull us away from God's path. That is why these very ideas were sold to us by the enemies of God. Remember, from our vantage point we do not see these as "bad" or "wrong" or "evil." We have embraced these things as good and right, even as the definition of truth. These things have become *our truth.*

As humans we have many important needs that are hardwired into us. Alongside these needs we cultivate appetites. We need to eat and be properly nourished. But what we like may not provide the best nourishment. Our preferred diet may be too much of one thing, not enough of something we need, and a slurry of toxins from a chemistry lab that masquerades as nourishment. Are these appetites part of our identity? Of course not. What are these? These are the products of our choices. People make the choice to eat differently all the time—if they have reasons to change. People who like sweets but now have diabetes often eat less sugar. But not always. Again, what are our reasons?

USING OUR POWER OF ASSENT AND DISSENT

Why do we study God's Word? One reason is to develop a whole new set of reasons for our decisions. But for anything in God's Word to find its way into our system of reasons, what must happen first? We must embrace this particular idea as our truth. In order to do this, we must have other reasons that we find compelling. In the case of God's Word, the most compelling reason to embrace any and all of its truths is that these writings represent revelation straight from God. Because our minds work in this way, it is imperative that we fully understand the nature of God's Word in contrast to any other ideas in all of life. If we have not answered the question, "What is the Bible?" to our satisfaction, we will inevitably base future decisions on ideas we *have already decided* are true, even if they are not.

As people begin to build a relationship with God, as the fine print says, "Results may vary." Why? Because individuals have different reasons for making different choices about this relationship. If this is so, what is one of our most important responsibilities in our relationship with God? To identify and embrace reasons that are true and real. To do this we must make whatever effort is necessary to find these reasons. That is, we must comb the Scriptures looking for every reason to follow God's path. We must then embrace these reasons as our own. Then we want to use these reasons to make one of the most important decisions we will ever make: to follow God's path or die trying. Is there any other way we can be faithful to God or our relationship with Him?

This is the vital step, but it is only the first step. Why? Because there are still many things in our character and guidance system that will pull us in the other direction. We have started the process of embracing truth. But what about the not-true ideas we have already embraced? Each idea pulls us in a direction. If we learned at some point that anger got us what we wanted, we honed our anger skills. We are in the habit of turning our anger loose when we want something, or doing so just to blow off steam. The decision we just made does not erase this pattern, does it? A bit later, we will see how to erase it. For now, watch the blueprint unfold.

USING OUR POWER OF ATTENTION

One of the pitfalls of modern life is the remarkable number of things which clamor for our attention. In a world filled with labor-saving devices with powerful capacities, like phones and computers, why do we have so little free time? As productivity has skyrocketed, work demands only increase. And the very tools which promise more leisure time clog that time with social media and other amusements. It takes time to get to work, to get children where they need to go, and get everything done so we get into bed at some point. In this world, in order to have any time and space for God we need well-honed powers of attention. We must realize that we are immersed in a world that is actually designed to keep us away from God via frenzy and fatigue. The relationship building, growth, and transformation we are describing take time and attention. How does all of this fit together? I cannot offer specific advice except to say that if we do not make time with God a priority and set time aside, we will not have time with Him.

There are myriad other important uses of this power, ones which greatly aid us. In relationships we benefit by focusing on some things and not on others. In circumstances we benefit from focusing on some things and not on others. During my life as a physician and surgeon I needed to tightly focus my time and energies just to get through my day and have any time with my family. But throughout my practice life, and even during surgical training, which required 12-to-18 hour days and spending every third night in the hospital, I still found time to continue to build my relationship with God, teach a home Bible study, and mentor several individuals. All this requires is a burning desire and fierce commitment, along with the realization that nothing in life is more important than God.

USING OUR POWER OF INTENTION

This brings us to our last power, the one that gets things done. If we are going to make the most of our lives we must take charge of our time and effort as much as possible. We need to learn to complete tasks which need to be done, and do these things to the best of our ability. We must become efficient. We must become relentless if this is needed. All of this is predicated on knowing what we need to do, and having reasons to do these things that provide sufficient motivation. This goes back to another important use of time: thinking things through. The more time we spend thinking, deciding, prioritizing, and planning on the front end, the less time we will waste with confusion and uncertainty. The more focused we are, the less we can be diverted by unimportant things. Building the willpower to be faithful to our Covenant also means we have increasing force of will that we can use in other important ways. The first step in building this power is being unwilling to accept doing anything less than our best. Then, do our best. Then, repeat this process. This pattern will take us far in life.

CHAPTER FIVE

PERSONAL GROWTH AND TRANSFORMATION IN COVENANT

"For He chose us in Him before the foundation of the world to be holy and blameless in His sight" (Ephesians 1:4).

"For we are God's handiwork, created in Christ Jesus to do good works, which God prepared in advance for us to do" (Ephesians 2:10).

"No one can lay any foundation other than the one already laid, which is Jesus Christ. If anyone builds on this foundation using gold, silver, costly stones, wood, hay, or straw, their work will be shown for what it is, because the Day will bring it to light. It will be revealed with fire, and the fire will test the quality of each person's work. If what has been built survives, the builder will receive a reward. If it is burned up, the builder will suffer loss but yet will be saved—even though only as one escaping through the flames" (1 Corinthians 3:11-15).

TAKE ANOTHER LOOK AT THE BLUEPRINT

Are you beginning to understand the tools God placed in our hands? We are to use these tools to build the life He intends for us. Can you see the task before us? We must simply replace deception with truth in our mind, heart, and will. And to do this we must *use* our powers of Assent and Dissent, Attention, and Intention. In other words, we must use our powers to develop these very same powers. Why? To build a new way of life, a new experience of life, and a new character with which we approach daily life. Does this sound like the transformed life we expect to have when we enter the Kingdom of God?

This is the sum of the transformation delegated to us in God's plan. Sounds like a big job. It is. Of course, we will only take this offer seriously if we want to build the life God planned for us before the foundation of the world. And this includes our best possible relationship with God, the largest collection of good consequences, the authentic life we were created (and re-created) to live, the greatest sense of reward and gratification in this life, and the greatest rewards in eternity. Do you believe God's offer is real?

BUILDING ACCORDING TO THE BLUEPRINT

What is a blueprint? Pictures on a piece of paper. For what is depicted to become real, though, what else must happen? We must build what is depicted. The plan of God is words in a book. At this point it is only present as *potential*. For this potential to be realized in our lives—for this transformed life to become reality—this life must be carefully constructed. Covenant organizes the injunctions of Scripture into a buildable blueprint. But we must build wisely. Blueprints offer details about what is to be built, with some instructions. But no blueprint includes details about use of nail guns, saws, and measuring instruments. A blueprint does not even detail the specific order in which things are to be built. What else is needed? Building skills. An experienced builder can take this blueprint and build it because he or she has *learned to build*.

Within the Body of Christ there are mature Christians. These people have built at least some of the things on the blueprint into their lives under the direction of God. How did these people learn to build these things? From *other people in the Body of Christ* who were examples, offered encouragement, and walked beside them, passing to them building skills learned from their own mentors. Another source for this understanding should be mentioned. For centuries mature Christians have recounted their own spiritual journeys and lessons they have learned in books. Some of my best friends and most important mentors lived centuries ago. Their books have inspired and instructed me in countless ways.

Unfortunately, I cannot walk alongside you. I cannot learn about your most pressing life issues. I cannot walk with you step by step through the process of transformation. What I *can* do is convey to you that this is the path to the new life you seek. We are far more the authors of our lives than victims of circumstances. And to the extent that we are victims of circumstances, the way we handle these circumstances can either break us—leaving us bitter and resentful—or lead to new maturity in our grateful, though wounded, heart.

THE THING THAT DETERMINES THE COURSE OF OUR LIVES

Many believe that the biggest factor forming their lives and their experiences is their circumstances. Do we have wealth, power, popularity, and all the other things that matter according to our world? Few of us can do much to change our circumstances. If our life is all about circumstances, how much hope can we really have? And even if something does change—say, we win the lottery—how much difference does this really make? God's answer to this question is altogether different from the world's. Consider how much hope this offers you. In fact, the greatest factor determining the life we build and our experience of life is something over which we have total control.

But how about another change of circumstance we thought was the answer: entering Covenant with Christ? Becoming a Christian was supposed to solve our quality-of-life problem, wasn't it?

"But when He, the Spirit of Truth, comes,
He will guide you into all the truth" (John 16:13).

"Sanctify them by the truth; your Word is truth" (John 17:17).

A very experienced builder would now like to offer you a few tips on how to actually build God's Covenant plan into your life.

TRANSFORMING OUR EXTERNAL LIVES TO MATCH OUR NEW IDENTITY

"Therefore, I urge you brothers and sisters, in view of God's mercy, to offer your bodies as a living sacrifice, holy and pleasing to God—this is your true and proper worship. Do not conform to the pattern of this world, but be transformed by the renewing of your mind. Then you will be able to test and approve what God's will is—His good, pleasing, and perfect will" (Romans 12:1, 2).

"You were taught, with regard to your former way of life, to put off your old self, which is being corrupted by its deceitful desires; to be made new in the attitudes of your mind; and to put on the new self, created to be like God in true righteousness and holiness" (Ephesians 4:22-24).

God's blessings are received while we are on a journey of preparation, study, training, growth, and transformation. This path leads to conformity to God's character and truth. This path leads to a growing ability to love. This path leads to growing obedience. There is nothing in Scripture that suggests we come to God, then remain where we are.

I would like to describe a series of steps to do what we are instructed to do in Romans 12:2. God says we are to be transformed by the renewing of our mind. We want to *put off* counterproductive things and *put on* the life God intends for us. In the above Scriptures, notice the things God does and the things we are to do (the underlined portions are things *we* are to do). Our identity and nature must be re-created by God. This occurs as we enter Covenant. Then we must go through a process of transformation of beliefs that produces a new guidance system and new elements of character. These are the two transformations in God's Covenant plan. Let's see how this plan actually works.

We must first understand that God's plan of growth and transformation is a slow, incremental, and progressive thing. Obedience is called for. Faithfulness is called for. Perfection is called for—yet perfection will not be attained in the moment, or ever in this life. So, what does God realistically expect? God is delighted by the same level of performance that delights us in our children. We aspire to perfection, but must be content to be where we are in His plan. We need to trust the process and become comfortable with the fact that it will be a bit messy—just like raising children.

As we let God search our hearts and minds in the midst of issues and conflicts, we will discover beliefs, feelings, and patterns which lead us away from God's will. Instead of employing the world's approach—"This is just me. Deal with it!"—we are to look within ourselves to find the reasons for these things. "What must I believe if I am this way?" If we can clarify *why* we are what we are, we can now change what we are. With God's help we can bring ourselves into alignment with His ways.

THE POWER OF OUR CHOICES

Most people highly value their ability to choose. Most have no idea *how powerful our decisions actually are.* Consider the impact of embracing and building one aspect of our lives after another upon ideas that are true versus lives that continue to be guided by ideas that are false. Can you now appreciate the power God places in your hands to transform your life based on His truth?

The enemy of God certainly understands the power of this power. For millennia he has been devoted to filling the minds, hearts, wills, characters, and guidance systems of individuals with deception. We see the outcome of his efforts on all sides. These ideas do not always appear overtly evil. Satan does not show up at our door selling lies. He shows up offering an upgrade for our lives. The pursuit of these upgrades and the destructive consequences of this pursuit have largely fashioned the history of humanity. These same ideas have done far more to fashion our lives than we realize, until we have spent time in God's school of love.

Of course, not everything within us is deception. God has also been at work through history revealing truth. We are made in His image and all live this out to some degree. So everything about us is not a candidate for change. As we said in *The Covenant of Marriage,* "We do not need to fix what is not broken." But within all of us are things that are broken. These things impair our ability to love and to follow God faithfully. Thus, we are to live out what is of God and transform what is not.

OUR AGENDA FOR GROWTH AND TRANSFORMATION

A few decades ago, in the pre-Internet era, I became convinced of the importance of reviewing and transforming my character and guidance system. So I cut up two Bibles (so I would have the front and back of each page for use). I collected every verse in Scripture that spoke to what I should *be* or *do*. That is, every verse about character or guidance. I collected these on note cards by topic, then used these cards to go through the process I am about to describe. This "whole Scripture" approach is the comprehensive approach to life change. I would not suggest you begin here. But considering I had a surgical practice and an enlarging family at the time, what could possibly motivate me to do something this time-consuming and difficult? I tasted the fruit of transformation at these deeper levels. I experienced the benefits of a life that was shifting to a foundation of truth. And I wanted more. I wanted these benefits in every part of my life, and I was willing to do whatever this required.

In the beginning, how do we know growth or transformation is needed? There may be a quality we want to see in our life but do not. We may see a behavior pattern we want to be rid of or one we want to become part of our life. We may want to disobey God or find we are unable to obey Him. This resistance means that we are being guided by a not-God idea. We have spoken of the importance of close relationships. In the messiness of relationships we find a rich agenda for growth and transformation. Daily life highlights other needs. There is no shortage of improvements we can make if we are willing to honestly look at ourselves. God is more enthused about our growth and transformation than we are. He will gladly point out things if we ask. The only question is: What are we going to *choose to do* about these things?

"Above all else, guard your heart, for it is the wellspring of life" (Proverbs 4:23).

There is a single doorway through which good things enter and become part of our lives, or through which deceptive and destructive things enter and shape our lives. Each of us holds this doorknob in our hands. Only we can open this door and invite an idea to enter our lives or eject an idea from our lives. We can hold this door shut and refuse to consider or reconsider something. One of the secrets of living is knowing when to open this door and when to bolt it shut more tightly.

This door is our agreement with an idea—our power of assent and dissent. The knob we hold is the choice we make to use this doorway. Just inside this door is our mind. Our mind is influenced and shaped by what we allow through the door. Just behind our mind is our heart. Our heart is shaped and formed by what our mind accepts as true. In turn, the power of attention in our hearts takes what we decide is true and forms our values, priorities, goals, and ideals. Then, just behind our heart is our will. Our power of intention—our will—then fashions our responses based on all of the above. As we go through the following exercise, we involve and impact all of these parts of us. People have the sense that our choices matter. They have no idea how much.

Over the last two thousand years of Christian history there have been many approaches to spiritual growth, or spiritual formation, or sanctification. Each of us will find one approach or another most useful. What follows is a process I have found to be uniformly helpful. It is one of the most powerful exercises we can engage in. This exercise can be applied in any circumstance to embrace truth (to grow) or to reject a false idea and replace it with a true one (to transform). I learned this pattern from the Navigator ministry. They taught it as a way to make specific Scriptural truths a consistent part of one's life. I have found this same pattern to be useful for this purpose, and also when dealing with deeper life issues—character, guidance system, and self-image. I pray this will be a life skill you can learn, apply, and benefit from for the rest of your life.

Let's first look at a five-step process to use this doorway. Then we will see the different ways this process can be used.

A FIVE-STEP PROCESS FOR TRANSFORMATION

Our goal is to shift our guidance system and character so that they are founded on God's truth. This requires that we identify God's truth about a matter. Usually, multiple Scriptures address any topic. It is vital to not just find one, but to survey *every* verse that speaks on this topic. We find these truths in lists of "do" and "don't do." We also find them in stories about people, parables, and object lessons. Each verse has a vantage point and may focus on only part of the overall topic. Therefore, to get God's full picture of truth we must assemble the full counsel of God—every Scripture on the matter.

Some view God's will as a path through the woods. They find this path and invite people to follow them in every respect. But a careful reading of Scripture shows a different picture. God's guidance is more like a playing field. There are definite boundary lines. Some things are clearly out of bounds. But within the boundaries there may be considerable latitude. There is *freedom in Christ* about things not clearly prohibited. Within this range of acceptable things God may want an individual to do one thing or another. Therefore, proper guidance consists of knowing the acceptable limits plus God's individual guidance at any point in time.

We must view the entirety of God's instructions before assuming we understand God's heart and mind. The balancing truth, voiced by the apostle Paul in 1 Corinthians 8, is to not allow our freedom to cause a brother to stumble, and certainly not to use our sense of freedom as a license for indulgence (Galatians 5:13).

COLLECT GOD'S ENTIRE TRUTH ON A MATTER

It is extremely helpful to copy all these verses in one place so they can be examined at the same time. Read them, study the context, and learn as much as you can about what God is saying. Then ask God to show you *His truth* for your life at this moment. What does God want to see in your life now?

Confine your approach to this portion of God's truth. It is extremely helpful to write this truth down as well as your answer to each question below. You should thoughtfully work over this material. By writing it as well, you will have access to your work in the future. This is essential if we are going to be accountable for life change.

STEP ONE: WHAT IS THE TRUTH?

Having engaged in the process of collection, study, and consideration, write in your own words the truth God wants to build into your life right now. Along with this, write the Scripture(s) in which this specific instruction is found. We want to imprint the exact wording of God's instruction to us.

STEP TWO: WHAT IS MY LIFE LIKE NOW?

Write down a description of what your life is like now in relation to this truth. Stay with this one for a few minutes. When God is tapping me on the shoulder about something and I get to this point, my first response often is this: "Pretty good on that one, in fact." Which raises this question: Why is God taking His time to engage with me on this issue? If I simply allow God's Spirit time to search my heart and life, a very interesting thing almost always happens. God's truths have layers, like an onion. There are superficial applications but also deeper and deeper layers. God's definition of truthfulness might be more exacting than the one I begin with. Even though my words might be technically true in a situation, I may be intentionally creating a false impression. The *words* are right, but only part of the story is. And the motive is usually wrong. As I allow God to search my heart, I begin to see applications of God's truths that were not evident at first. I am often near tears by the time God is finished with even this superficial review of my life and character. This exercise always leaves me something to work on.

STEP THREE: WHAT SHOULD MY LIFE LOOK LIKE?

Now write a description of what applied truth would look like. In other words, what should my life look like? This should be written in as much detail as possible.

STEP FOUR: WHAT IS MY PLAN TO MOVE FROM STEP TWO TO STEP THREE?

Next, write a step-by-step plan to move from step two to step three. This might include memorizing one or more pertinent Scriptures so that you'll have God's *specific words* on this topic available at all times. As we seek to apply God's Word to our lives, we all encounter a curious reality. We find ourselves playing with wordings and definitions as we try to keep doing what we are used to doing. If we know God's specific words, instead of just having a general sense of what we should do, we will shut down much of this strategy. There will be an internal voice saying, "Yes, that may be true, but in *this* case ..." This inner voice will try to negotiate to continue the status quo. This voice will continue

As I allow God to search my heart, I begin to see applications of God's truths that were not evident at first. I am often near tears by the time God is finished with even this superficial review of my life and character.

to assert our former truth and reality against God's. It is this inner negotiating strategy that we need to unplug. We do so by affirming to ourselves that its underlying beliefs are lies. We now see through the deception that we formerly embraced as true.

This process is intended to produce a step-by-step plan, thought out well in advance, to which we are committed. One of the most important elements of success is identifying a problem situation on the front end. We want to recognize the scenario as it is developing, before we're thoughtlessly repeating our old pattern. Our plan should include this "early warning system." Then it should involve a series of steps that results in correct action. Perhaps pausing and thinking about a response, perhaps praying, perhaps reciting a pertinent Scripture for clear guidance. Then, take action that is truly appropriate in the situation.

STEP FIVE: CHECKUP AND ACCOUNTABILITY

Last, plan a checkup point. Depending on how frequently the issue occurs, you want to pick a time when there has been opportunity for changed behavior on several occasions. Note on paper how things went, and perhaps schedule another checkup.

It is helpful to involve a trusted friend as an accountability partner. Perhaps your spouse, but in issues related to your spouse there are advantages in a same-gender friend. Hopefully you will begin building such friendships, ones centered on personal and spiritual growth.

Depending on the issue, its complexity, and the strength of old behaviors, it may take several repetitions for a new habit pattern to begin to form. For this to become our *only* behavioral choice, more follow-up may be needed. For more challenging situations, refined approaches and more support may be required. The key is to do whatever is necessary to produce the desired behaviors on several occasions.

As we engage in appropriate behaviors, what should we expect? First, they will feel unfamiliar and uncomfortable. You may feel vulnerable. But you will get through the "awkward phase." Then you will begin to experience the positive consequences of this new behavior.

God may bless you in ways that relate to the situation or ways that seem unrelated. Still, you will have the sense that your faithfulness is being rewarded.

THE OUTCOME OF THIS EXERCISE

What have we just accomplished? We have affirmed and embraced a new truth, one directly from God. As we do this, as we have said, far more than a behavior is at stake. Other things in our being begin to align with this truth. Elements of our character shift. Our frame of reference shifts. Or emotions may shift, along with values and other things.

One such exercise does not an excellent character make, but we now have one real and true brick in place in our foundation. As we add one after another, our character grows and strengthens. As we employ this pattern in area after area, larger and larger parts of our lives begin to shift. We will gain confidence in the benefit of applying God's truth to our lives. Or, as this Scripture puts it: "Taste, and see that the Lord is good" (Psalm 34:8). After we have engaged in this process in a formal way for a year or so, we will begin to internalize this pattern of growth so we no longer need to write these things down, though this is always helpful. God intends this pattern of growth itself to become our habit.

This is a life skill. We get better at any skill with practice, and it gets easier. Notice how our three powers are being used. Not only Assent and Dissent, but Attention. To follow this plan, we must *pay attention.* We must direct our attention from old patterns to new patterns. We must recognize the importance of change. Then our Power of Intention gets a workout. Pushing through internal and external resistance to create a new life is difficult. At first, we may be easily swayed or diverted. This is why *accountability* and *checkups* are important, so we can stay at this until we succeed. To be successful, then consistently successful, means we are strengthening this power. You will be amazed, as you exercise these powers over time, how powerful they become. And you will be amazed at your ability to consciously direct these powers.

MOVING FROM "BEGINNING TO LIVE TRUTH" TO "SCRIPTURAL CONVICTIONS"

But we need to take note of still another reality. Why did we have our former patterns to begin with? Because, at some point, we affirmed that *not-God* was our best option. We liked the results enough to continue the pattern until it became part of us. Having affirmed a new truth, what happens to the old idea, the not-true one upon which our way of life was based? This idea is *still there* at this point, and still capable of guiding our behavior in certain situations.

Have you ever noticed that people who should—and do—know better will on occasion do really uncharacteristic things? A prominent Christian leader has an affair with an office worker, for example. This person could speak for hours about why no one should ever do this. Yet *they* do this. What is going on here? Somewhere in the depths of this person's mind and heart is the idea, "Yes, that may all be true, but in this case … " We always choose to act according to *our perception of our best interest*. For a reason we deemed sufficient, we concluded that *in this circumstance* this is our best move.

When we now insert actual truth, this is not our only "truth." The new one is simply added to a group of allowable options for behavior, alongside every behavior we previously agreed was acceptable. If you ask this person what they believe about this matter, they may quote an applicable Scripture. But if you watch how they behave over time, these other behavioral choices will be part of the picture. Scripture has a word that describes someone guided by opposing ideas: "double-minded" (James 1:8). It is significant that James says this person is not to expect anything from God. He or she is, he says, "unstable in all they do." The Scripture in James cites a variant of conflicting beliefs: asking God for something and yet doubting at the same time. Doubt is not disbelief. Nor is it belief. It is a confused mixture of the two. God calls us to sort this situation out so that we obey only Him.

For every issue, each of us has a list of responses that are allowable in certain circumstances. We also have a list of responses that are never allowable under any circumstance. God's plan is that we go through the process of adding every important element of love and obedience to the "will do" list. And we are to place every counterproductive idea—*not-God*—on the "never in any circumstances" list. Is there a name for this process? Yes. "Developing convictions."

How do we remove every item based on deception from the "acceptable behavior" group? First we identify them. This cannot happen at one time. In any moment it is difficult to answer the question, "What might I choose to do in any situation?" We may not discover some of these until we feel an urge to stray from God's path. Behind every such urge is an idea. We deal with these ideas by thinking them through again. We look past any supposed benefit of this course of action and find the lie. Our power here is the power of Affirmation *and* Dissent. We have the power to decide that something is not true. By affirming that something is a lie, we move this idea within ourselves from the "acceptable in some circumstances" list to the "never acceptable" list. We will not follow a lie if we know it is a lie. We will only follow a lie if we are not aware that it is a lie. That is, we only follow lies if we are deceived. If we continue to be deceived, these ideas continue to feel like truth.

A person thinks he or she has just found "true love," though this person is already married. Every other consideration fades, for isn't finding true love the most important goal of life? However, instead of finding true love, how many people commit adultery and simply blow their families and lives apart? This is the enemy's point: to separate us from God and damage us in the process. Rather than just considering the falseness of a lie, we need to focus on the promises that go with these lies. These promises are the true power that drives us to sin (Ephesians 4:22). These promises are also lies, but we tend to overlook this because these benefits are something we believe we need. This highlights the last step in the process of rejecting deception. What do we really need? And how do we best go about meeting our needs? If we go back to God's truth to answer these questions we now find that our old approach, based on Satan's deception, is *the last thing we would do* given the opportunity. We now have a Scriptural conviction on this matter.

GROWING AND REVISING OUR GUIDANCE SYSTEM

To understand our guidance system, let's envision obedience to God as walking on a path. This path goes in two directions. It is the path toward God and also away from Him. If we are not moving toward God on this path *we are headed away from Him.* We often think of "sin," or disobeying God, as a single act. But it never is. Rebellious choices and acts always occur in groups. Why? Because obedience is not an act. Obedience is choosing a path. Obedience is a plan that we follow. We are always moving on this path, either toward God or away from Him. If we decide not to move toward Him our rebellious direction will be evidenced by a series of disobedient acts.

> How do we remove every item based on deception from the "acceptable behavior" group? First we identify them.

Let's apply this picture to building our guidance system as God intends. The point is to follow God's path for the rest of our life. Our guidance system ideally guides us down the path toward God instead of in the opposite direction. Though we seem to have many possible paths as we travel through life, in reality there are only two: God's path, leading to growth and transformation, producing the best relationships and the best us, and "other." God's plan moves us toward being more and more loving. He wants us to learn to build with both hands, not build with one hand while tearing down with the other. We are guided down God's path by His truth.

If we are going to take a comprehensive look at our guidance system it would help to make a list of all the parts which make up this system. Then, take a look at our current thinking in each area. Our guidance system consists of our ideals, goals, priorities, and values, as well as our hopes and dreams for our life. Each of these elements points us in a general direction, and within each category are many specifics. What are our most deeply held values, for example? It is a wonderful idea to make a list of the specifics in each category, then spend some time considering why we hold these views. Often, many individual beliefs go together to form each value. It is good to compare all of our beliefs in each area with God's Word. And, as we are reading God's Word, to be attuned to guidance system directions as we read. The more we adjust our belief system on the front end, the less damage control we will need further down the road.

Our guidance system is organized around self-interest. This is actually not a bad thing if we properly define "self" and understand what is truly in our best interest. We spend our lives trying to figure out what is best for us. We spent our lives until the time we entered Covenant developing a finely honed sense of what is best for the old us. In Covenant, since our *new self* is joined to another, how does this impact our self-interest? We are now joined with God. His interests become our interests, and the interests of our new self become His concern. How does this translate to daily life?

It is in our best interest to look after God's interests with the same enthusiasm we show for our own. He is doing the same for us. We now have the life of God—His Spirit—within. Obedience to God is our new native language, an authentic expression of this new being. Rebellion was part of our old life, but is merely a holdover of deception in our new life. Any benefit we think we obtain from *not-God* is a destructive illusion. So how do we take the best care of this new life? We walk on God's path, hand in hand with Him, taking off the old life, putting on the new life, learning one new way to love after another as we grow into the person God created us to be. Do you see the difference between this life and one based on confusion about who we are and what is truly best for us?

Our best interest is achieved by building and rebuilding our guidance system based on the whole counsel of God on every issue. As we consider obeying everything Jesus commanded (Matthew 28:20), we are not called to try to cram a square peg of obedience into the round hole of our nature where it does not fit. Instead, we are invited to authentically express the *being we became as we entered Covenant through obedience.* The peg (what we are told to do) fits perfectly in the hole (our new identity and nature). But we may not realize this. We may have a different view of obedience. If we do, we will struggle to walk God's path.

> In Covenant, since our new self is joined to another, how does this impact our self-interest? We are now joined with God.

Early in my Christian life, some things God says to do and be in His Word seemed completely out of sync with common sense and the way I thought the world worked. We have already seen why our embraced ideas create this point of view. But an even bigger problem for me was the perception that God's instructions violated the very essence of who I thought myself to be as a person. This felt like I was being instructed to try to ram a square peg of obedience into a round hole of "me," into which it definitely did not fit. However, it occurred to me that "me" had become different when I entered Covenant. I decided to try an experiment. I would give God the benefit of the doubt and try doing something on the "not me" list. Though something within me continued to resist, as I actually did what God said a remarkable thing happened. Once I obeyed, it seemed that this is what I had wanted to do all along. I simply had not realized it. I had just experienced living an authentic life. My actions now correctly expressed the new life God had placed within me. This experience powerfully confirmed to me the reality of the new life we receive in Covenant and the limits of my ability to accurately understand this new life apart from God's revelation. This experience also revolutionized my view of obedience.

This motivated me for decades to do exactly what I am recommending here: to systematically study and apply God's Word. Take one issue after another under the heading, "What should I do or be as a Christian?" Go through the above five-step meditative process for each truth until this truth becomes a functioning part of your life. Then move to the next one. Life is long, so we have time to build many of God's truths into our lives and remove many of Satan's roadblocks that we put in our own way.

For the five-step process we can also use as our new truth the principles and practices of Covenant. What priority do we give our Covenant and our God in our life? What are our Covenant responsibilities to God? What is our plan to fulfill each consistently? It is remarkably helpful to write down such meditations and stay with these things until God becomes the true center of our lives.

I have been engaged in this process for decades, yet I still find beliefs that need adjustment. This is a lifelong process. As we go through processes of growth and transformation they often operate so slowly it seems not much is happening. Early in my own journey I questioned the benefit of this commitment of time and energy. However, when I looked back over the previous year it became evident that my life had shifted more than I realized. Looking back over decades, it is clear that this is the best way I could have possibly invested my time. More good things have flowed from these efforts than any other effort in my life. The reason I have the relationship with God, the Marriage, and the life I now have is because of the transformations which have occurred—first in my identity, then in my character, guidance system, and self-image. This has allowed me to follow God and cooperate with Him instead of resisting Him.

BUILDING AND REBUILDING CHARACTER AND SELF-IMAGE

How would you define yourself? Who are you? What are you? What about you is fixed in stone, and what can change? Based on our perceptions, the answers to each of these questions will be different from the answers we find in Covenant and God's Word.

If we want to begin understanding our character and revising it as needed, it is helpful to make a list of the character qualities we have. If we are not clear about these, consider the question: "How would I describe myself, in as much detail as possible?" Are we honest, loyal, punctual, and easygoing? Or, do we cut corners, use people, show up when we feel like it, and frequently complain? There are no wrong answers on this list. We all have issues and the more honest we are about them, the better. If we make a list of as many qualities as we can, we will be able to search the Scriptures and note God's plan for us. Whatever our issues are, there will be a standard for godly character in Scripture. We can start by simply trying to be more like Christ in each area. Soon, though, we will find ourselves defending our current ways. Now it is time to look at our reasoning. Why do we think being assertive and angry is essential? In a certain relationship or environment this may have served us well. But now these qualities are not appropriate in most situations. Perhaps we could not trust anyone but ourselves to look after us. This is reasoning we can reconsider within Covenant. God has taken responsibility for us. It is still a good thing to defend ourselves and stand up for appropriate things. But we do these things as ambassadors of Christ. His honor is on the line, as well as our own.

If we begin looking at ourselves in this way and comparing our qualities with Scripture, we will also become more attuned to character guidance as we read Scripture. The more we understand about godly character, and the more benefits we see from shifting to these qualities, the more motivated we will be to make this revision process a high priority. For more serious issues, like troublesome anger issues, it is helpful to spend a significant amount of time working over the five-step process we have discussed. It is especially important to explore the reasons why we use anger to relate to people. We need a firm foundation on this topic in Scripture. And we need a step-by-step plan to build a new pattern of relating and dealing with problems. Occasionally, professional help may be in order, but God's Word and God's Spirit have more power than we often realize to empower life change.

Many in our culture believe we are defined by our preferences, or our desires, or our choices, or our beliefs. Many believe feelings are expressions from the very core of our being. Everyone wants to express who they are—to be authentic—but what do we express to do this? Everyone wants to be loved for who they are—but what part of us must be loved for this to occur? If our answer to this question is our preferences, or choices, or beliefs, or the things we do in the interest of self-expression, we invite serious problems into our life. Many of our choices, preferences, feelings, urges, attitudes, and behaviors are destructive to self and others. Our culture teaches that "true love" means to accept someone as they are. Does true love therefore mean we must embrace and even celebrate these destructive things? This misguided view of love causes some to view people who disagree with a person's choices as a "hater." Is this view based on truth or deception? We should not let two vital questions be obscured in this discussion. What part of us does need to be loved and accepted? How do we learn to love one another in this way?

How do we know who we are? The most important step in our transformation is determining who we think we are at this moment. It is helpful to make a list of everything you think you are. These would not be individual character qualities, but a more overall description of ourselves. Where do we fit into the big scheme of things—family, peer group, society, and church? What potentials do we have? What are our strengths and weaknesses? Are we loved, and do we know how to love? After considering how we view ourselves, ask how any view of ourselves might be limiting us or directing us away from God's best for our lives. Now we can go to the Scriptures with some actual questions about who we are in Christ.

THE PUZZLE OF SELF

There are several pieces to this puzzle. **First, we have a *true identity and nature.*** This includes every fixed, unchangeable thing about us. We cannot change our identity. God can, and does, but only as we enter Covenant. Our identity directs the course of our life in several powerful ways. Despite the popular saying "You can be whatever you want to be," we can only become what we are created to be, or something less than that. We cannot be a better athlete than it is genetically possible for us to become. We can recognize and fully develop this potential. Or we may not, in which case our life is less than it might be. Though none of us can look within and fully define ourselves, we have a good sense over time for what is us and what is not. We can try to be something we are not, or be forced to play a role unsuited to us. If so, we feel frustrated and unfulfilled. Developing and authentically expressing ourselves is one of the keys to a deeply fulfilling life. If we know who we are, one of our strongest drives is to be this person in every way possible.

The second piece of the puzzle is *our perception of who we are.* We all spend years trying to figure out who we are and where we fit into the big scheme of things. One key source of information we draw from is how others react to us. We hear much from parents and other family about who and what we are. We also draw from experience. When we try to do something athletic or artistic, what happens next? What could possibly go wrong as we assemble our view of ourselves from these sources? For one thing, other people are often a very inaccurate mirror. Negative responses and words may not always be about us. Other people may project their issues on us.

Discouraging words can keep people with real aptitude from pursuing their gifts. On a larger scale, we can get the message that we are unfit overall. "You can't be loved because … " "You are a loser, ugly, worthless." We have all heard these things spoken over people, and we've all seen discouraged and insecure people withdraw from the life they could be living. They think the best life is denied them because of "what I am." In fact, this is due to what they have been told they are, and have accepted at face value.

Insecurities come from many sources. All of these have to do with an incorrect view of self. Have you noticed it is virtually impossible to encourage someone out of their insecurity? Presenting evidence of someone's true capabilities may do nothing to erase their insecurity. Why? Because *our self-image is one of our most firmly held beliefs.*

How many people in our world live down to an incorrect image of themselves? The second most powerful factor driving the course of our lives—and if badly distorted, the most important—is our belief about who we are.

A third piece of the puzzle is *our character.* Are we warm and friendly, sarcastic and brooding, a depressed victim, a pushy manipulator, withdrawn? Are we responsible, dishonest, violent? Our character is the sum of the qualities we express to the world. Often people confuse character and nature, but these are formed in completely different ways. Our nature is created by God and given to us. Our character is created by us, by our decisions. Our character may reflect aspects of our nature—introversion is a wiring thing, but the shyness often seen in introverts is a character quality. Introverts can be trained to be socially engaging; they just do not enjoy these interactions the way an extrovert does. For the most part, our character is formed as we try out various approaches early in life. If generosity works, we do more of it. If defiance gets us what we want, others get more of it. This is why disciplining children at critical ages is so important. We do not want wrong lessons about what works to take hold. Lying in a three-year-old may be cute, but it is also extremely dangerous. We continue to build layer upon layer of our persona, or character, into adulthood. We base our decisions about what we will be on what we think we are supposed to be, need to be, or want to be. We attempt to meet other's expectations or our own, or we notice what best serves our interests. Or we try to emulate someone we admire.

We run into problems when things that worked earlier in life—say, in our junior high peer group—do not impress our employer or our spouse. What if one believes "this is just who I am"? People often defend their character as they would defend their life. Given that our world is full of deception, and much of this deception has found its way into counterproductive and destructive character qualities, ridding ourselves of such things would be more like removing a cancer-filled kidney. In order to benefit from God's plan, we first need to realize we need to change these counterproductive character qualities for best results. Then we need to figure out what about us needs to change, and how this occurs. Armed with this information, we are on the way to a better life.

THE PROCESS OF BUILDING AND REBUILDING

We keep returning to the same point, don't we? "Decide what is really true, and truly beneficial." The first set of truths to consider is what is truly *us*. We have described our new life in detail, one now joined to God in Covenant. You can fill in the details of your specific makeup and subtract every part that feels like "self" that came from your decisions. It is a remarkably powerful thing to embrace this truth, and the other truths of Covenant, as *our truth.* Why? Because the new life that God wants us to build with Him requires changes in us that *we will vigorously resist.* When we sense this resistance, if we understand the big picture we can overcome our own resistance and actually carry out God's plan.

After spending countless hours beside people who would benefit from one life-change or another, it has been fascinating to see how strongly some people resist beneficial and needed changes. This inner resistance is the sole reason that many people choose not to follow an aspect of God's Word or to engage in the process of transformation at all. Why have we have painted this big picture so extensively? The natural resistance to change that is built into our wiring system *will* keep us from making the changes that are *absolutely necessary* if we are to carry out the rest of God's plan unless we are armed with certain key pieces of information. Our world has sold us on myriad ideas which directly oppose these needed changes. Our own minds and hearts believe some of these ideas to be real and true. If we are to be faithful to God and live the life God intends we must know what about us can change; what about us must change; the resistance we will face as we try to make these changes; and why we should make the effort to push through our own resistance. Then we need to know how needed transformation occurs and the role we must play.

Early in my mentoring experience I noted two responses to God's truth. Some agreed with these ideas in conversation during a Bible study, but did not build these ideas into their lives. Others embraced these truths enthusiastically, like they had just found water in a desert. These people did begin to live out these truths. The difference going forward in the lives of those who *embraced* truths, versus those who did not, was striking. I spent considerable time trying to understand why a person had one response or another. During those years I noted something even more important. When people embraced certain truths, more happened than a change in behavior. These truths took root in these lives, and lives began to change in more powerful ways. Then God began to use these people in more powerful ways. Understanding these phenomena, then learning to apply this understanding, led to the strategy for growth and transformation found in this book. What did God show me about these things?

First, knowing what we should do is important. But we still may not do it. Why? Because of the reasons we already have for not doing it. If the correct reasoning was already in place we would already be doing what we should be doing. So, the strategy shifted from merely teaching what we *should* do to looking carefully at the reasons *why* we should do so; then examining the reasons for our resistance and identifying the flaws in this reasoning. We must effectively deal with our resistance if we are to follow God.

Second, there are foundation stones of understanding upon which everything else rests. Envision a group of upside down pyramids next to each other. The point at the bottom of each pyramid is a foundational belief. Resting atop this idea is an expanding set of beliefs and practices. The broad base of this pyramid consists of all the ways we live—the "superficial things" of life. We can talk about who empties the dishwasher in a Marriage. This will get the dishes clean. Or we can look at the nature of the joining of lives in Covenant. If one gets a foundational idea right, all the things which rest upon this foundation will shift. The dishes still get clean, and many more issues are cleaned up. What are the foundational ideas in our relationship with God?

FOUNDATION STONES FOR OUR LIFE IN CHRIST

It is good to take this list and make sure your own foundation stones are true and strong. Confusion about any of these topics will create a shaky foundation. We can build something large upon a solid foundation. If we try to build the same structure on a shaky foundation, what happens? It is worth the time to develop convictions about the following foundational topics.

1. The nature of God, and the identity and mission of Jesus.
2. The nature of our relationship with God (which is the topic of this book), including our new identity and nature.
3. The truth of God's Word, and the fact that it is the only source of ultimate truth.
4. The nature of sin—which is more than simple misdeeds—and the nature of deception which leads us to sin.
5. The nature of forgiveness—which is more than a get-out-of-jail-free card.
6. The nature of faith and faithfulness and the imperative of obedience. This, plus an understanding that obedience also relates to growth and transformation, not just behavior.
7. The nature of love: the way this is defined in God's Word and by Covenant.

Please note that we cover each of these topics in this book. But also note that there will be one outcome if we hear, nod, and smile when we read these things. There will be another outcome altogether if we search out these things, embrace these as our truth, and eject any dissenting ideas. You do not just want to get a firm hold on these ideas. You want these ideas to get a firm hold on you. Upon these foundation stones all else is built.

SELF-IMAGE

One view common to humans is, "I cannot be loved because … " If we are burdened by thoughts and feelings of inadequacy, we can go through the process we outlined. Fill in the truths of Scripture and Covenant about who you are. God first says to love others as we love ourselves. How well are we loving ourselves? Do we realize that God wants us to love ourselves as *He loves us*? Not only are we loved and benefited by this, properly loving ourselves helps us love others. These are the kinds of thoughts we can embrace as our truth once we understand the truth of God. But do not stop at affirming them. Go through the process of making these real in your life. Attack insecurities with truth; round up and brand lies for what they are. Lay out truth, embrace it, and live it.

Along with building a real love relationship with God, one of the most important things we can do is collect a growing list of reasons to follow His plan. This is actually part of honoring and worshipping Him. The more our minds become sharpened to identify truth in all its forms, and the more heightened our senses become to identify deception and deceptive patterns, the more enthusiastic we will become about following God in every detail of life. We move out of the fog of the spiritual war and into the light of God's Word and His love.

CHARACTER

As we go through Scripture we may see many qualities we would like to see in ourselves. As in every other realm, there are many good qualities already within us. Some of these can be strengthened and others added. The process is the same. Embrace the truth, find sufficient motivation to change, formulate a step-by-step plan to become one thing, and then to become another. Have an accountability partner or at the least a self-check plan.

> *"They perish because they refused to love the truth, and so be saved"* (2 Thessalonians 2:10).

For every misformed and dysfunctional aspect of character there is a lie we embraced that put it there. Behind every insecurity, and every wrong view of ourselves, there is a lie we chose to embrace. In Scripture there is a truth that rebuts each lie. In Covenant there is an understanding of the new creature we have become that brings these Scriptures to life. One of the most important things we can do in this life is fall in love with truth, then begin to use it to transform our minds.

"But I am afraid that, just as Eve was deceived by the serpent's cunning, your minds may somehow be led astray from your sincere and pure devotion to Christ" (2 Corinthians 11:3).

Genuine fulfillment comes from authentically expressing our identity into the world. Consider the quality of life when one's guidance system, self-image, and character are all working in opposition to one's nature. Our obedience, and therefore our best life, is sabotaged by ideas Satan has already loaded within us. Even if we enter Covenant with God, the life we could live before God is reduced to nearly nothing. This is Satan's plan B in case we escape his kingdom and enter the Kingdom of God. How many Christians do you know who are living this meager life in the Kingdom of God instead of the powerful and abundant life offered us by God?

Attack insecurities with truth; round up and brand lies for what they are. Lay out truth, embrace it, and live it.

DEALING WITH MORE CHALLENGING LIFE PATTERNS

Most issues of behavior and character can be adjusted with the above strategy. But some require additional measures. Serious addictions and some mental health issues require professional help and perhaps medical intervention. But two insights may help unplug the power even of things with a physiologic or "mental health" component.

When we look at not engaging in destructive (e.g., "sinful") behaviors through the contractual lens, we are left with only willpower versus a drive that predictably overcomes our willpower. "I want to not do this, but I cannot stop myself" becomes the mantra. Yet in Covenant we know we are capable of effectively resisting any rebellious behavior because the rebellious nature of Satan no longer drives us uncontrollably toward such behaviors. The balance of power has shifted. God's Spirit is within. We have a new and different nature driving us toward godly behavior. Our legitimate interests have become God's vested interests. We can pray for power from Him over these issues in a new way. We also understand that any dysfunctional behavior ultimately requires our *assent and permission*. This can also be withdrawn by us at any time if we have sufficient reason to do so. But sometimes we still want to give ourselves permission to do destructive things. Why?

The second insight involves our view of sin. Most view rebellious behavior as simply "bad," as something we "should just stop doing." Yet as we dig our heels in there is a huge power pushing us in the other direction. We talked about one kind of deceptive lie, but there is another form of deception in play in these situations.

Each of us has a unique set of deepest emotional needs. These are part of our true identity: the old one or the new one. These needs are created within us by God. We all need to be loved, but each of us needs to be loved in specific ways. This is related to our various love languages (see Gary Chapman's book series). When a tenacious pattern of sin is present, outside spiritual forces may be strongly influencing us in various ways. That topic is beyond the scope of this book. But another thing is almost certainly in play. This behavior or pattern is *our* plan B to meet one of our deepest needs.

These deepest needs are some of the strongest forces in our being, like needing to eat or breathe. This is why meeting these needs is such a powerful experience. But not meeting these needs is also a very powerful experience. Often during our formative years one of these core needs is not met. Far worse, the person may conclude that this need can never be met. This sentence usually begins with "I will never be loved because … " Our remarkably strong need to be loved is designed to drive us into God's arms or into the arms of a husband or wife. Then it is meant to energize us to build healthy families and relationships. But this huge force can be redirected. Instead of moving toward healthy intimacy—which we believe for some reason we cannot have—we may choose promiscuity to gratify our need to be loved. Or the camaraderie of the drug culture or a street gang may offer acceptance to one who craves it.

The deception? That this substitution is a desirable long-term strategy to meet one of our most important needs. Here the need is real, not manufactured. It is the strategy to meet this need that is deceptively billed as a working alternative. Instead, such lifestyles lead to the death of many things—and perhaps even of the person. In order to unplug the power that drives these behaviors, one must look at not merely the rebellious behavior and say, "Stop it." One needs to look for the pressing, *legitimate* need the person is trying to meet in a destructive way. One needs to determine why the person concluded that a healthy path to meeting needs is not possible for him or her. This is the ultimate lie that needs to be confronted and replaced with God's truth. If a person is given hope that their deepest needs can be met in a godly way, he or she can begin building life patterns that allow this to happen.

One of the greatest truths we can ever learn is that God loves us. He loves us not because of what we are but because He created us, and He wants to *re-create us in connection with Himself.*

SPIRITUAL GROWTH

GOD'S PLAN MEETS DAILY LIFE

We now have what we have called a "together-life" with God. Our life is not our own to do with as we please. We now have a Marriage-like relationship with a perfect and all-powerful Being who loves us more than we love ourselves. This should soften the blow of realizing we are no longer in charge.

An understanding of Covenant should greatly aid our spiritual growth. Our growth should always involve four areas: prayer, the Word, fellowship with believers, and outreach to non-believers. We spoke earlier of investing our public and private efforts in these directions. We have also spoken of deep truths and powerful processes of change in Covenant. But these deep truths and powerful processes happen in the context of day-to-day life.

"He who is faithful in a very little thing is faithful also in much" (Luke 16:10, NASB).

Growth and transformation are demonstrated in our daily lives through simple things. We invite someone to eat with us. We listen carefully and take great interest in the life of one person, then another. We are more aggressive about identifying and meeting needs. We are more encouraging. We offer a word of truth to someone that means something to them. Our schedule changes, making more room for God and other people. Our money goes in new directions. Our interests point in new directions. Our perception of God's workings in the world sharpens, and our desire to be with Him in these things grows. It is said of Marriage: "It's the little things." So it is in relationships in the Kingdom of God.

THE PATH OF SPIRITUAL GROWTH

We have just gone through the detail pages of the blueprint. We have looked at our tools: our Three Powers and a pattern of Scriptural meditation to use these powers. We have seen how to apply these tools to individual choices as well as to our guidance system, character, and self-image. Why are we doing all of this? Let's go back to the first page of the blueprint, the one that shows the finished factory, and what this factory is going to produce.

God loves us and wants the best for us. He loves others inside and outside the body of Christ, and He wants us to play a key role in some of their lives. God wants us to tell the truth with our lives. What does this mean? He wants us to live authentic lives. He wants our expressions of life to reflect the life of God within us. He rewards us for living this way: through consequences, through gratification, through satisfaction, through peace of mind and heart, through eternal rewards, and through new opportunities we are now prepared for.

Let's consider a bigger picture. Our world is a battle of ideas, between the ideas of God and those of the enemies of God. God tells us that our best life comes from being joined to Him and following Him. Satan tells us that God and following Him are a sham. He claims that he offers the path to true satisfaction and gratification. Satan's deceptions are vulnerable. Truth, reality, and consequences all testify against his lies. His only hope to keep the con alive is to obscure the truth. If there were an army of people on all sides living godly lives and experiencing the good fruits of God's plan in full measure, it would blow Satan's lies to shreds before a watching world. Therefore, Satan has been doing everything possible to prevent God's truths and God's plan from being lived out within the Body of Christ. To truly honor God and fulfill our Covenant responsibility to Him, I believe we must play our individual role faithfully so that our lives serve as a compelling witness of the truth of God. Our witness will not be perfect but it should be powerful, and powerfully reflect the Lover of our souls.

THE GOD OF OPPORTUNITIES

When Holley and I cooperate with God and a new thing is built into our lives, it is amazing how often an opportunity soon appears. To make the most of this opportunity, we need the foundation just built. The importance of an opportunity is difficult to assess at first. Some do not appear to be major things, but later prove to be. One never knows until one pursues them. Of course, not all opportunities are from God and we must be discerning. But a clear pattern has emerged: preparation, then use of what is prepared. What if we had not made the most of the opportunity to prepare? Either the next opportunity would not have come our way, or we would not be equipped to make the most of it when it does.

So we have learned to pay careful attention to two things. First, to any prompting from God to grow or prepare. This, by the way, almost always comes in the form of a problem or an issue we must deal with.

Second, we carefully examine any opportunity that comes our way. After prayerful consideration, if we believe this opportunity is from God, we have learned to pour heart and soul into whatever this opportunity might be. This may become the next big thing, or a small thing, or another building block, or something that benefits someone else. Regardless of the outcome we have the strong sense that we are participating with God, who is the Lord of opportunities.

Now go back to the front page of the blueprint. This is your life journey. You begin where you begin. This path leads to God. Fortunately, God is everywhere. Thus, He can walk with you on this path to Himself. Why the journey? To *become like Him* in every way that matters. Now that I'm far down this road (but nowhere near the endpoint, by the way), I have had the joy of becoming close to people who are also far down the road. I cannot relate with words the joy of being in the presence of those who love God deeply and are noticeably transformed toward His image. This is but a taste of what eternity will be like.

"Son though He was, He learned obedience from what He suffered" (Hebrews 5:8).

"No discipline seems pleasant at the time, but painful. Later on, however, it produces a harvest of righteousness for those who have been trained by it" (Hebrews 12:11).

THE CURRICULUM OF LIFE

Our lives are puzzling at times, disconcerting at times, beautiful and glorious at times, and stunningly painful at times. Why? Because God wants to use all these things to *refine us into His image*. If we are deeply committed to building our relationship with God, and to studying and applying His Word, how do we know what we need to learn and what to study? We should be on two tracks of study. First, a systematic study of God's Word. The second agenda is driven by what is happening in our lives. We will routinely encounter life issues. We need to develop the reflex of looking to the Word for help with these issues. We need to learn how to locate pertinent Scriptures. We need to learn to apply them. The five-step pattern for applying Scriptural truths presented in this book is a wonderful application tool. Use it or employ one you prefer more.

When studying chemistry, part of the process is reading, part is lecture, and part is going to the laboratory and doing what you are reading and hearing about. In the same way, God wants us to always be learning the basics at deeper and deeper levels. Then He wants us to apply these lessons in our lives. This combination over time will lead to a deep knowledge of Scripture and a finely honed ability to apply it.

Through this curriculum of life God offers us an opportunity to grow our new life to maturity. Our new identity contains one or more "spiritual gifts." These are special capabilities we can develop for ministry in the Body of Christ, some of which are described in Romans Chapter 12. He offers us a chance to develop our relationship with Him. He offers us a chance to learn how to love as He loves. He offers us the opportunity to come alongside Him as He accomplishes His purposes in this world. We just need to become prepared to make the most of each opportunity. Every day will present opportunities to make progress in one way or another.

"But solid food is for the mature, who because of practice have their senses trained to discern good and evil" (Hebrews 5:14).

We also benefit greatly from focusing on building our Three Powers. We need to strengthen our ability to separate truth from deception. We need to practice focusing on spiritual realities, honing in on what is most important in life, developing correct values and priorities, and following through on our commitments. Building our Three Powers is one of the most important steps toward building good character overall. By these we learn to make proper choices and build the right things. It is helpful to choose one of these powers each week and focus on strengthening it.

"I know what I was feelin', but what was I thinking?"
—Dierks Bentley[18]

We have a life, but how do we make the most of it? Before we find the answers in life, we must first learn the right questions. Noted theologian and country music artist Dierks Bentley posed perhaps the most important question we will ever ask if our lives are to reach their potential. "What was I thinking?" As we go through the issues of daily life our reflex response is to blame others for whatever problems occur. If we want to grow to our potential, though, we do better to avoid blaming others. Instead, we should ask two questions. What was I thinking? And, what is God trying to teach me?

"But solid food is for the mature, who by constant use have trained their senses to distinguish good from evil" (Hebrews 5:14).

When we consider the life of Jesus, or see things in the lives of matured godly people we admire, do we realize that this can be *our* life? In the case of Jesus, it is our life, a life waiting to be built and expressed. The power of the Living God is squarely behind this effort. God's truth and our Three Powers are the tools used to build this life into our character and guidance system. This is the life we are created to live and created to enjoy. First, though, we must see the lies we now live. We must cultivate a deep distaste for counterfeit things we previously chose to love and embrace.

THE ROLE OF GOD'S WORD AND GOD'S SPIRIT IN OUR TRANSFORMATION

We must also recognize the work of God's Spirit in our transformation. We have talked a lot about our responsibility in the process of life transformation. We have focused on *our role* in this way because most Christian teaching assumes that we play little or no role in our transformation. The results of this misunderstanding are evident on all sides. We have looked at the role God assigns us in this process. But this situation has a few more moving parts; it is vital to understand the entire process if we are to harness the power of God's plan.

"I keep asking that the God of our Lord Jesus Christ, the glorious Father, may give you the Spirit of wisdom and revelation, so that you many know Him better" (Ephesians 1:17).

"For the Word of God is alive and active. Sharper than any double-edged sword, it penetrates even to dividing soul and spirit, joints and marrow; it judges the thoughts and attitudes of the heart" (Hebrews 4:12).

"The Word became flesh and made His dwelling among us. We have seen His glory, the glory of the one and only Son who came from the Father, full of grace and truth" (John 1:14).

"But they did not understand what this meant. It was hidden from them, so that they did not grasp it, and they were afraid to ask Him about it" (Luke 9:45).

Have you ever looked at a passage of Scripture several times? Then, while reading it again, something you never noticed before literally jumps off the page at you? These words address something important in this moment. Though you read these same words before you completely missed this point. What just happened? God has just opened your eyes to a particular truth. Your eyes saw these words before, but you did not grasp God's truth or see how this applied to your life. Until, that is, God pointed this out to you. This is God functioning as the "Spirit of revelation."

Let's consider what just happened. You came before God to read His Word. You desire to examine your life in light of God's truth. But our perception has limits. Paul asked God to give the Ephesians the Spirit in the role of *revealer*, One who would show them what they will not see on their own. The Word of God is beautifully described above as a living thing that engages with us and reveals to us our true nature.

Remember, Jesus is the Word of God. He came to live on earth as the Word in living form. In Covenant, we are *in Him,* and He is *in us.* If it is beginning to dawn on us that reading God's Word is different from reading any other literature, we are grasping a vital truth. If we realize that in Covenant we now have a new relationship to this Living Word, we grasp another exciting truth. This is not only to *be* our life. It is our life.

"But the Advocate, the Holy Spirit, whom the Father will send in my name, will teach you all things and will remind you of everything I have said to you" (John 14:26).

"Do not quench the Spirit" (1 Thessalonians 5:19).

The life of God is now within us. But we live based on many deceptions. As we read God's Word, the words of life (as Peter termed them in John 6:68) are right in front of us. But our lack of perception, or mis-perception, must be penetrated. This is the real-time role played by God's Spirit. He takes the truth of God and shows us how it applies in our lives in specific situations. But only if we put ourselves in His presence and seek His truth. Though God's Spirit is literally within us, He does not invade the parts of our lives left untouched by His truth without our invitation. And if we ignore or reject His truth He stands back and lets us have our way until we find our way to be intolerably painful. Then we will return with a more receptive heart and mind. So how can we choose to engage most constructively with the Living Word and the Spirit of God? This is a working relationship we must build as we go through the issues of life.

FINDING TRUTHS TO GRAFT IN AND DECEPTIONS TO EJECT

Now that we realize all of these things, let us take a final look at developing our agenda for transformation. I have found four general ways God brings these issues to my attention. First, important truths become apparent while reading His Word, or listening to teaching or even in a song. Conveyed in whatever way, I feel this truth of God impact me very strongly. Our next move is crucial when this happens, for many simply enjoy this brush with the Almighty and then move on. If we are to build our lives, we must ask why God is speaking this thing to us: *what was I thinking?* At this point we do well to search out the whole counsel of God's truth. Then determine the specific truth He wants us to apply in our lives. Then apply this truth in the manner of the five-step process outlined earlier.

The second way a need for transformation may come to our attention is through conflict with others. We may be the initiator or the responder. In either role our approach may benefit from revision. As music artist Bentley noted above, the key question is not what we did or did not do, but *why*. What was I thinking? What do I believe, what do I want, what do I value, what are my priorities, what do I believe is a "win" in this situation? If this is a person with whom we are in Covenant, we can examine the relationship issue in light of God's truths surrounding Covenant. If not, we can search out His truths related to our heart and conduct in general. Again, once we see a discrepancy between our beliefs and His truths, we have narrowed the question to: "Lord, what truth do you want me to apply in this situation?"

The third way to identify needed transformation is by looking at our life patterns. For instance, do we have patterns of failure due to "others"? Are we perpetual victims? We can look for any pattern that characterizes our life that differs from the growing victory we would reasonably expect in a life joined to the living God. Again, we must be careful to define "victory." This is not a growing bank account or group of social media followers. Instead, victory is defined as the growth of our new being in Christ, and by increasing fruit produced by this life. If we are "living down to" who we have been told we are (loser, stupid, ugly, unlovable, and more) or subliminally sabotaging our own success (finding reasons to break off relationships "before the other person sees who we are and walks away from us"), or note any other pattern of defeat in our lives, we have an issue of belief to work on. We may not be able to look within and identify this belief. We often do not recognize our role in these dramas. We usually view ourselves as victim, not author. But the question to ask is this: "What must I believe about myself if this pattern exists in my life?" Then, "What does God say is true of me?" The answers to these two questions can lead us back to the Word and to our identity in Christ in Covenant. We can embrace a new belief about ourselves in the depth of our being using the five-step process mentioned above.

A fourth way to identify needed transformation is our feelings. I vividly remember being in a Promise Keepers meeting. Strong emotions began to well up. At the time I was being grievously abused and wounded by someone. This was a relationship, so there were also issues on my end and I was in the midst of trying to sort all of this out. I am a guy, and guys generally view strong emotions like this as an annoyance that can keep us from doing what we need to do to fix things. So I shut down these emotions and directed my attention elsewhere. Men, this is a serious mistake if we are trying to learn and grow.

From this beginning point God took me on a two-year journey through my own heart in light of His Word. I learned about my wounds, needs, hopes, fears, and pain, things I had been sidestepping while trying to handle a difficult relationship. Here is the pattern I learned. I can only briefly describe it here. This kind of thing is more in the realm of mentoring, in the context of a years-long process with someone we trust deeply.

Our emotions are a sensory apparatus that help us understand interactions and people at deeper levels. We feel some things during a conversation and feel other things later as we review what was said. What was meant, and what was this person trying to do by saying these things? Our emotions inform us, or perhaps misinform us, of these things. Emotions also inform us about ourselves. What real impact did a situation have on us? We may not initially understand the importance of something. We must process things to better understand them. This means listening as our heart explains to us the impact and importance of an event.

For massively important things in life—abuse, neglect, violations of various sorts—in relationships where other major considerations are also in play (such as not destroying a relationship with the people who provide our food), our emotional reactions can be buried deep within so we can survive. If we are beaten as a child, or molested by a family member, we may keep silent and pretend things are OK. Why? Our very survival, from our perspective as a child, may be on the line. Or it may *literally* be on the line. In less extreme situations we can also bury our feelings and reactions to keep the peace or for other "good" reasons. But these emotions, reactions, and realities do not disappear. They nestle down within us and become something called "baggage."

Baggage is a term commonly used to describe something we carry forward from previous experiences. Something about these past experiences can cause dysfunction in our current life, though we may not make this connection. These dysfunctions may manifest as codependency, emotional issues, addiction, or other pain-killing strategies. Or trauma may manifest as overachieving or emotional isolation. Basically, according to the psychologists, most unhealthy emotions and dysfunctional coping strategies can be traced back to former life experience.

But I would add one more thing. These dysfunctions can be traced back to deceptive beliefs about self, other people, or life. These are ideas we embraced based on these experiences. Every trauma or neglect of an important need carries with it a message about us. "How important must I be if … ?" "What do I deserve in this life … ?" If we make peace with these situations, without realizing it we may also accept these messages within the depths of our being. These are lies from Satan that damage and wreck lives like cancers. They devour our being from within. Unless, that is, we pry them out of our mind and heart and send them back to their author.

When we experience a feeling that is out of context with what is going on in the moment, emotions from our "baggage car" are tapping us on the shoulder. These emotions remind us they are there, and await "processing." This can be anything from an unreasonably angry response to someone who "reminds us of … " to a more pervasive feeling of fear, anxiety, sadness, or loneliness that colors our whole being for no apparent reason. These out-of-place emotions are a doorway to needed transformation.

If we simply take the time to "let these emotions go"—allow ourselves to fully feel them—something important begins to happen. This process often occurs in a psychologist's office, but we benefit more if we take these things before the Lord. Once we turn our attention to these feelings and allow ourselves to feel them, memories will begin to surface. Things done and said will become attached to these emotions. The importance of these situations becomes evident from the depth of our emotional response. As we feel these things, the lessons we "learned" about ourselves through these situations come to light. These lessons, we will find, are the deepest source of pain. And when we examine them, each one of these painful things we have come to believe about who we are, or what we are—all of these are lies from the pit of hell sent to further damage our lives! When we see such a lie, what is the truth? How do we reject and eject the lie and embrace God's truth? We already know the answers to these questions, do we not?

I awoke with unpleasant feelings of various types: sadness, anger, pain, loneliness. I opened my mind and heart before the Lord and waited. Soon a flood of emotion followed, sometimes so powerful it felt as if I would explode.

After the Promise Keepers event, I spent some time with a Christian psychologist trying to sort out a number of things. I learned how to listen to my emotions and made some serious progress understanding my situation. But God had more in mind for me.

Soon after I began to be awakened by God an hour or two before I would normally arise. This occurred two or three mornings per week for the next nine months. I awoke with unpleasant feelings of various types: sadness, anger, pain, loneliness. I opened my mind and heart before the Lord and waited. Soon a flood of emotion followed, sometimes so powerful it felt as if I would explode. And with the emotions came memories from throughout my life. Things that deeply impacted me that I did not understand at the time they happened. After an hour or so of what felt like an internal tornado, a lesson would crystalize—a truth would emerge. These lessons were in contrast to the lies I had embraced, usually without realizing it, in each situation. As this process continued over the course of about nine months a theme became evident: "What is love, and what is it *not*?" God was giving me an intense course in His school of love. Everything about love could not be taught. But what God did through this process prepared me for the next opportunity and chapter in my life. These lessons were proven true as I lived them out. I took these false beliefs from the very depths of my being—about my self-image, character, and guidance system—and employed the process that was becoming so familiar to grind new truths into the fabric of my life.

One other point bears mentioning. Our baggage is a finite thing. Emotions trapped "in process" create dysfunction. So do the lies we embrace that misform our character, self-image, and guidance system. When we allow ourselves to experience these emotions we learn the lessons they have to teach. If we also *un-learn* the lies we accumulated in the process, these dysfunctions disappear. A part of us ceases living in the past. We come into the light of God's life and love.

CHAPTER SIX

BUILDING AN ABUNDANT LIFE

LEARNING TO POWERFULLY USE OUR POWER OF ATTENTION

God wants us to have a wonderful, powerful, transformed, and abundant life even more than we do. He went to considerable personal trouble to make this relationship available, including watching His Son die an agonizing death on a Roman cross. He wants us to be faithful so we can build wonderful things in our lives. Why? To show a watching world what it looks like when the power of the living God is poured out in and through a human life. This honors God and the Covenant we entered with Him. Anything less does more than squander an opportunity for individuals. It impacts God's reputation, for we are His ambassadors on this earth.

At several points in Scripture God instructs us to focus on *this* instead of *that*. Or, to make this matter a priority. God has laced the Scriptures with promises, always in the form of "If you do this, I will do that." Thus we must make it a priority to do what we are instructed to do so that God will do what He promises to do. Many things in Scripture are not about right and wrong per se, but about balancing things properly. All of these involve our Power of Attention, and they require sharpening and strengthening this power.

Let's look at three of the many areas where use of this power is required. What is at stake here? Our quality of life hangs in the balance. A vast amount of our experience of life flows directly from where we direct our attention. Among the first things we must pay attention to are God's instructions about how to use this power for best results. As we go through this section, see how many of these instructions you can find.

CONTENTMENT VERSUS DISCONTENT

One of the most important choices we can make is to be contented. What? Isn't contentment about enjoying pleasant circumstances and constructive relationships? Isn't contentment our experience when things are going well, at least for the moment? Actually, contentment is not about circumstances. This is one of the great secrets of life. The apostle Paul summed up this reality nicely:

> "*I am not saying this because I am in need, for I have learned to be content whatever the circumstances. I know what it is to be in need, and I know what it is to have plenty. I have learned the secret of being content in any and every situation, whether well fed or hungry, whether living in plenty or in want. I can do all this through Him who gives me strength*" (Philippians 4:11-13).

How would you describe contentment? It is the experience of being pleased, being satisfied, having enough, or of the situation being enough? Why is finding contentment in life so important? Think for a moment about times we have been discontented. What is discontent? We are not pleased, not satisfied, the situation is not good enough, or we do not have enough. Said another way, our *expectations* have not been met.

Our entire society, thanks to advertising, media, work, and our peers, seems determined to produce discontent. How? By convincing us how important it is that we have *more*. If embraced, these ideas form our expectations. We become convinced that having certain things in our lives will lead to contentment. The right job, right house, right car, right education, right spouse, and on it goes. Success, money, fame, meeting expectations, fitting in, and on it goes. Or, the right party is in power, the right policies are in place—the right politics, we think, will make our lives *enough*. Whatever sales pitch we happen to embrace, the thing to note is that we have embraced a sales pitch. Thus, until the right thing occurs, we will not be content. We will not settle!

Let's think for a moment about the nature of discontent and contentment. If we are discontented, this is a statement that what we now have is insufficient. Our world teaches us to not settle for less than what we want. We deserve the best, after all. High expectations equal the best life. We will be content if, and only if, our expectations are … finally met. If we were satisfied with our lives, after all, we would be content, not discontent. So is the answer to lower our expectations?

Of course, there are some things about which we should be discontented: our own character deficiencies and immaturity, for example. It is good to desire a better life and to desire that other people be better. But do we want to be better in an *absolute sense*, as in being better at our job or our Marriage? Or do we want better in the sense of *being better than other people*? One path is God's desire for us, the other reflects Satan's urge to falsely elevate himself. The next question becomes this: Do we want to actually find contentment in life or just use discontentment as leverage?

> Superiority over others is a game no one can win for more than a while, then they lose badly. Our internal experience is more powerfully created by what is in our heart than what is in our wallet.

Here are a few more questions to consider: Do we want situations to meet our expectations—whatever those happen to be—or do we want our expectations to be in sync with reality? What actually produces contentment? And perhaps the most important question: What does it say about our God if we are deeply dissatisfied with our lives?

Does having more than others produce contentment? Someone famously asked John D. Rockefeller, one of the wealthiest men who ever lived (with net worth of more than $400 billion in today's dollars), "How much is enough?" Rockefeller's answer? "Just a little more." Superiority over others is a game no one can win for more than a while, then they lose badly. Our internal experience is more powerfully created by what is in our heart than what is in our wallet; by the virtue we possess rather than the image we display; by the value we create in the lives of others rather than the value of our house. No one can take away our good character. Circumstances change and things come and go. But even doing good things does not ensure that we are content.

> *"And my God will meet all your needs according to the riches of His glory in Christ Jesus"* (Philippians 4:19).

To be truly content, we must realize that our vital interests are secure. No earthly circumstance can damage the indestructible and eternal life within us. Nothing can take away the things that are truly important. What is truly, vitally important? Our relationship with God. This relationship is the wellspring of our life on earth—and of the one to come. Every other blessing flows directly from God. His highest priority for us is that we be faithful, and by this to become mature. No human and no circumstance can stand in the way of this. This is not to say that we will not suffer loss, feel pain, grieve, and wish things were otherwise as we go through this life. But if everything that matters is secure, can we now be OK with our current situation, whatever it is?

For this state of mind to become real in our lives, we must understand our vital interests. Our world makes more of an effort to misinform us about this than any other topic. We must realize the source of supply for our vital needs. The source for everything truly important is God and our relationship with Him. Covenant is His vehicle for uniting with us, displaying His love for us, and requiring our love in return. Thus, to truly understand our vital interests, we can look to what God has committed to us in this relationship.

How important is contentment? More than we realize. God has given us the life we have now. When we feel discontent, what is happening? Very often, our dissatisfaction is due to the lack of something we are convinced we need. This is a very vulnerable position from a spiritual standpoint, for this is the *first* step toward turning from God's path. If we really need nothing beyond our current life—if we are satisfied now—then we are not open to temptation. Satan's first move with Eve was to create dissatisfaction. She became dissatisfied with God, who she "just learned" was keeping her from her best life. She was dissatisfied with being merely human instead of "as God." She was certainly dissatisfied with a God who apparently lied to her instead of loving her as she thought. She needed a new god—obviously—so she chose one. Can you think of any things about God our culture urges us to be discontent with today? Are there any things outside the will of God that our culture promotes as necessary for our best life?

Our culture, with more material wealth, technology, equality, and education than any culture in history, is perhaps the most discontented collection of people on the planet.

Our culture, with more material wealth, technology, equality, and education than any culture in history, is perhaps the most discontented collection of people on the planet. Though having more of almost everything than anyone else, our populace wants still more of one thing or another. But what of people who are genuinely deprived? People who are victims of disaster, serious illness, or other life-threatening or life-changing circumstances? What of Christians who are going through the most trying of circumstances? Can we expect anyone to be content in a life like this? See 2 Corinthians 11:23-29. In this passage Paul details the challenges in his life. If you have this question, please read this passage, then refer back to the passage from Philippians 4 quoted at the beginning of this section.

> *"Endure hardship as discipline; God is treating you as His children. For what children are not disciplined by their father? If you are not disciplined—and everyone undergoes discipline—then you are not legitimate, not true sons and daughters at all. ... God disciplines us for our good, in order that we may share in His holiness. No discipline seems pleasant at the time, but painful. Later on, however, it produces a harvest of righteousness and peace for those who have been trained by it"* (Hebrews 12:7-11).

To be content in extreme circumstances we must realize that pain, loss, deprivation, and other adversities are actually part of God's training process. This process is designed for our benefit. One cannot become a good football player without getting beat up and exhausted in practice, getting yelled at, and at times being humiliated. None of this feels good. If football only consisted of practice, no one would play the game! But practice is not the point. Games are the point; practice is the necessary preparation for these games. The discomfort of practice is the price one pays to become a good football player.

In a more expansive (and important) way, the pains and problems we encounter in life are but training tools in the hands of a loving God. This is the truth; all we need to do is recognize God's love for us, His power in our lives, and the ways He uses these things for our ultimate good. Then we can relax into the process. We can accept these as necessary and beneficial. When we learn to see adversity in this way we receive the most benefit from God's plan, for we cease resisting it.

All we need to do is recognize God's love for us, His power in our lives, and the ways He uses these things for our ultimate good. Then we can relax into the process.

At the beginning of this section I said contentment was a choice. What is that choice, exactly? We can choose to affix our hope for happiness and contentment upon life meeting our expectations. We can fix our hope on a human institution, from our job to the political system. We can choose to define our conditions for happiness and settle for nothing less. This is like locking up our own happiness and holding it for ransom, demanding that the world meet our terms or we will never let our happiness out of prison. We can spend our lives trying to motivate and manipulate others to meet these expectations. How is this plan working?

Or we can realize we are living in the middle of a mess that we had some part in creating. We can be OK with ourselves the way we are, and we can be OK with others the way they are. We can desire something better for all, but not allow discontent to destroy our happiness in the meantime. We can focus on the deeper truths of God's love and provision. We can choose to keep current issues in perspective. Today's issue is one of many we will confront over a lifetime. The secret ingredient of contentment is thankfulness as we turn to God and ask Him to supply our real needs. We can choose to thank God for our life right now, whatever that life might be.

DEALING WITH ADVERSITY

"Be anxious for nothing, but in everything through prayer and supplication with thanksgiving make your request known to God. And the peace of God will guard your hearts and minds in Christ Jesus" (Philippians 4:6, 7).

"If God really loved me, He would … " We have all thought this, usually in the middle of a painful situation. It is very difficult when we are dealing with a significant threat or loss to envision God's loving hand allowing such things for our good. When people speak of their "crisis of faith," it often involves such a situation. We begin to question God more seriously, then fault Him for allowing … whatever it is He has allowed. When faced with a threatening situation, which we often are in this life, God tells us to pray. We are to ask for what we want, find something to thank Him for, and then be *filled with His peace.*

And in the hands of our loving Father, we expect things to turn out "well." Many are praying for healing, but the child dies, or the cancer recurs, or the disability proves to be permanent. Or some other worst-case scenario plays out. Can we really not trust God with these "big things"?

This question deserves a thoughtful answer. Holley and I have faced a number of challenges. In a few, the worst-case scenario did happen, despite working and praying as hard as possible for a different outcome. Our lives were deeply impacted. Real losses and serious pain occurred. We got through these things, but getting past some of them was harder than we expected. Where was God? In the moment, I did not have a good answer.

> *"And we know that God causes all things to work together for good to those who love God, to those who are called according to His purpose"* (Romans 8:28, NASB).

We all carry a ruler in our pockets. When we look at any issue of life, we pull out this ruler. It measures the extent to which something is in our best interest—in our perception of things. If the issue looks beneficial, it is "good." If it appears to threaten our interests, it is "bad." If it poses a serious risk to life as we know it, it is "horrible."

But as Holley and I have looked back over the decades, something clearly stands out: often these worst-case scenario outcomes were the ground from which grew some of our choicest blessings. Some of these changes led to the most precious things in our current life. So when we look back and see major benefits flowing directly from these times, were these things in truth bad? Painful, yes. But were they *bad*? Or, were they actually good? We still would not have chosen these things. But looking back we are grateful for what God has done. Adversity makes us dig much deeper for answers: deep into ourselves and into the things of God. It often strips away counterfeit things we lean on.

But often there is a very important purpose behind stripping these things away in God's larger plan.

Holley and I have learned from experience to put no confidence in what our personal rulers tell us. In fact, we have seen the "blessing from adversity" pattern so strongly over time that we no longer fear situations that appear threatening. We have learned through experience that even a devastating loss is not the end of the story. Even the end of an earthly life is not the end of the story.

Think for a moment about the bigger picture of adversity. We are fixed to one outcome—the one we think is best. But who has a better vantage point to know what is best for us in the end: you and I, or God? On one hand, God has an agenda and a plan. Is there another strategy behind all of this? Through serious adversity Satan seeks not just to damage us but cripple us.

We have learned through experience that even a devastating loss is not the end of the story. Even the end of an earthly life is not the end of the story.

We live in a world filled with adversity because we live in a world awash in rebellion and not-love. As we face adversity, proper use of our Three Powers is critical. Faithfulness is critical. It is good to understand real risks and the damage that may occur. But we want to maintain balance and perspective. We even want to maintain a certain quality of life in these crises. In adversity all good things come from realizing that God is in control.

If we view only one outcome as acceptable, we will fixate on trying to bring this about. We will be extremely anxious and even feel that our life hangs in the balance. This issue will literally take over our emotional lives.

The opposite of this approach is to *trust God and His love.* If we do, we can do as the above Scriptures say and find *something* to thank God for as we ask for our desired outcome. While we should work hard for best outcomes as we understand them, we must keep in mind the limitations of our understanding. We must always keep in mind *Who* holds everything that is truly essential in His hands. Rather than fixating on the risk, think for a moment about what we believe. Do we believe we understand what is best, not only for ourselves but for everyone else in the situation? Or does God know the answers to these questions in a way we could not possibly know? Does God love us? Does He love us more than we love ourselves—and even more than we love everyone else in the situation?

Another excellent question for God in such situations is this: "What are you trying to teach me?" This is a much better question than "Why me?" or "Why this?" If we understand our Covenant with God, we know that God's plan is not centered on our good feelings or our desires. He wants us to grow the new life He gave us to maturity; He wants us to put away the deceptions of our past and avoid embracing new ones. Are you aware that adversity is, inevitably, an attack from our enemy? How can this enemy do more than wound us in the moment? How can he cripple us for the long term? He can do this by leading us to embrace a lie about God's love for us, His nature, or His power.

So in these high-pressure, high-stakes situations we need to be extremely careful to guard our heart and mind (using our Power of Assent and Dissent). We need to provide ourselves reasons to affirm God's love, character, and power. We need to shift our focus from the risk of loss to what God may do in everyone's lives who are involved, and commit ourselves to pray for these benefits. If you have lived long enough to have seen the adversity-blessing pattern I mentioned earlier, you can thank God with a high degree of confidence for what He will do going forward. You can always thank God that you are offered an opportunity to know Him better and trust Him more deeply.

"His Master replied, 'Well done, good and faithful servant! You have been faithful with a few things; I will put you in charge of many things. Come and share your Master's happiness!'"
(Matthew 25:21)

Satan can get us off balance for the rest of our lives if we sustain a significant loss. At times he even convinces us that our lives are over. Nothing can "undo" the damage, nothing can replace the loss, and our future will never be the same. Do you know people in just such a chronic state of mind? They are full of blame and bitterness. This is a self-fulfilling prophesy, for their lives have been irreparably damaged, as has their relationship with the God they no longer trust. But the culprit was not the circumstance. The deepest damage is done by the one who embraced a lie in the midst of a difficult situation. On the other hand, in the same situation, though we acknowledge any loss that occurred and deal authentically with pain, grief, and other emotions, if we can also find things to thank God for, this will completely change our attitude. In fact, we will have peace in our hearts instead of bitterness. Life will not feel like it has come to an end. We are still moving forward, though perhaps wounded. But even these wounds may prove to be a gift in the long term.

"Shadrach, Meschach, and Abednego replied to him, 'King Nebuchadnezzar, we do not need to defend ourselves before you in this matter. If we are thrown into the blazing furnace, the God we serve is able to deliver us from it, and He will deliver us from Your Majesty's hand. But even if He does not, we want you to know, Your Majesty, that we will not serve your gods or worship the image of gold you have set up'" (Daniel 3:16-18).

How would you describe maintaining your trust in God and belief in Him even when you do not understand what He is doing or what the outcomes will be? The term I use for this is *faithfulness*. This is the word used to describe one who lives out the realities of Covenant. In the furnace we still honor our God. Life is a furnace, adversity is inevitable, but our response to adversity is our choice. Covenant shows us the right choice, but it shows us something else as well. We are obligated to a certain set of responses to God in Covenant. Do you realize that God has bound Himself to us in this same Covenant? It is

His honor to love us in action. We need never doubt His love, power, or faithfulness.

FORGIVENESS

It is helpful to understand the uses God makes of adversity and to be willing to embrace these things—as Scripture says in Hebrews 12—as a form of discipline and a teaching tool. But there is another issue in play that we must often grapple with: the role played by others in these scenarios, or perhaps the role we played. How many of us remain stuck in the past because we were deeply wounded? We seem not to be able to get past the trauma, pain, and loss. We hold *someone* responsible: another person, or on occasion God Himself. Or we may be stuck in the past because we did the wounding. We may be responsible and remain mired in shame and guilt.

One thing is certain. We will experience pain, frustration, and loss in this life. And we will wound others and at times cause them serious loss. What then? We will disappoint God in these scenarios, either by causing them or by the way we react and respond to them. Fortunately, God has a plan: forgiveness.

If a loss deeply impacts our life, what do we want? We want the responsible party to assume responsibility for the damage. We want this party to fix the damage, to make it like it never happened. If this is not possible, we want them to make the situation right in some way.

What do we do? We put this person in a special category in our mind and heart: "You owe me … " And we will not rest until this debt is paid. We can hold a person in this place in our heart and mind for the rest of their lives, or even after they have died. This person is "the reason my life is less than it could have been and should have been." Our life is, in our mind, irreparably damaged. What happens next? Unforgiveness plus time equals bitterness. Over time our being becomes infused with resentment, malice, and hatred. We have all been around bitter people, those who are always eager to tell us *why*.

For less grievous matters, we can still choose not to forgive. In these cases our hearts are still set against another person. They still owe us a debt they have thus far refused to pay. Relationship, in this case, is always damaged or broken.

How does God want us to deal with these situations? Before we look at specifics, one fact must be understood: two people sustaining precisely the same loss can have radically different life outcomes. For instance, a couple can lose a child in a tragic accident and be devastated for a lifetime. A family can (and often does) disintegrate. Siblings' lives can be tragically misdirected. Or, with the exact same loss, a Marriage can grow deeper and more powerful and a family grow stronger. What is the difference? How this tragic loss is viewed and handled. We keep coming back to the beliefs we embrace about a situation, our lives, and God.

Two people sustaining precisely the same loss can have radically different life outcomes.

"Though He was God's Son, He learned obedience through what He suffered" (Hebrews 5:8).

"Jesus said, 'Father, forgive them, for they do not know what they are doing'" (Luke 23:34).

"But if you do not forgive others their sins, your Father will not forgive your sins" (Matthew 6:15).

We must realize when dealing with any loss that God is always at work, always trying to teach us important things—even if these are excruciatingly painful lessons in the short run. But how are we to view the parties responsible for the damage, pain, and loss? God says to forgive others or He will not forgive us. This is the starting point and endpoint of the conversation. We need to determine how to get from where we start—experiencing pain, loss, and anger—to the point that we can forgive. Also, what does forgiveness actually mean?

"In your anger do not sin" (Ephesians 4:26).

When our self-interest is compromised deeply by someone, our natural response is anger. What is God's approach? Is it to refrain from being angry? No. Is it to patiently endure all things and simply pray for the other person? Rarely would this be the right approach. When we are offended or wounded, God's approach involves three things: *properly diagnosing the problem, speaking truth in love*, and *forgiveness.*

When we feel our interests are violated, we should ask ourselves several questions. "Why do I have this response?" Is this about a moral issue, a Covenant violation, a violation of integrity, or a display of malice? Or is this situation really about my expectations, my desire to be in control, or some value that really does not reflect God's priorities for me or the other person? Do I need to learn something in this situation before I try to teach someone a lesson? Our ultimate objective is to restore unity and build relationship.

If, after reflection, we believe this is an issue of moral significance, it is beneficial to speak the truth clearly about what was done and why it is a problem in addition to relating how we feel about it. Then we listen. It is surprising how often there is an element of misunderstanding and miscommunication involved. We may not know the whole story. Thus, the third key skill to master is termed *reflective listening.* This means we hear the other person out and reflect back to them what they are really saying. If they do not agree with our reflection of their point, we keep discussing until they agree that we understand what they are saying. They do the same for us. At this point we have subtracted the problem of misunderstanding. And we have subtracted perhaps 80 percent of the conflicts we encounter between people. For the 20 percent in which a real issue exists, we have at least clarified the details.

"Do not seek your own revenge, beloved, but leave room for the wrath of God. For it is written, 'Vengeance is mine, I will repay,' says the Lord" (Hebrews 10:30).

When major misconduct and significant loss is involved, the facts may be obvious. The issue then becomes what to do with these facts. If we have not forgiven, we are still holding the other person responsible to make the situation right. Perhaps this person can do something to restore what is lost. Or perhaps they either will not or cannot. What then? They may fully understand what they caused in our life, or be oblivious. Or, worse, they may know and not care, or even be pleased that we are wounded. What then? There is something within all of us that simply wants revenge at this point.

"... in all things God works for the good of those who love Him, who have been called according to His purposes" (Romans 8:28).

"... the Father of compassion and the God of all comfort, who comforts us in all our troubles, so that we can comfort those in any trouble with the comfort we ourselves receive from God. For just as we share abundantly in the sufferings of Christ, so also our comfort abounds through Christ" (2 Corinthians 1:3-5).

God's injunction that we forgive says nothing about the response of the other party. Why? We hold this person in the place of owing us. But what do they really owe us? To make our pain go away? They cannot. To restore our loss? How can they? Who is responsible for the quality of our life going forward? Who can redeem what was lost, not by replacing it but by giving us something valuable instead, like maturity, growth, and transformation? And we may be blessed in other areas of life. Through painful situations we are given new ways to help others—and new opportunity for ministry. We learn to comfort others in the ways we have been comforted in our loss.

If, that is, we allow God to comfort us instead of requiring comfort from the hand of one who cannot give it. Instead of asking "Why me?" we should ask, "Lord, what are you trying to teach me?" And instead of requiring something from the offending party, we should step aside and allow God to have His way with them. He is more interested in justice than we are. He is more capable of reaching into someone's life and impressing on them the wrongs they have done than we are, and He is more capable of bringing them to repentance. And if anyone does not repent, God is in charge of handling this situation as well.

"As far as the east is from the west, so far has He removed our transgressions from us" (Psalm 103:12).

"Though your sins are like scarlet, they shall be white as snow" (Isaiah 1:18).

We hear the phase "forgive and forget," as if forgiveness is to *pretend it never happened* or *does not matter.* We hear that God forgets our sins for the sake of Christ, that our transgressions are separated from us as far as the east is from the west. But this statement refers only to the *judicial* aspect of our sins, the sentence of eternal separation from God that hangs over all of us because we joined in the original rebellion with Adam and Eve and shared the nature of the author of that rebellion. There are other levels of consequence when we do wrong or someone wrongs us.

There are four types of consequence when we do wrong. There is the *judicial consequence* noted above. God judges everyone at the White Throne judgment (Revelations 21). There He determines our eternal destiny according to whether we are in Covenant with Him or not. In Christ our sins are no longer held against us in this judgment because He paid the penalty of death for our sins on Calvary. This forgiveness extends to sins committed before we came to Christ and after we entered Covenant with Him.

"For no one can lay a foundation other than the one already laid, which is Jesus Christ. If anyone builds on this foundation using gold, silver, costly stones, wood, hay, or straw, their work will be shown for what it is, because the Day will bring it to light. It will be revealed with fire, and the fire will test the quality of each person's work. If what has been built survives, the builder will receive a reward. If it is burned up, the builder will suffer loss but yet will be

saved—even though only as one escaping through the flames" (1 Corinthians 3:11-15).

There are three other kinds of consequences for sins. There is the *judgment of the behavior of believers.* Next, there are *temporal consequences* woven into the fabric of our universe. Finally, there are *relational consequences.*

Though believers will not be eternally separated from God for sins, our faithfulness will be rewarded, and our lack of faithfulness will cause loss, as shown by the verses in 1 Corinthians 3 (above) and 1 Corinthians 4:5. This judgment occurs at the time of "the Lord's coming."

But there are more immediate consequences. Any violation of God's moral law sets in motion myriad *temporal consequences*, some immediate, some long delayed. We may be forgiven for lying, but trust is destroyed and our reputation damaged. We may be forgiven for theft but perhaps lose a job or spend time in jail. Depending on the nature of the wrongdoing, there may be less severe but still significant consequences. God's judicial forgiveness does not erase temporal consequences. We may get a second chance or we may not. But even if we do, now we are in the role of having to prove we have repented. We must demonstrate we will not repeat our wrongdoing or its consequences will multiply going forward.

> If, that is, we allow God to comfort us instead of requiring comfort from the hand of one who cannot give it. Instead of asking "Why me?" we should ask, "Lord, what are you trying to teach me?"

Another type of consequence is *relational.* When we offend someone deeply enough there is always this question: Will this person remain open to us and allow continued relationship, or will this person turn his or her back to us, ending the relationship? If the relationship continues, will it be forever changed, or can it be restored through our repentance? And what happens to a relationship when serious harm is done and there is a lack of repentance?

In the Christian community we have confused God "remembering our sins no more," at the great White Throne judgment, with other consequences which do not disappear. The outcome of this confusion is a widespread belief that *our sin really does not matter anymore*. We can live our life doing what we please regardless of God's heart, direction, or Law—and our sins are simply ignored in the big scheme of things. "God's grace and forgiveness are sufficient to cover my sins." We assume there are never going to be meaningful consequences for our sin. We then hear that we are supposed to take the same "like it never happened, like it doesn't matter" approach when someone sins against us. "Forgive and forget." "Turn the other cheek." The same Jesus who said this, though, also advised His disciples who did not have a sword to sell their cloak and buy one (Luke 22:36). Oddly, the "forgive and forget" strategy is far more palatable to the offender than to the one who is offended. Obedience matters. Offenses matter. The way we treat each other matters, and we help each other by reinforcing this reality. This is the way people learn to love more perfectly, or should learn.

"Do not quench the Spirit" (1 Thessalonians 5:19).

What about God? How does He respond in relationship when we sin? Our sins quench the Spirit of God. These disrupt the *experience* of our relationship with God. He is waiting with open arms if we repent. But what if we do not? Does this impact our working relationship with God? Absolutely. If we are truly in Covenant with God we will not in the end be eternally separated from Him. But if our relationship is damaged by disobedience, we build less in collaboration with God than He desires, and we will be less rewarded than we would have been. God does not erase this loss.

"But Jesus would not entrust Himself to them, for He knew all people. He did not need any testimony about mankind, for He knew what was in each person" (John 2:24, 25).

Jesus was highly selective about His intimate associates; He knew what was (and is) *in the hearts of people.* He does not lavish His choicest blessings indiscriminately but reserves those for people who are devoted to Him and follow Him. When we sin, which we all will, He waits for us with open arms. But we will not experience the warmth of His embrace until we repent. This is the model of the father of the prodigal son (Luke 15). This is the model for us as we relate to others.

What does it mean to *repent*? In our culture today it seems this means to apologize in a way that causes people to restore relationship, often without any real change of heart and mind about what was done. Saying "I'm sorry" and true repentance may be very different. The biblical picture of repentance is to understand the wrong we have done and feel remorse. But there is more. We are also to understand, then embrace, God's view of the situation. That is, our mind and heart change from defending what we have done to the role of prosecuting attorney—one who clearly outlines the crime. Then we assume full responsibility for committing it. Then we give this situation to Jesus and accept His forgiveness. Remember, the word "repent" means to turn and walk in the opposite direction, not to simply regret doing something, perhaps because we got caught.

"For the sorrow that is according to the will of God produces a repentance without regret, leading to salvation, but the sorrow of the world produces death" (2 Corinthians 7:10).

In Covenant there are many life exchanges. If our life is now joined with Christ, our life becomes *His*—including our mistakes. If we give these things to Him, we no longer possess them ourselves. While we may have the consequences of our sins, this burden is shared by Jesus. He does not take consequences away; He bears them with us. If we have given these things to Him and have been transformed by embracing His truth and rejecting the lies of the enemy that guided us to sin, this sin is *no longer ours*. We have changed. The sin is part of our story, but it is no longer a part of us. This is the genius of Covenant and the plan of God.

In Covenant there are many life exchanges. If our life is now joined with Christ, our life becomes *His*—including our mistakes. If we give these things to Him, we no longer possess them ourselves.

The approach God takes is the one He wants us to emulate. We are not to continue to open ourselves to those who abuse us or would destroy us. Remaining in an abusive relationship, continuing to "forgive" while we suffer physical or other abuse, is not God's approach. What is His approach? To speak the truth in love. To have boundaries and conditions for a relationship that are healthy. To always remain open to a restored relationship, but not to pretend that unrepentant abuse is a relationship. We are to help people and walk beside them in their difficulties. But we are to be clear about another's heart. If someone is determined to pursue sin, we are not to stand between them and the consequences of their actions in a misguided attempt to "love." We want to convey the impression that sins do matter. We are to speak God's truth and stand aside while consequences play out so the person can realize one of life's most important lessons: sin has consequences that are ultimately unbearable. A person must turn from his or her course to survive, and certainly to thrive. God never indulges a heart of sin, nor should we.

FORGIVENESS IS A CHOICE WE MUST MAKE

Regardless of what else is occurring, though, we choose to forgive. We choose to cease holding another responsible for fixing the consequences of his or her sin. We allow God to restore and bless our lives as He desires. We allow Him to teach us through these things as He desires. We remain open to those who sin against us and extend our hearts to those who repent. But we are realistic about the person on the other side of the relationship, and about the nature of the relationship. We do not continue to act like a person's sin never happened, or as though it is not happening if it is. We do not stand in the way of God's consequences, bailing unrepentant people out of their difficulties. We do not assume the consequences for unrepentant people, like our children, in the misguided assumption that this is God's approach. Instead we speak the truth in love and continue to love. We stand on God's side on the question of right and wrong and wait for others to join us.

We also receive the forgiveness of God. In the same way we no longer hold others responsible for fixing the impact of their sin, we allow God to do the same thing in the lives of others for our sin. When we sin, we repent and learn God's lessons. We are transformed. Our story is still our story—and this includes *our sin*—but we no longer *own* our sin or its effects. We have given these to Jesus. We make recompense and do what we can to repair damage. We seek to understand the depth of the damage we caused. But we allow our Lord to bear the burden of these things going forward instead of remaining crushed by a weight of guilt or shame. This is part of God's plan of transformation and the sharing of burdens in Covenant.

Our story is still our story—and this includes our sin—but we no longer *own* our sin or its effects. We have given these to Jesus.

AN OUTLINE OF GOD'S PLAN IN SCRIPTURE

Let me cite a lengthy passage from the book of Colossians. Based on our discussion, see how many parts of God's Covenant plan you recognize in this passage. See if terms we formerly glossed over now come to life (e.g., "powers and authorities" are the fallen angelic hierarchy that has ruled over humanity since Eden; "circumcision" is the removal of the nature of this enemy from within us).

Beginning with the foundational realities of Covenant—the transformation of our nature and our new bond with Christ—watch the progression in these verses. Do you see the way this sequence forms into a step-by-step plan? Note the many roles played by our Three Powers as we respond to God and follow His plan.

This is not the entirety of the plan we detailed, however. An even better exercise is to read the entire New Testament (or, more correctly, "New Covenant") and see how long it takes to find *everything* we have discussed. As you do this, keep in mind the highest priority of Covenant: faithfulness, and the intended outcome of Covenant, which is love in action. Do your plans for your life align with God's?

"For in Christ all the fullness of the Deity lives in bodily form, and in Christ you have been brought to fullness. He is the head over every power and authority. In Him you were also circumcised with a circumcision not performed by human hands. Your whole self ruled by the flesh was put off when you were circumcised by Christ, having been buried with Him in baptism, in which you were also raised with Him through your faith in the working of God, who raised Him from the dead.

"When you were dead in your sins and in the uncircumcision of your flesh, God made you alive with Christ. He forgave us all our sins, having canceled the charge of our legal indebtedness, which stood against us and condemned us; He has taken it away, nailing it to the cross. And having disarmed the powers and authorities, He made a public spectacle of them, triumphing over them by the cross" (Colossians 2:9-15).

****

"Since you have been raised with Christ, set your hearts on things above, where Christ is, seated at the right hand of God. Set your minds on things above, not on earthly things. For you died, and your life is now hidden with Christ in God. When Christ, who is your life, appears, then you also will appear with Him in glory.

"Put to death, therefore, whatever belongs to your earthly nature: sexual immorality, impurity, lust, evil desires and greed, which is idolatry. Because of these, the wrath of God is coming. You used to walk in these ways, and in the life you once lived. But now you must also rid yourselves of all such things as these: anger, rage, malice, slander, and filthy language from your lips. Do not lie to each other, since you have taken off your old self with its practices, and have put on the new self, which is ***being renewed in knowledge in the image of its Creator****. Here, there is no Gentile or Jew, circumcised or uncircumcised, barbarian, Scythian, slave or free, but Christ is all, and is in all.*

"Therefore, as God's chosen people, holy and dearly loved, clothe yourselves with compassion, kindness, humility, gentleness, and patience. Bear with each other and forgive one another if any of you has a grievance against someone. Forgive as the Lord forgave you. And over all of these virtues put on love, which binds them all together in perfect unity.

"Let the peace of Christ rule in your hearts, since as members of one body you were called to peace. And be thankful. Let the message of Christ dwell among you richly as you teach and admonish one another with all wisdom through psalms, hymns, and songs from the Spirit, singing to God with gratitude in your hearts. And whatever you do, whether in word or deed, do it all in the name of the Lord Jesus, giving thanks to God the Father through Him" (Colossians 3:1-17, my emphasis added).

WHY DOES IT MATTER HOW MUCH WE GROW OR WHAT LIFE WE BUILD?

We have just covered God's plan to transform us and build many things. This plan obviously requires much from us. In fact, it requires all that we have, all we can do, and all we can become for best results. But we may like much about our life now. There may be things we do not want to give up. Or we may wonder, "Why bother?" There is one last reality we will do well to keep in mind. We will all look into the eyes of Jesus one day and be judged for what we chose to do with the opportunities He entrusted to us. Choose wisely. Your choices will impact you for all eternity.

"Behold, I am coming soon. My reward is with me, and I will give to everyone according to what he has done" (Revelation 22:12).

"For we must all appear before the judgment seat of Christ, that each one may receive what is due him for the things done while in the body, whether good or bad" (2 Corinthians 5:10).

"If anyone is ashamed of Me and my words, the Son of Man will be ashamed of him when he comes in His glory and in the glory of the Father and of the holy angels" (Luke 9:26).

BUILDING A HEART OF LOVE FOR GOD AND OTHERS

"Of all the commandments, which is most important?" "The most important one," Jesus replied, "is this: 'Hear, O Israel: the Lord our God, the Lord is One. Love the Lord your God with all your heart and with all your mind and with all your soul and with all your strength.' The second is this: 'Love your neighbor as yourself.' There is no commandment greater than these" (Mark 12:28-31).

Think of the most loving experiences in your life. A newborn asleep on your chest. A deep need unexpectedly met by someone who cared. Looking into the eyes of one you deeply love and seeing a door, open wide, into each other's lives. Catching your breath and holding each other close after marital intimacy. Or considering, for the first time, what God actually did for you and me two thousand years ago and opening ourselves to receive Him on His terms. As Holley and I recalled many such moments the very morning I wrote this, I asked her what she felt most at these times. Her answer: "Oneness." Why does this *oneness* nourish our souls in a way nothing else can?

What is love? This word encompasses many things and has many dimensions. Love is feeling, and it is understanding. It is knowing, and it is caring. It is receiving and giving. It is simply *being there* for each other. We must have the capacity to love and make the choice to love. We choose to trust, then entrust ourselves to another. We recognize a sincere offer of love, then commit ourselves. We must receive and embrace in order to feel and enjoy. We must give, and we must offer ourselves. Love is trusting, valuing, honoring, protecting. Love is the soil in which we can grow to our potential. A life full of love is synonymous with abundance.

What does love require? We must clearly see the truth about another, and also the reality of the relationship. Early in a relationship there are many questions about the other: intention, heart, and the meaning of what is said and done. There are always mixed signals to sort out. What happens next depends on what we decide to believe about the other. And what drives these decisions? Is what we *decide is true* always actually true? The turning point of love is always what we believe about another. We cannot believe in another, or entrust ourselves, or commit ourselves, or invest ourselves unless we believe certain things.

How does it feel to be a defiant and destructive young adult? Is this person's life abundant, or is he or she starving? Now think about a couple falling in love. Is theirs an abundant life? Suppose the defiant young adult has two parents who love him or her just as deeply as this couple love each other. Is being loved the question, or is a person's ability to receive love also at issue? Why does this point matter? We cannot live an abundant life without experiencing love in deep ways. Can we be deeply loved yet not realize it? In romantic literature there are many stories of love that was not recognized and returned; instead, the opportunity of a lifetime slipped away.

What about our relationship with God? Do we feel His love? Is our life filled with His love in a way that nourishes us? If not, why not? What do we really believe about Him? Do we understand His heart toward us? If we are not experiencing His love in a way that ignites our heart, is the issue God's love or our assumptions and beliefs? If we do not understand or recognize or embrace what God has done and wants to do in our lives, how can we *feel* loved by Him? If we do not feel deeply loved by God, what now? What keeps us from experiencing Him as He is? Is the issue what we *assume to be true* about God, or ourselves, or life? Where did these assumptions come from? From what we decided is true … but these are things that may not be true at all. Why did we decide these things in the first place? Why did we make these decisions that keep us from experiencing love? Of course, the real question is, "Will we *un-make* these decisions and shift the foundation of our viewpoint to actual truth?"

Our world is a hard place. We all have embraced ideas that we meant to guard our hearts. This is the only reasonable response in a world full of dangerous people. We have all been hurt, dismissed, ignored, betrayed, and abused. How can we find our way to abundance in this world? Or is it best to continue hiding behind the wall we built to protect us?

Love is what we most need in life, but our attempts to love have often been our most painful experiences. Few in our world truly love us. We may have trouble believing that anyone does. We may have strong feelings and label them "love," yet the relationship may provide little evidence of true love. Even if two try their best to love, do they know how to build an intimate, love-for-a-lifetime relationship? Many have never experienced anything close to the pure form of love that God intends. For most of us love is elusive. So elusive that many conclude pure love itself is but a childish illusion. Why then is the yearning for love so deep and pervasive in human hearts? Who put this hunger—this need—in our hearts? And why?

For many years I was puzzled by the two greatest commands of God: that we love Him with essentially every fiber of our being, and that we love other people as ourselves. It is one thing to say, "I should." And to this we may honestly also say, "I want to." But it is another thing altogether to say, "I do love God with every fiber of my being."

In my experience, I like things or I do not. Turnip greens, for instance, are something one either likes or deeply dislikes. It is one thing for someone to instruct me to eat something I do not like. I can do that. But what if they instruct me to like something I do not like? How is that even possible? It is the same for how one feels about a person. If I simply do not like someone, how do I *make* myself like him or her? Far more, how can I possibly compel myself to love a particular individual if I do not love them now? Love, in the common perception—and in my perception early in my Christian life—seemed a powerful but mysterious force. This force seemed to be directing me far more than I was able to direct it. So how can I make myself feel love for God?

On one hand, this must be possible, for God does not hold us accountable for things that are beyond our control. Yet for many years I was completely baffled about how I could possibly obey these two greatest commands. As I began to learn about Covenant, then learned the lessons of deeper personal transformation, the answer became clear. It also became clear that learning to give and receive love is a huge part of the abundant life God desires for us. In Covenant we are to build a real love relationship with God and loving relationships with others in the body of Christ. Then, once we have learned to love, we are to extend this love to all who are made in God's image.

This invites two questions. The answers may seem obvious, but in reality they are not. First: What is love? Can we do better than "I'll know it when I see it"? Second: Is God really serious about His commands? The correct answer begins with the realization that God wants an abundant life for us, not a life that is dysfunctional and deprived.

I would give everything I own,
I'd give up my life, my heart, my home.
I would give everything I own,
Just to have you back again.
Just to touch you once again.
David Gates and Bread, "Everything I Own"[19]

For all of us, love is somewhere in our field of view or somewhere over the horizon. In their 1972 hit song cited above, David Gates and Bread captured this beautifully. What would one trade for love once we realize its worth? The answer: everything.

We often think of love only in romantic terms. I listened to this song for years assuming it was about a romance somehow lost. Romance, though, is only one facet of a much broader picture. Gates actually wrote this song about his relationship with his father after his father's funeral. What was it about that relationship that was worth … everything?

What the world needs now is love, sweet love.
It's the only thing that there's just too little of.
Jackie DeShannon, *What the World Need Now is Love*[20]

Think about love in Marriages and families. Think about the love received by a child, or not received. Think about the love between a husband and wife, or its lack. Then the relationships with extended family, or among those in a church body, or among people in general. Think of all the damage in your life caused by the lack of love from others. Now multiply that by nearly eight billion and consider the cumulative consequences of *not-love* within ourselves, our families, and our world throughout history.

God's most prominent and important command is that we love Him and each other. We see through history, or in our society, or in our circle of family and friends, both the importance and benefits of love and the loss and devastation that flow from not-love.

"Love does no harm to a neighbor. Therefore, love is the fulfillment of the law" (Romans 13:10).

We need a bigger view of love. If asked whether we love someone, the first place we check within ourselves is how we *feel* about this person. Let's pause and really think about that idea. Is love primarily a feeling? Are loving actions primarily driven by feelings? Are love-for-a-lifetime relationships built on feelings? Feelings are part of the picture, and they are clearly important. They energize our expressions of love and form a big part of our experience of love. But what is love at the most fundamental level? What is its foundation? How is it nurtured and grown? If God says to love Him, how do we comply? If God says to love our brothers and sisters in Christ, how do we comply? And if God tells us to love everyone, including our enemies, how in the world is this possible?

TAKING THE FIRST STEP ON THIS JOURNEY

We must return to the most basic definition of love noted in the Scripture above. Love *does no harm to a neighbor*. Whatever else we may think, feel, or want, if we simply confine ourselves to doing constructive things for others—and ourselves—we are on God's path. As we travel this path we must learn more about what is, and is not, constructive. We must overcome much resistance within ourselves to do even this one thing. But if we commit ourselves to this first step of God's plan, our commitment becomes the ground from which will grow a deeper capacity to love. As we walk God's path, feelings will come. Blessings will come. Better relationships will come. Greater fulfillment and joy will come with each additional step along this path.

Covenant is God's answer. Covenant is the vehicle through which God displays His love toward us. Covenant is the vehicle through which God requires our love in return. Covenant is His school of love. What are we to learn in this school?

1.) **Love and *not-love* in our hearts and our world are reflections of a spiritual war**, one between God and the one who seeks to depose

God and rule in His place. If this war did not exist, we would still be in the original state of connection, unity, and harmony with God and each other. This battle entered our hearts because humans chose the guidance of the enemy of God. This choice ushered death, disobedience, and *not-love* into every human heart by inserting within us the unloving nature of the enemy of God.

Ever since that initial event, human character and guidance systems have been further corrupted because individuals continue to embrace the guidance of God's enemy. As long as the nature of this enemy remains in one's heart, this person is literally incapable of obeying God, including loving as God instructs. This person will spend eternity in the company of the leader he or she continues to choose to follow, in an existence characterized by *not-love*. But what if this individual comes into Covenant with God? Does guidance from this enemy still continue to misdirect that person? We have seen that it does. Given the vital role love plays in human lives, might this enemy have directed special attention to loading minds and hearts with ideas that block us from loving and experiencing love? As we look around at the lives of Christians, how much of his *not-love* agenda do we see in action? What, of this agenda, do we see in our own lives?

2.) **To love, we must understand the truth about the other person and the reality of the relationship.** The condition for entering Covenant is to believe God, then to choose to *believe in* Him. Covenant is God's plan to give us new life and a new nature joined to God. We are indwelled by His Spirit. He is in us and we are in Him. This is the ultimate expression of God's love for us and the ultimate reality of oneness. If we are in Christ, the issue is not whether we are loved (or not). We most definitely are. Instead, it's whether we embrace the reality of God's love. God *is* truth. God *is* love. We are connected in the deepest way possible. In turn, God invites us to totally entrust ourselves, commit, and invest.

With new life and a new nature (one that no longer includes the nature of His enemy), we become capable of learning to love. The issue of love now shifts from a question of one's *nature* to a question of one's *beliefs*. We cannot change our nature; only God can, and God does. But we can change any beliefs that stand in the way of love.

To learn to love as God loves, we must grow the new being we have become to maturity. We must subtract the deceptions of God's enemy, for these still misform our character and misdirect our life. Within Covenant we find everything needed to learn to love as God does, as much as our finiteness allows. All that remains is to choose to follow God's plan. Since loving in this way is the pinnacle of following and emulating God, developing the capacity to love in this way requires that we embrace the entirety of God's plan and devote ourselves to carrying it out in every detail. How have you decided to approach your relationship with God?

3.) **Four elements combine to create loving feelings toward another. These are trust, connection, commitment, and investment.** The Covenant relationships which are the topic of this book series have four characteristics that correspond to each of these elements. Think of your relationships that have had one, two, or three of these elements, but not all four. If trust is missing, or there is no investment by the other party, or one person is not fully committed, our hearts may still want a loving relationship. But something vital is missing. Our hearts can only experience the fullness of love if we totally trust in each other, are firmly connected, are firmly committed, and if both people are fully invested in the relationship. Are you experiencing the fullness of God's love in your heart? If not, what steps can you take right now to begin to experience this reality?

"For you died, and your life is now hidden with Christ in God"
(Colossians 3:1).

4.) **Covenant is the closest and most intimate of connections.** We are literally joined at the level of nature and identity. In the New Covenant we are joined in this way to our Creator. We are one with Him. He said He will "never leave us or forsake us"—because He cannot. He is literally within us, and we are within Him. We are fully accepted *by* Him because we have been fully accepted *within* Him. What heart experience does this acceptance create? Do you understand how God has accepted you? How does this make you feel toward Him?

We are in this same bond with others in the Body of Christ. By accepting Christ into ourselves we also accept all who are in Him into ourselves. What is this reality supposed to look like in relationships within the Body of Christ? What experience of acceptance are we supposed to create for each other? What heart response can this create?

5.) **In Covenant we now have a life conjoined with our Covenant partner.** That is, we enter the life of God, and God inhabits every part of our life. This is the ultimate in a trust relationship. We spoke in *The Covenant of Marriage* about fully inhabiting each other's lives, and about the necessity of being constructive as we do. Humans can be wrecking balls. Yet this kind of trust is an inherent part of Covenant. This level of access to each other's lives is part of God's plan for this relationship. But such trust must also be earned in order for us to *want* the other person in every part of our life.

When it comes to giving God this access, He loves perfectly and is all-powerful. We have heard these things, but in order for our hearts to warm to God's presence we must experience His love, care, and protection as we do life together. This is understandable, for we have been let down and hurt before by those we trusted. We want to guard our hearts from disappointment and protect our lives from damage. People must prove themselves to us. This is a more interesting question with God, for we are invited to fully trust a Being we cannot see clearly or understand fully. At first, we have only heard *about Him* in Scripture and from other people. For our hearts to engage, we must gain experience in a relationship with Him.

At the same time, consider what this is like from God's perspective. He is also entrusting His honor and reputation to us. He is entrusting the care of His children into our hands. We want God to prove Himself before we are comfortable trusting Him with everything in our lives and hearts. Do we have the same sense of urgency to prove to God we can be trusted with the things of God? We now have access to the resources of the Creator of the universe. In return we are to offer God anything He desires. If we approach our relationship with Him in this way, and find that we can totally rely on Him, what happens in our hearts? Have you built this kind of trust relationship with God? If not, what is necessary to do so? Will you take these steps?

I find it extremely interesting that, along with accepting the life of a perfect God within myself, God's plan also joins me to the lives of a vast number of very imperfect people. It's much like the family members you did not choose, and perhaps would not have chosen. Here we must keep in mind that we are not free to accept or reject these people on their individual merit or based on our individual preference. We accept these people for Jesus' sake in the *same way that Jesus accepts us*. If any of these have a need we can supply, from where do these resources ultimately come? If we suffer loss at the hands of a brother or sister, who is ultimately responsible for providing for our every need and protecting all our vital interests?

When it comes to others in the Body of Christ we should each feel a keen sense of responsibility to earn the trust of our fellow Christians. We are to learn how to be a constructive influence in any life with which we intersect. In the plan of God we are to help each other become this kind of influence. Beyond entrusting our lives to other Christians, we are to trust God to guide, provide, and bless in the midst of what will inevitably be a messy growth process for all of us.

6.) **People in relationships may be connected but not committed.** Inherent in the historic understanding of Covenant is the highest possible level of commitment. This relationship comes with an array of duties, obligations, and responsibilities that require our total commitment to fulfill. The highest priority of Covenant is faithfulness: totally committing ourselves to fulfill every role assigned to us in Covenant. We are to devote everything we have, are, or can become in order to love our Covenant partner in action.

Being in this relationship does not ensure that we are totally committed to it, however. In Covenant we can be assured of God's total commitment to us. The question is, will we affirm and embrace our commitment to Him? It is vital that we recognize, then embrace, God's plan in whole, as well as every part. If we do, how does this impact our heart? Have you committed yourself to God and His plan in this way?

In addition, we are to affirm and embrace these same Covenant duties and obligations in our relationship with all in the body of Christ. In our culture, few ideas can create more apprehension than such an open-ended commitment to even one person, much less all of our brothers and sisters. Yet this is God's plan. We can be assured that He will help us and bless us as we follow Him, even if we are not sure where the path leads.

"For where your treasure is, there your heart will be also" (Matthew 6:21).

7.) **We must do more than commit ourselves to God's plan. We must follow through.** This always involves learning how to be more consistent in our love. This in turn involves removing impediments within ourselves to loving God and others. It involves developing deeper understanding, better priorities, stronger levels of commitment, and more willpower. In other words, to build this life we must grow up. Many things within us must grow, and many must be transformed if we are to be faithful. We must also realize that building faithfulness is a lifetime task. Though we should aspire to perfection, we must be content with growth and progress.

"We love because He first loved us" (1 John 4:19).

Consider what happens if we are devoted to someone to this degree. We pour our life into the life of the other. Covenant is intended to be reciprocal—both pouring into each other's lives in this way—if this is possible. But what if this reciprocity is not possible? With, say, a special needs child or disabled adult, if we pour our lives into bettering the life of another, how do we *feel* about that person?

What does it mean to pour our life into the life of God? Or to pour our life into the lives of our brothers and sisters? Or for God and His children to pour their lives into our life? This is what eternity will be like in the Kingdom of God. We pray, "Thy Kingdom come, and Thy will be done, on earth as it is in heaven." Understand, it is this mutual investment we are asking for among other things. How would you feel if this back-and-forth love characterized your existence? In this world it clearly does not. What then? We are the ones charged with bringing the life of God to a lost and dying world. It is sad that we are not loved as we should be. It would be even more sad if we never learn to love as we could, and should, though we have been given the opportunity to do so.

"*... until we all reach unity in the faith and in the knowledge of the Son of God and become mature, attaining to the whole measure of the fullness of Christ*" (Ephesians 4:13).

"*Instead, speaking the truth in love, we will grow to become in every respect the mature body of Him who is the head, that is, Christ*" (Ephesians 4:15).

If we want our hearts to become energized to love, we can start by recognizing and appreciating the love we have received. What has Jesus done for our sake? What has the Father done, and what does the Spirit of God do on our behalf? At the outset, it is we who cannot reciprocate the love of God. Given the realities of our relationship with God, how can our hearts not be on fire for Him?

"*The thief comes only to steal and kill and destroy; I have come that they may have life, and have it to the full*" (John 10:10).

Why did I spend the hundreds of hours it took to write this book series? The short answer: Because God led me to do so. But the heart motivation for this effort comes from seeing what is available to each of us in a relationship with God or in a Marriage. Then, seeing the contrast between what is possible and what most people build in these relationships and their lives. What is going on? Most Christian teaching makes no mention of a specific plan we must follow to build these relationships. There are no reasons given for the many things God tells us to do, nor is there any guidance about how we can become able to do these things.

The understanding of Covenant related in this book series has been the integrating point of my spiritual life for over thirty-five years. There have been vast benefits when these concepts were lived out in life and family. I have interacted with many people during these years. I have seen great benefits when people are shown an intelligible plan for building a relationship with God or a Marriage, and offered compelling reasons to follow this plan. This knowledge is not common knowledge. But over time I have become convinced that it is very important knowledge. Few teach anything about the nature of these relationships. I have never seen this topic approached in the depth offered in this book series. This is truly remarkable, because I am convinced that Covenant is the heart of God's plan for every human being. Transformation is the heart of Covenant; understanding our two transformations is the key to building these relationships.

If we do not understand the nature of our relationship with God or our Marriage, much less the rules and principles which govern these relationships, how can we build them to their potential? In the absence of this understanding I am not sure that we can. Therefore, in this book series I have attempted to convey what I have learned. I hope others build upon the solid foundation of understanding that has been carried forward by H. Clay Trumbull and other teachers. May this understanding bless your life. May your life become a testimony to the beauty of God's truth and His plan. As you understand and live these things, may you convey these things to others.

THE LIFE PRODUCED BY FAITHFULNESS TO COVENANT

What kind of life is produced by actually following God faithfully for many years? Our experience of life is transformed. Though we are still impacted by circumstances, we are content with the life God has designed. We are at peace with God and ourselves. We have joy, for we see God working in and through our lives on a daily basis. We face anything in our future with confidence because we know that everything that matters about us and our lives is in the all-powerful hands of our loving God. We have a level of confidence in all these things because we have experienced God's love and care in every situation.

We live and relate differently. We do not have pressing needs which must be met by others. We are free to build relationships devoid of manipulation, and we feel no resentment when people do not do what we want. Why? Because everything in our lives that matters and all of our deepest needs are in the hands of our Loving Father, not undependable people. We are free to love and expect nothing in return because we are already loved perfectly, and will always be. We are still to build things and do things in life. Far from passive and detached observers, we wisely apply our efforts and express our potential in many ways. We build things that are truly important for ourselves and others.

Outcomes in our lives are different. We have spent years building good consequences into our lives. We have spent years building quality relationships. When we love many people, many people love us back. God blesses our efforts and rewards us in the depths of our heart in ways only He can. At the same time, we will continue to experience trials, pain, and loss. But we see these differently now. These things continue to be part of our lives in order to spur further growth and build deeper maturity. We have an enemy that strongly opposes us, and on occasion his weapons land a blow. When this occurs we can thank God. Though the enemy means these things for evil, God can redeem even the most grievous loss and use it for our good.

Our future is different. We are assured a place in eternity with God, but the experience of eternity expands to our present. We are in His Kingdom now. Today we pay forward blessings to others that will last for eternity. We have compelling reasons to get out of bed each day. We have a life to build here. We have a relationship with God and others to build now. And we have an eternity to enjoy the good fruits of every good effort we make.

How do we build this life? One step at a time. One idea at a time. One decision at a time. One embraced or rejected belief at a time.

One changed value or priority at a time. One decision to act at a time, and one completed task at a time. Our decisions matter. Our commitments matter. I pray you will make the decision to follow God's plan, in whole and in every part, and carry out this commitment faithfully. I will personally guarantee you that this will be the best life you could possibly live, as it has been for me. How do I know this? Because I have come to know the God who wrote your plan and mine from experience. I believe in Him. I pray that you do also.

"But to you who are listening I say: Love your enemies and do good to those who hate you" (Luke 6:27).

LOVING EVEN YOUR ENEMIES

This is the hard one. This is the one that makes no sense to our heart and mind. Again, it must be emphasized that this is not a command to submit to ongoing abuse, nor is it to place ourselves in danger unless we are specifically instructed to do so by God. Here too we must distinguish *feeling* love from *acting in a loving way.*

"If your enemy is hungry, feed him; if he is thirsty, give him something to drink. In doing this, you heap burning coals on his head" (Romans 12:20).

We are to do good toward those who hate us. Why? Because those who hate are living in deception and delusion. They are people like us, made in the image of God, and therefore loved by God. And, at a point, while still separated from God, we were like these people. Not everyone will enter Covenant with God. This is clear from Scripture. But some will, and we cannot see

We are to do good toward those who hate us. Why? Because those who hate are living in deception and delusion. They are people like us, made in the image of God.

who will respond and who will not. We can never know the impact of a display of godly character or an undeserved kindness. In offering these we reflect God and throw a lifeline to the lost and dying.

"I tell you, my friends, do not be afraid of those who kill the body and after that can do no more. ... Fear Him who, after your body has been killed, has authority to throw you into hell" (Luke 12:4, 5).

We contend with people because we fear they stand in the way of our best life. We fight with others over "important" issues. Yet if the things vital to our life are eternally secure, in the arms of the most powerful of beings, what do we have to fear from any human?

"Whoever believes in Me, as Scripture has said, rivers of living water will flow from within them" (John 7:38).

"Love your enemies and pray for those who persecute you, that you may be children of your Father in heaven" (Matthew 5:44, 45).

If our hearts are already full of His love, what do we need from any human? Jesus offered that we may have "springs of living water" flowing from within us. That is, the life-giving love of God and the Word of God is to flow from us into a lost and dying world. By this we clearly demonstrate that the life and love of God are within us.

1 CORINTHIANS 13

(1) If I speak in the tongues of men or of angels, but do not have love, I am only a resounding gong or a clanging cymbal.

(2) If I have the gift of prophecy and can fathom all mysteries and all knowledge, and if I have a faith that can move mountains, but do not have love, I am nothing.

(3) If I give all I possess to the poor and give over my body to hardship that I may boast, but do not have love, I gain nothing.

(4) Love is patient, love is kind. It does not envy, it does not boast, it is not proud.

(5) It does not dishonor others, it is not self-seeking, it is not easily angered, it keeps no record of wrongs.

(6) Love does not delight in evil but rejoices with the truth.

(7) It always protects, always trusts, always hopes, always perseveres.

(8) Love never fails. But where there are prophecies, they will cease; where there are tongues, they will be stilled; where there is knowledge, it will pass away.

(9) For we know in part and we prophesy in part,

(10) but when completeness comes, what is in part disappears.

(11) When I was a child, I talked like a child, I thought like a child, I reasoned like a child. When I became a man, I put the ways of childhood behind me.

(12) For now we see only a reflection as in a mirror; then we shall see face to face. Now I know in part; then I shall know fully, even as I am fully known.

(13) And now these three remain: faith, hope, and love. …

But the greatest of these is love."

ENDNOTES

INTRODUCTION

1. H. Clay Trumbull, *The Blood Covenant, a Primitive Rite and Its Bearing on Scripture*, second edition, Forgotten Books, London, 2011 (Originally published in 1893).

2. Kay Arthur, *Covenant Study*, Precept Ministries International, Chattanooga, Tn., 1983.

3. Trumbull, *The Blood Covenant.*

4. Peter R. de Vries, *End of the Spear*, Rocky Mountain Pictures, 2005.

5. Matthew Crawford, "Where Did the Terms 'Old Testament' and 'New Testament' Come From?" standingonshoulders.wordpress.com, 2009 (accessed November 2020).

CHAPTER TWO

6. Sam Parnia, MD, *Erasing Death* (HarperOne, 2014), p. 39.

7. Jonathan, Sarfati, PhD, *The Greatest Hoax on Earth,* Creation Ministries International, Powder Springs, Ga., 2014, p. 247.

8. Phillip Johnson, *Darwin on Trial,* Intervarsity Press, Downers Grove, Il., 2010.

9. Jonathan Sarfati, *The Greatest Hoax on Earth.*

10. *The Book of Enoch,* Defender Publishing, Crane, Mo., 2004

11. Zecharia Sitchin, *The Twelth Planet*, Harper, 30th Edition, 2007

12. Keith Green, "No One Believes in Me Anymore," For Him Who Has Ears to Hear, Sparrow Records, 1977.

CHAPTER THREE

13. Axe, Briggs, et. al., *The Price of Panic,* Regnery Publishing, 2020.
14. Sitchin, *The Twelth Planet.*
15. Wedding Paper Divas, @WeddingPaperDivas-newleyweds.com, accessed May 2019

CHAPTER FIVE

16. Dierks Bentley, "What Was I Thinkin'," Dierks Bentley, 2009
17. David Gates and Bread, "Everything I Own," Bread, Sony/ATV Music, 1972.
18. Jackie DeShannon, "What the World Need Now Is Love," Imperial Records, 1965.
19. McDowell, Josh, *Evidence that Demands a Verdict,* Thomas Nelson, Nashville, Tn. 2017
20. Brother Lawrence, *The Practice of the Presence of God*, Image, Inc. 1977.

BOOKS BY MARK JOHNSON, MD

Beware the Raised Eyebrow: Are Cultural Expectations the Path to the Good Life?
Carpenter's Son Publishing, Nashville, Tn., (2017).

What Is a Covenant?
Carpenter's Son Publishing, Nashville, Tn., (2020).

The Covenant of Marriage,
Carpenter's Son Publishing, Nashville, Tn., (2020).

The Covenant of Marriage Study Guide,
Carpenter's Son Publishing, Nashville, Tn., (2021).

The New Covenant,
Carpenter's Son Publishing, Nashville, Tn., (2021)

Distributed by Ingram Publishers.

Books may be purchased from the Author's website, from your local Christian bookstore, or from Amazon in paperback or e-book.

To Learn More About These Books or the Author
To Access the Author's Blog Page
or
To Purchase a Book

VISIT THE AUTHOR'S WEBSITE

MarkJohnsonMDAuthor.com

CPSIA information can be obtained
at www.ICGtesting.com
Printed in the USA
JSHW041041221121
20654JS00003B/5

9 781952 025358